Scribe Publications
A CERTAIN MARITIME INCIDENT

Tony Kevin retired from the Department of Foreign Affairs and Trade in 1998, after a 30-year public service career during which he served in the Prime Minister's Department and was Australia's ambassador to Poland and Cambodia. He is currently an honorary visiting fellow at the ANU Research School of Pacific and Asian Studies, and has written extensively on Australian foreign, national security, and refugee policies in Australia's national print media.

Tony Kevin began researching the sinking of the asylum-seeker boat that he named SIEV X in February 2002. The resulting book, *A Certain Maritime Incident*, was first published in August 2004. It won the 2005 ACT Book of the Year award and the Community Relations Commission for a Multicultural NSW award in the 2005 NSW Premier's literary awards, and was shortlisted for the 2005 *Age* Non-Fiction Book of the Year award, a 2005 Queensland Premier's literary award, and a 2005 NSW Premier's literary award.

For more information about this book and its author, visit www.tonykevin.com.au

INDONESIA: SINKING OF ILLEGAL IMMIGRANT VESSEL   1/4

O.JA25691 1049 23.10.2001 ~~CLA-FIRST-SENSITIVE~~ (M)

TO.
PP CANBERRA/

RP.
PP GENEVA UN/

DECLASSIFIED

FM. JAKARTA/ FA

~~RESTRICTED~~ (M)

INDONESIA: SINKING OF ILLEGAL IMMIGRANT VESSEL

~~THE FOLLOWING CONTAINS SENSITIVE INFORMATION.~~ (M)

START OF SUMMARY

A SUSPECTED ILLEGAL ENTRY VESSEL (SIEV) CARRYING 397 POTENTIAL ILLEGAL IMMIGRANTS (PII) SANK ENROUTE TO CHRISTMAS ISLAND DURING THE AFTERNOON OF FRIDAY 19 OCTOBER. THE SIEV IS BELIEVED TO HAVE FOUNDERED IN ROUGH SEAS TO THE SOUTH OF SUNDA ST WITHIN THE INDONESIAN MARITIME SEARCH AND RESCUE AREA OF RESPONSIBILITY. 45 SURVIVORS WERE RESCUED BY TWO INDONESIAN FISHING VESSELS AND RETURNED TO JAKARTA LATE ON THE AFTERNOON OF 22 OCTOBER. THERE HAS BEEN CLOSE INTEREST BY THE INTERNATIONAL MEDIA IN THE STORY.

END OF SUMMARY

[redacted]

CHRONOLOGY (U/L)

2. TUESDAY 16 OCTOBER- APPROXIMATELY 430 POTENTIAL ILLEGAL IMMIGRANTS (PII) DEPARTED CIPINAS (SOUTH OF JAKARTA) AND TRAVELLED TO SUMATRA VIA JAKARTA AND MERAK. THE SURVIVOR SAID THAT ON ARRIVAL IN SUMATRA, THEY THEN TRAVELLED ONE AND A HALF HOURS BY BUS TO A HOTEL. THEY REMAINED OVER NIGHT IN THAT LOCATION (POSSIBLY BANDAR LAMPUNG)

3. WEDNESDAY 17 OCTOBER - ABU QUASSAY INFORMED THE PIIS THAT THEY WERE TO PACK THEIR BELONGINGS AS THEY WERE DEPARTING THAT EVENING. LATER THAT DAY THEY MOVED FROM THE HOTEL TO THE POINT OF DEPARTURE, ONLY A FEW KILOMETRES AWAY. THE VESSEL WAS WAITING FOR THEM. THE DIMENSIONS OF THE VESSEL WERE REPORTED AS 19.5 METRES LONG WITH A BEAM OF 4 METRES. A MAKESHIFT UPPERDECK HAD BEEN ADDED, WITH THE AFTER DECKS ENCLOSED BY CHIPBOARD (PRESUMABLY TO ENHANCE

INDONESIA: SINKING OF ILLEGAL IMMIGRANT VESSEL

SEAWORTHINESS).

4. THURSDAY 18 OCTOBER - THE VESSEL DEPARTED BANDAR LAMPUNG AT APPROXIMATELY 0130. AT THIS TIME, DUE TO THE SIZE OF THE VESSEL, 10 PIIS REFUSED TO EMBARK, LEAVING 421 PIIS ON BOARD. APPROXIMATELY ONE HOUR AFTER DEPARTURE, PIIS APPARENTLY BECAME APPREHENSIVE ABOUT THE ABILITY OF THE VESSEL TO REMAIN AFLOAT WITH THE NUMBERS ONBOARD. THE VESSEL STOPPED APPROXIMATELY 5 KILOMETRES FROM THE POINT OF DEPARTURE, DURING WHICH TIME THE CREW WAS IN RADIO CONTACT WITH ABU QUASSEY. THE VESSEL THEN RESUMED ITS PASSAGE AND ABOUT 0900 AGAIN STOPPED NEAR AN ISLAND "DUE TO HIGH SEAS". A NEARBY FISHING BOAT CAME ALONGSIDE THE VESSEL TO REMOVE 24 PIIS (397 PAX REMAINING).

5. FRIDAY 19 OCTOBER - AT ABOUT 1400 THE VESSEL BEGAN TAKING WATER. THE CREW SOUGHT TO REASSURE THE PASSENGERS BY TELLING THEM THAT THIS WAS A SMALL PROBLEM. THE PIIS ASSISTED THE CREW TO BAIL THE VESSEL, USING IMPROVISED SCOOPS FASHIONED FROM THE HULL TIMBER. AT THIS TIME, THE VESSEL WAS OUT OF SIGHT OF LAND.

6. AT 1500, THE VESSEL BEGAN TO LIST HEAVILY TO PORT. WITHIN FIVE MINUTES, THE VESSEL CAPSIZED. IT SUNK COMPLETELY AFTER MOMENTARILY REMAINING NEUTRALLY BUOYANT. DEBRIS SOON SURFACED AFTER THE SINKING. THE MAJORITY OF THE PIIS DROWNED IMMEDIATELY, WITH SOME 120 INITIAL SURVIVORS. THERE WAS A HEAVY SEA RUNNING, AND IT COMMENCED RAINING AFTER THE SINKING. THE EXACT POSITION OF VESSEL AT THE TIME OF SINKING IS UNKNOWN, BUT IT IS JUDGED AS NO FURTHER SOUTH THAN 8 DEGREES SOUTH LATITUDE ON A DIRECT LINE FROM SUNDA ST TO CHRISTMAS IS.

7. SATURDAY 20 OCTOBER - THE SURVIVORS REMAINED IN THE WATER FOR APPROXIMATELY 19 HOURS, WITH MANY OF THE SURVIVORS PERISHING DURING THAT PERIOD. AT APPROXIMATELY 1000, THE REMAINING SURVIVORS WERE APPROACHED BY TWO INDONESIAN FISHING BOATS. ONE VESSEL TOOK ON BOARD 44 PIIS (41 ADULTS AND 3 CHILDREN), WITH THE SECOND BOAT PICKING UP 5 PIIS. OF THESE, 4 WERE ALREADY DEAD AND THE REMAINING SURVIVOR WAS A FEMALE.

8. THE CREW OF THE FIRST BOAT (44 PIIS) CONTACTED THEIR CHINESE OWNER FOR INSTRUCTIONS. THEY WERE SUBSEQUENTLY DIRECTED TO PROCEED TO JAKARTA WITH THE PIIS. THE TIME OF ARRIVAL IN JAKARTA WAS APPROXIMATELY 1800 ON MONDAY 22 OCTOBER.

9. A VESSEL OVERDUE ALERT MESSAGE WAS ISSUED BY RESCUE COORDINATION CENTRE AUSTRALIA ON MONDAY 22 OCTOBER AND FORWARDED TO INDONESIAN SEARCH AND RESCUE COORDINATION CENTRE (BARSARNAS) IN JAKARTA.

GENERAL (U/L)

10. LOSS OF LIFE - 353 PERSONS (INCLUDING 70 CHILDREN). THE SAFETY EQUIPMENT CARRIED ON BOARD WAS ENTIRELY INADEQUATE CONSISTING OF 70 NON SERVICEABLE LIFE JACKETS.

INDONESIA: SINKING OF ILLEGAL IMMIGRANT VESSEL   3/4

11. IT IS ASSUMED THAT THE 10 PASSENGERS WHO REFUSED TO BOARD THE BOAT AT BANDAR LAMPUNG REMAIN IN SOUTHERN SUMATRA. THE WHEREABOUTS OF 24 PIIS REMOVED FROM THE VESSEL PRIOR TO SINKING ARE UNKNOWN. THE WHEREABOUTS OF THE 1 FEMALE PII ON THE SECOND RESCUE BOAT IS ALSO UNKNOWN.

12. THE SURVIVORS HAVE BEEN TAKEN BY IOM TO ACCOMMODATION IN BOGOR AREA AND ARE THE SUBJECT OF CONSIDERABLE ATTENTION BY THE INTERNATIONAL MEDIA.

XC. O.JA25691

XC.

ACTION: DR.A.CALVERT (DFAT)

DR A HAWKE (SEC DEF)

ADM C BARRIE (CDF)

MR W FARMER (DIMCA)

MR M M-WILTON (DPMC)

PRIME MINISTER	MIN FOREIGN AFFAIRS	MINISTER FOR TRADE
ATTORNEY GENERAL	MIN DEFENCE	MIN IMMIG+MC AFFAIRS
MIN JUSTICE+CUSTOMS	MR R CORNALL (A/GS)	MR RICHARDSON (ASIO)
COMM.M.KEELTY (AFP)	MR L WOODWARD (ACS)	RADM M BONSER (NSC)

INDONESIA: SINKING OF ILLEGAL IMMIGRANT VESSEL   4/4

MR F LEWINCAMP (DIO)   MR C R JONES (CNA)

ACTION: MR.R.SMITH(IOB)

DR.A.CALVERT(SEC)   MS.P.GREY(D/S)   MS.P.FAYLE(D/S)
DR.A.THOMAS(D/S)   MR.D.RITCHIE(D/S)   MR.J.FRYDENBERG(MIN B)
MS.S.BORCHERS(MIN F)   MS.A.HAWKINS(MIN.G)   MS.L.MANTON(MIN H)
MS.C.MILLAR(EXB)   MR.P.GRIGSON(SED)   MR.G.LADE(KRB)
DR.G.RABY(ILD)   MR.P.DOYLE(PS TF)   MR.I.MCCONVILLE(LGB)
MR.B.PATERSON(ISD)   MR.C.SPARKE(GCB)   MR.B.MILLER(STB)
MR.L.ROWE(PCD)   MR.C.DECURE(PMB)   MR.B.DAVIS(DG-AUSAID)
MR.C.TAPP(PHI)   MR.P.FLANAGAN(HCB)   MR.M.DILLON(APNG)
MS.A.O'KEEFFE(SPA)

ACTION: ;
INFO: :

To my family

A CERTAIN MARITIME INCIDENT

the sinking of SIEV X

Tony Kevin

SCRIBE
Melbourne

Scribe Publications Pty Ltd
PO Box 523
Carlton North, Victoria, Australia 3054
Email: info@scribepub.com.au

First published by Scribe 2004
Reprinted (with minor corrections) 2006
Reprinted (with corrections) 2008

Copyright © Tony Kevin 2004, 2006, 2008

All rights reserved. Without limiting the rights under copyright reserved above, no part of this publication may be reproduced, stored in or introduced into a retrieval system, or transmitted, in any form or by any means (electronic, mechanical, photocopying, recording or otherwise) without the prior written permission of the publisher of this book.

Cover design by Miriam Rosenbloom
Typeset in 11/15 pt Fairfield by the publisher
Printed and bound in Australia by Griffin Press
Only wood grown from sustainable regrowth forests is used in the manufacture of paper found in this book

National Library of Australia
Cataloguing-in-Publication data

Kevin, Tony.
A certain maritime incident : the sinking of SIEV X.

ISBN 9781920769215

1. Refugees - Australia. 2. Refugees - Government policy - Australia. 3. Illegal aliens - Australia. 4. Illegal aliens - Government policy - Australia. I. Title.

305.9069140994

www.scribepublications.com.au

Contents

	List of Illustrations	x
	Preface	xi
Part One	THE SINKING	
ONE	Context for a Human Tragedy	3
TWO	Embarkation	31
THREE	The Voyage	53
FOUR	Rescue and Return to Jakarta	80
FIVE	Where the Boat Sank	95
Part Two	THE INVESTIGATION	
SIX	A Presumption of Regularity	107
SEVEN	The Thirteenth SIEV	129
EIGHT	Accidental Whistleblowers	148
NINE	Opening Pandora's Box	164
TEN	Defence Strikes Back	183
ELEVEN	Questions about Disruption	201
TWELVE	Out of the Loop	226
THIRTEEN	Can We Handle the Truth?	238
FOURTEEN	Epilogue	255
	Notes	259
	Glossary and Abbreviations	285
	Cast of Characters	291
	Website Sources	298
	Appendices	299
	Acknowledgements	305

List of Illustrations

FIGURE 1
This 'thumbnail' map was published in *The Australian* on 24 October 2001, accompanying front-page stories on the sinking, and was the first map published of where SIEV X sank [page 5]

FIGURE 2
Sydney Morning Herald artwork by Rocco Fazzari, 15 February 2002 [page 6]

FIGURE 3
Australian Financial Review artwork by Ward O'Neill, 20 September 2003 [page 16]

FIGURE 4
Canberra Times artwork by Geoff Pryor, 13 December 2001 [page 19]

MAP 1
This map was drawn professionally by www.sievx.com, using the same template as the Operation Relex surveillance maps that Defence submitted to the CMI committee in July 2002 [page 101]

MAP 2
This map, developed by Marg Hutton, dramatically casts into question both the Defence Review of Intelligence Related to SIEV X submitted on 4 July 2002, and part of the ADF testimony on 30 July 2002 [page 197]

Preface

THIS STORY FALLS NATURALLY into two parts. First, there is what happened in Indonesia surrounding the sinking of SIEV X, based on close analysis of the public record. Second, there is the extent to which Australian government agencies' prior knowledge of and possible implication in this maritime disaster was systematically camouflaged, lied about, or withheld from Senate investigative committees—our main accountability mechanism over national government performance in this country—for almost three years. And that cover-up continues to this day.

The early part of the book, after some scene-setting, is an analytical narrative of the recruitment of 430-odd passengers by Abu Quassey's people-smuggling enterprise, their journey through western Java and across Sunda Strait to southern Sumatra, their forced embarkation on SIEV X, its voyage and sinking, and the rescue of 45 people and their return to Jakarta. This part concludes with a discussion of the available public evidence on where the boat sank.

The second part is an account of the blocked Senate investigation, which began with my questions in February 2002. This has been a fierce struggle, waged through Senate investigative committees and the national media, and also by more subtle means. The contestants were the national security system, which closed ranks in its determination to hold onto its secrets, and a few courageous individuals determined to get at the truth of how 353 people, mostly women and children, died while seeking to reunite their families and rebuild their lives in Australia.

In this investigation, government ministers and senior officials played fast and loose with facts and repeatedly misled the Senate about what they knew and when.

This book is for the dead, and for the survivors and their grieving kin, many of whom live among us in Australia. It is also for the rest of us, because we need to get to the bottom of the SIEV X tragedy to regain our national honour. It is a kind of detective story, dealing with a great crime that is in the process of discovery because some people cared enough to lay themselves on the line for the sake of truth.

I have taken some chronological liberties in terms of introducing important information that only became known later. These aspects are clear, and readers will be able to follow the timelines. I don't claim the omniscience of hindsight, but it is important at crucial parts of the story to record when government ministers and officials were lying or obfuscating, and how we can now be sure that they were. All cover-ups rely on short public memories, and one aim of this book is to compensate for that.

This story will not be finished until a full-powers judicial inquiry, as demanded by the Senate, obliges or liberates public servants, police, and defence officials who know something about SIEV X to come forward. Sooner or later, in one form or another, this will happen, and the true story will be pieced together.

Secrets about large-scale state crimes cannot be covered up permanently. One only has to look at the eventual uncovering of Soviet responsibility for the Katyn Forest massacre of Polish army officers in World War II; the truth being exposed about 'Bloody Sunday', the British army killings of peaceful civil rights demonstrators in Londonderry, Northern Ireland, in 1972; or the failed cover-up surrounding the sinking in 1964 of HMAS Voyager.

Until whistleblowers or a judicial inquiry reveal the truth about SIEV X, I rely on the method of adducing the highest-probability hypotheses that best explain the accumulations of facts that cannot reasonably be explained in any other way. In a situation like this, one must rely on the laws of probability in applying methods of scientific induction or deduction, rather than the laws of courtroom proof. A lot of this book follows the method, 'If it looks like a duck and walks like a duck and quacks like a duck, it probably is a duck', rather than, 'Here are the fingerprints of A on the trigger of the gun that we know killed B'.

So my method is vulnerable to the criticism that I have not proved my hypotheses. But until there is a judicial inquiry with the power to send people to jail if they lie or refuse to testify — a power that Senate committees are loath to use — or until people in the national security system voluntarily disclose facts known to them, this is the best I can do. Readers will judge for themselves the credibility of my case.

At any rate, my main purpose in writing this book is simply to get it down on paper and thereby help keep this public issue alive. Even in the internet age, printed books have a special weight and permanence. They sit on library shelves, and they go into reference bibliographies. This book had to be written, because the sinking of SIEV X is too important an issue to fade away now, after so much evidence has been amassed. I don't try to 'prove my hypotheses'. I do, however, try to mount a case that supports the Senate's rightful demands for a comprehensive, independent judicial inquiry into the sinking of SIEV X.

Part One

The Sinking

Chapter One

Context for a Human Tragedy

ON 19 OCTOBER 2001 there was a mass drowning in the seas between Indonesia and Australia. Three hundred and fifty-three people—146 children, 142 women, and 65 men—perished when their vessel, a boat that later became known as SIEV X, sank in the Indian Ocean 50–60 nautical miles south of Sunda Strait. The victims had been trying to reach Christmas Island to request asylum in Australia as refugees. The grossly overloaded 19-metre SIEV X had set off on 18 October 2001 from a bay in southern Sumatra, at the northern end of Indonesia's Sunda Strait, with 421 passengers on board. After having somehow sailed for 33 hours and 130-odd nautical miles down the full length of Sunda Strait and out into the Indian Ocean, it finally lost engine and pump power, quickly filled with water, capsized, and sank in international waters about one-third of the way to Christmas Island. It sank well inside Australia's declared and intensively patrolled Operation Relex military border-protection and surveillance zone, which covered almost all the sea/air gap between Java and Christmas Island.[1]

The sinking happened at the height of the Australian government's war against people smugglers, which had begun about two years earlier. Most of this campaign was kept secret until 2002, when the government found it politically expedient to start releasing selected and highly sanitised portions of the record, under pressure of questions from the Senate's 'children overboard' inquiry (which was the first subject of investigation by the Senate Select Committee into a Certain Maritime Incident, referred to in this book as the CMI committee). However, key parts of the story of the government's covert war in Indonesia against unauthorised boat people—known as the people-smuggling disruption program—are still secret.

David Marr and Marion Wilkinson, in their book *Dark Victory*, uncovered a little of the truth about key events in this secret war, but they did not closely deal with SIEV X, or the possible extent of the people-smuggling disruption program in Indonesia. This book will begin to fill in some of those gaps, but much of the story is still to be told. It is hidden behind blacked-out paragraphs in available official documents and obscured by an official refusal to answer senators' questions about what really happened, or by untrue official answers.

This tragic and shocking event was a pivotal moment in Prime Minister John Howard's election campaign. It summed up all the covert ruthlessness of his 'dark victory' at the polls three weeks later. Most people at the time thought it was just a dreadful accident, and accepted it as further proof of the dangers of the people-smuggling trade. Howard and his ministers quickly turned the tragedy to political advantage, saying it proved the need for robust border-protection policies to prevent such unsafe boats from setting out.

John Howard's war against boat people was well planned, timed, and executed. Its primary domestic political purpose was to win back one million One Nation voters, who saw strong border protection as a test of national leadership.

Three days after SIEV X sank on 19 October, 44 survivors were landed back in Jakarta on a fishing boat. Overnight, the disaster

Context for a Human Tragedy

Fig 1: This 'thumbnail' map was published in *The Australian* on 24 October 2001, accompanying front-page stories on the sinking, and was the first map published of where SIEV X sank. I tabled this map when testifying in the Senate CMI committee on 1 May 2002, and it was published as a CMI document.

There are still no official maps of where SIEV X sank, and government ministers and officials still falsely claim that the sinking location is unknown. [Map reproduced courtesy of News Ltd]

became front-page international news. Initially, it was not seen particularly as a story with Australian connections. Howard said firmly and repeatedly that the boat had sunk in Indonesian waters, and that it was not Australia's responsibility. Both claims were accepted at the time. Both were later shown to be untrue — even by the Australian government's reluctantly provided evidence.

This event had immediate and profound international consequences. Within two days, Indonesia acceded to Australia's long-standing demand to accept the return of asylum-seeker boats that the Royal Australian Navy towed back to the edge of Indonesian territorial waters (12 nautical miles from the Indonesian shoreline). Howard needed this Indonesian concession to show the electorate that his tough border-protection policies had worked. The sinking of SIEV X gave it to him. Indonesia also finally agreed to Australia's long-standing demand for an international diplomatic conference against people smuggling, and it was held in Bali in February 2002. Almost immediately, the boats stopped coming; the sinking of SIEV X finally deterred the trade in unauthorised asylum-seeker voyages from Indonesia to Australia. Most analysts have concluded that Howard gained re-election because his border-protection war had proved his credentials as a strong national leader. Would he have won without SIEV X?

In February 2002, I opened up the question of SIEV X as an issue for public inquiry. I asked the Senate committee that had just begun investigating the scandal of the misrepresented photographs of 'children overboard' to also examine unexplained, obvious questions about the sinking of this other asylum-seeker boat a few days later. I wanted to know how and why 353 asylum-seekers had died in this way, who within the Australian government and its agencies had known about the tragedy, what they knew about it, when they knew it, and what, if anything, they did or could have done about it. In March, I gave a working name to the nameless boat—SIEV X, or 'suspected illegal entry vessel, unknown'.[2] It was a convenient borrowing from the Department of Defence acronyms SIEV 1 through to SIEV 12, denoting the twelve asylum-seeker boats whose interception histories were being detailed by Defence in evidence to the CMI committee. My

Fig 2: *Sydney Morning Herald* artwork by Rocco Fazzari, 15 February 2002

proposed name was at first resisted; the preferred official usage was 'the Quassey boat', after the people smuggler who had, according to media reports, organised the voyage. However, my suggested name soon became official, because it was short and (I realise now) because it blurred the link between this story and Quassey.

Until we are told the real name of the boat it will continue to be known as SIEV X. The survivors don't know its name or its owner, though it must have had a registration name in Indonesia. Any name signs must have been erased or removed before the passengers boarded.

OVER THE PERIOD from March to September 2002, the CMI committee questioned official witnesses closely and received much written evidence on SIEV X. From the start, the committee was handicapped by official misrepresentations and by official refusals to provide information. For a few weeks in May and June, the SIEV X cover-up was front-page news. However, deft spin by the Defence Minister's office then took the issue off the boil. The turning point came when the CMI committee accepted the Defence Department's untrue written claim (submitted on 4 July) that 'Defence can only speculate as to where the vessel foundered', and did not insist on an appearance by the author of that advice (Rear Admiral Raydon Gates, who had prepared a review of Defence intelligence on SIEV X under instructions from the Defence Minister, Senator Robert Hill) for oral examination.

From that moment, the CMI committee's examination of whether the Australian Defence Force (ADF) might have failed in its responsibility to try to rescue the SIEV X passengers lost urgency and momentum. The ADF was let off the hook by the committee's tacit consensus. The committee's report, released on 23 October 2002, effectively exonerated the ADF from any blame for the failure to search for and try to rescue the SIEV X passengers. As Part Two of this book will show, we know now that this exoneration is highly questionable.[3]

The attention of opposition senators by July had shifted to Australia's people-smuggling disruption program in Indonesia. Australian Federal Police (AFP) Commissioner Mick Keelty was grilled on this by Senator John Faulkner, Labor's forceful leader of the opposition in the Senate, on 11 July 2002. Keelty revealed to the CMI committee startling evidence regarding this virtually unknown program's operations in Indonesia—evidence that greatly concerned Senator Faulkner and the committee's chairman, Senator Peter Cook.[4]

Faulkner was not going to let this issue go. He followed up his intense July interrogation with blistering Senate chamber statements on 23, 24, 25, and 26 September questioning the disruption program. For example, on 25 September, he said:

> I ask these questions: was Enniss [an informant paid by AFP who had purported to be a people smuggler] involved in the sabotage of vessels? Were others involved in the sabotage of vessels? Do Australian ministers, officials or agencies have knowledge of such activities? And what about the vessel now known as SIEV X, part of the people-smuggling operation of the notorious people smuggler Abu Quassey? That vessel set sail on 18 October 2001 and sank on 19 October 2001, drowning 353 people, including 142 women and 146 children. Were disruption activities directed against Quassey? Did these involve SIEV X? I intend to keep asking questions until I find out. And, Mr Acting Deputy President, I intend to keep pressing for an independent judicial inquiry into these very serious matters. At no stage do I want to break, nor will I break, the protocols in relation to operational matters involving ASIS or the AFP. *But those protocols were not meant as a direct or an indirect licence to kill.* [my italics]

Then, on 10 and 11 December 2002, the Senate, by agreement of non-government parties (Labor, Democrats, and Greens), passed two SIEV X motions that in important respects superseded the CMI committee's report. The first called for an independent judicial inquiry into the sinking of SIEV X and into the people-smuggling disruption program.[5] The second called for the alleged people smuggler Quassey (then in prison in Indonesia on minor passport offences, having never been charged by Indonesian authorities in relation to the sinking) to be brought to justice in Australia for his alleged role in the 353 deaths.[6]

The government treated Faulkner's speeches and the two Senate motions with contempt. It did not respond, and it took no steps to set up a judicial inquiry. It never tried to bring Quassey to trial in Australia or Indonesia on a charge of homicide (murder or manslaughter). The only alleged crime by Quassey that belatedly stirred the AFP into a little action was the Australian offence of 'people smuggling', which is not a crime in Indonesia.

One searches in vain for any official references at this time by the Minister for Justice and Customs, Senator Chris Ellison (responsible for the AFP), or Keelty to any operational consideration of homicide proceedings in respect of Quassey and SIEV X. Quassey could have been brought to Australia under discretionary provisions of the extradition treaty. The Indonesian Justice Minister, Yusril Mahendra, said on 1 February 2003 that he had been ready to hand Quassey over.[7] It seemed that the AFP was not interested in pursuing the death of 353 people who had immediate family members in Australia. To speak, as Ellison and the AFP did, of trying to bring Quassey to account for people smuggling was grotesquely inappropriate: it was like proposing to charge Martin Bryant for illegal possession of firearms after the Port Arthur massacre. In any case, the AFP never succeeded in bringing Quassey to Australia to face any charge. It was all smoke and mirrors.

Important additional items of SIEV X evidence became public early in 2003, but by this time the issue had been judged as pretty well over by the mainstream media in Australia. The conclusion by Marr and Wilkinson (*Dark Victory* came out in March 2003) that 'Australia did not kill those who drowned on SIEV X but their deaths can't be left out of the reckoning entirely' was not helpful. Their book gave credibility and an authoritative context for greater public understanding of the ruthless nature of Australia's border-protection war, but its conclusion on SIEV X did not seem to be based on close study of the evidence. Indeed, some facts first revealed in *Dark Victory* added further weight to my concerns.[8]

In 2003, references to SIEV X were infrequent in the mainstream media. But Marg Hutton's scrupulous archival and investigative website www.sievx.com, and my own speaking and writing campaign, kept the subject alive for those who cared to follow it. The highlights were the vigorous www.sievx.com public campaign following the Senate motions pressing Ellison and the AFP to bring Quassey to Australia for trial. Then came the public release in February 2003—16 months late, and eight months after the Senate had learned of its existence and asked to see it—of a crucial reporting cable from the Australian embassy in Jakarta that had been sent four days after SIEV X sank. This is the cable that is reproduced in the front pages of this book.

On 20 May 2003, www.sievx.com published 'SIEV X and the DFAT Cable: The Conspiracy of Silence', a research paper by Marg Hutton analysing the cover-up of official knowledge of the sinking position. In June the *Canberra Times* published two new www.sievx.com maps showing quite accurately where SIEV X had sunk in the Operation Relex zone, and how an RAAF Orion surveillance aircraft had flown directly overhead the next morning (both maps are reproduced in this book). Yet it had been claimed the previous July, in maps submitted to the CMI committee in the Gates review, that no wreckage, and no Indonesian fishing boats (which were rescuing survivors at the time), had been detected by this RAAF flight.[9]

The government's tactic in 2003 was to ignore anything to do with SIEV X in the hope that people would forget about it. I was derided as a conspiracy theorist, but my work on SIEV X led to some public recognition and approval: an International Whistleblower of the Year award, inclusion on the list of Just Australians of the Year, and inclusion in *The Bulletin's* 'Newsmakers of 2003' list. All this helped to keep the story alive.

Labor continued to pursue a low-key investigation in Senate Estimates committees during 2003–04 but seemed loath to go public with the issue. However, new evidence gradually built up in the Hansard records in response to probing from Senators Faulkner, Jacinta Collins, Andrew Bartlett, and Bob Brown. Government ministers and senior officials frequently answered evasively or declined to answer, on grounds that senators could not contest. The official lack of cooperation became more confident and brazen. Hutton and I kept track of answers and supplementary documentary evidence, recording and analysing its accumulating log of discrepancies and inconsistencies, but it seemed that no one else was listening. As one national journalist said: 'All you are doing now is just putting new flakes onto a layer cake. Nobody is interested any more in SIEV X.'

THIS BOOK highlights the wealth of disturbing on-the-record Senate testimony (and questions arising from this testimony) that I believe invited the following propositions and questions:

- It is likely that the alleged people smuggler Abu Quassey was a police disruption or 'sting' agent. This is suggested by the sustained high-level of Indonesian and Australian protection before, during, and after the sinking of SIEV X, as well as by subsequent AFP attempts to help minimise his sentence in his 2003 trial in Egypt and render him immune from further prosecution.
- As Commissioner Keelty reluctantly admitted, the conduct of Indonesian police people-smuggling disruption teams — initially set up, trained, equipped, and funded by the AFP — was out of AFP control, and criminality in Indonesian disruption operations (for example, the deliberate sinking of boats) could not be ruled out.
- There was a pattern of disruption operations in Indonesia before SIEV X, involving frequent sinkings and voyage failures in Indonesian waters, and of the progressive elimination of autonomous people smugglers from the Indonesian market in order to clear the way for 'sting'

operators in contact with disruption programs.
- The strikingly precise official and media reporting soon after the sinking of SIEV X, covering, for example, the boat's size, structure, fuel capacity, and passenger details, could not have come from survivors; it must have been provided by sources close to the organisers of the SIEV X voyage.
- Tracking devices may have been fitted on board; if so by whom?
- Reports of radio distress-messages sent from SIEV X remain unexplained.
- Survivors reported the appearance of military-type vessels which failed to rescue survivors. Where did they come from?
- The arrival of a well organised rescue operation the next day and the return of survivors by boat to Jakarta, along with the close management of news and information, is suspicious.
- What is the provenance and significance of a photograph of SIEV X, taken before it got into trouble, and allegedly shown to two survivors by Australian police officials?

My close study of the SIEV X public record leads me to ask whether there was from the beginning an undeclared 'back channel' of tasking and information management. Did such a channel run, possibly through intermediaries, between Australian national-security agencies working from the Jakarta embassy—the AFP and perhaps the Australian Secret Intelligence Service (ASIS)—and Indonesian police disruption-teams working with or through Quassey?

There may be another explanation, but we will never find out if there is no full-powers judicial inquiry, and if government agencies continue to block Senate questions. The record of resolute official covering-up suggests that something dishonourable, and probably illegal, lies at the centre of this story.

QUASSEY FLEW HOME to Egypt in April 2003 under Egyptian police protection after the AFP failed to have him brought to Australia.

He went on trial in Cairo in September that year for manslaughter related to the SIEV X sinking. The AFP quickly inserted itself into the process, delivering six boxes of documentary evidence to the Egyptian embassy in Canberra and insisting that it be sent to law enforcement authorities prosecuting the trial.[10] Soon after this evidence was provided, the charge was apparently reduced to accidental manslaughter. The Australian embassy in Cairo took a close interest in the trial, which was reportedly held in a closed national security court. There was little reporting of proceedings. On 27 December, Quassey's sentence of seven years imprisonment was announced — two for people smuggling and five for the accidental manslaughter of 353 people. This meant about one week in prison for each death. No details of the evidence presented, or of witnesses (testifying in court or in sworn written testimony), have been made public.[11]

By blocking full transparency on the sinking of SIEV X, at the Senate investigative level and at the criminal justice level, Australian government agencies are helping to shield what may be capital crimes by Abu Quassey and his Indonesian associates. Government agencies or their supporters might respond that no crime has been legally established, but this profoundly misconstrues public-accountability obligations. 'You can't prove anything' is not a proper response from a government agency to well-founded questions from the Senate about possible Australian agency associations with criminality in a matter of 353 deaths.

The responsible ministers have backed evasive tactics by officials, shrugging off the issue with rhetoric. AFP minister Ellison in May 2003 repeatedly challenged the relevance of questions on 'events over two years ago' to AFP budget estimates for 2003–04,[12] and Foreign Minister Alexander Downer in December 2003 airily dismissed Senate motions on SIEV X as 'just a political stunt'.[13]

The cover-up of the drownings is a systemic problem for Australia, because the SIEV X issue is about justice for all who come within our national security authorities' proper duty of care. If the lives of asylum-seekers don't matter — people drowned inside Australia's declared border-protection zone in a boat that had been monitored by Australia's people-smuggling disruption program—none of our lives matter. And that should concern even the most hard-nosed among us. Justice is indivisible.

LIVING THROUGH THE SIEV X inquiry process for two years has shaken my trust in the integrity of Australia's machinery of government. As a former senior public servant who worked for 30 years in two sensitive national security departments (Foreign Affairs, and Prime Minister and Cabinet), I had always assumed there was some bedrock of honour that would impose moral limits on what government agencies might do—that there were administrative safeguards and implicit value-based understandings that certain kinds of conduct would be recognised as intolerable and quickly brought to public attention by responsible officials. (Senator Faulkner must feel the same, as he has pursued this case at no apparent political gain to himself or Labor.)

However, after the blocked SIEV X inquiry, that faith has gone. I now think that practically anything is possible at the national security level. Many senior people can be induced or pressured to help sustain a whole-of-government cover-up, as long as they can convince themselves that the issue is about national security. This applies to not only the less accountable intelligence agencies like ASIS, but also the fully accountable organisations such as the ADF, AFP, the Department of Immigration (DIMIA), and the Department of Foreign Affairs and Trade (DFAT). There are no longer meaningful checks and balances if a prime minister, the national security ministers, and their senior advisers are prepared to manipulate information to cover up politically inconvenient truths.

Prime ministers now have enormous influence over their ministers and backbenchers, and over senior officials in federal agencies. The power to make or break careers is wielded vigorously, and those who lead federal agencies transmit that power down to the rank and file. Holding the line for the boss means special rewards, and vice versa.

The agenda-setting reach of executive power even extends to opinion makers outside government—editors and commentators, leaders of research institutes and think tanks, heads of professional and service associations, and so on. Institutions that depend in various ways on the public purse, or government patronage and support, now more frequently tailor their contribution to public debate to what they feel is acceptable to government.

The rules have changed: the imagined protections of our informal, plural system of governance are fading away. The unthinkable becomes thinkable, and exposure of official wrongdoing can no longer be taken for granted. It has to be fought for by people prepared to take risks.

When I started my public work on SIEV X, I hoped that it might become an Australian Watergate, that it might be the lever that would pry open the Howard government's manifold cruelties towards boat people. I was wrong. An Australian Watergate is probably impossible, because we don't have the political culture that enabled the exposure of President Richard Nixon's crimes: a true separation of powers between the national leader and the legislature, a tradition of independent investigative journalism, and financially self-supporting public institutions that are not dependent on government appointments or access.

Bob Woodward and Carl Bernstein, the journalists who broke the Watergate story that eventually ended Nixon's presidency of the United States, took personal risks, but they had enormous institutional backing. The experience of Andrew Wilkie in 2003, the Office of National Assessments whistleblower who resigned from his job as senior intelligence officer in protest at the Howard government's allegedly dishonest use of intelligence in committing Australia to the invasion of Iraq, showed that Australian officials who speak out don't get that kind of support.

A closer analogy to SIEV X is the HMAS Voyager disaster of 1964. During routine night manoeuvres, an intoxicated captain steered his destroyer into the path of the aircraft carrier HMAS Melbourne, which sliced his vessel in two. Eighty-two seamen, including those on HMAS Voyager's bridge, perished. Under political pressure, a compliant royal commission ordered by prime minister Robert Menzies set up the blameless captain of HMAS Melbourne to take the fall. It took Captain Ronald Robertson and his supporters four years of lobbying, culminating in an unprecedented second royal commission set up by Menzies' successor, Harold Holt, for the truth to come out. We may have to wait for John Howard's successor for the truth on SIEV X.

Once my questions on the sinking of SIEV X were raised publicly in 2002, the matter should have alerted us to the poison seeping into our system of governance — a poison that would lead to more abuses of executive power.

Since SIEV X there have been many instances of government misuse of power. These include the attempt (fortunately bungled) to destroy Justice Michael Kirby's reputation and tenure as a High Court judge; Foreign Minister Alexander Downer's curiously neglected duty of care during the 13 months before the Bali bombings in October 2002 to pass on to Australian travellers three well-founded generic intelligence warnings of possible terrorist

Fig 3: *Australian Financial Review* artwork by Ward O'Neill, 20 September 2003

incidents in Indonesia in bars frequented by Westerners; the misrepresentation of intelligence on Saddam Hussein's weapons of mass destruction to convince the public of the urgent need for a war in Iraq without United Nations authority; the use of Australia's SAS forces in secret pre-emptive combat in Iraq before the war was officially under way; and the manipulation of Al-Qaeda terrorist threats in Australia to frighten us into acceptance of laws giving the Australian Security Intelligence Organisation greater arrest and interrogation powers. All these pressures have led to the undermining of the nation's civil liberties and multicultural values.

We should have recognised the importance of the SIEV X disaster as a signal of how ruthless the Howard government was prepared to be.

Once political pressure pushed the agencies' senior officials onto the slippery slope of helping to block the SIEV X investigation, it was difficult for them to turn back. To do so would have been to admit the initial wrong-doing. This is how lies become locked into bureaucratic systems. The corruption of public institutions starts small, then grows as more people become incriminated and compromised. Service loyalties, and a concern to protect careers, do the rest. And lies are much harder to resist down the line if they have started from the top.

The blocked investigation of SIEV X extends even to concealing the names of the dead. Here is how Senator Ellison replied in August 2003 to a request from Greens Senator Bob Brown to make public the list of names of those drowned in the SIEV X sinking, a request that had been put six months earlier:

> A list was provided to the AFP from a confidential source after the vessel sank. Provision of any details of that list would compromise that source. It may also compromise a current ongoing investigation in Indonesia. The list purports to contain some details of passengers, but its veracity has not been tested. The AFP believes it is unlikely that a full and comprehensive list of those who boarded SIEV X or those who subsequently drowned will ever be available.[14]

Imagine how Australians would respond to being told that the names of its dead in Bali would be withheld, possibly forever, and for such spurious reasons. The reluctance by Ellison and the AFP to release the names of passengers, survivors, and victims—a list to which they almost certainly have access—is understandable. It would have raised awkward questions as to when, how, and from whom the AFP was able to obtain such detailed and precise information.

Hence the verbal gymnastics of the Ellison answer, a fairly typical example of the way Senate questions on SIEV X have been routinely fudged by government agencies. Officials would rather not lie if they can help it, so the art of verbal sleight-of-hand, the '90 per cent lie', is increasingly practised by career-conscious bureaucrats in John Howard's Canberra. The drafters of the above reply could not be said to have lied were the passenger list ever produced, for instance, in response to a demand from a full-powers judicial inquiry. Enough semantic escape clauses have been written into it to protect AFP officials from possible perjury charges. They have carefully avoided claiming that no such list exists.

With every such craftily worded reply to Senate questions our formally accountable government agencies dig themselves deeper into a systemic cover-up. Technically they may seem to be winning, yet many decent people inside and outside these organisations must know by now that serious questions are being evaded.

WHY THE PUBLIC APATHY in Australia about SIEV X, even as the truth is gradually being pieced together? We are mostly silent because to acknowledge what may have happened would be unsettling and shaming.

Part of our SIEV X denial mechanism is the claim that Australians could not do such bad things because 'we are not like that'. So it is important to say that evil-doing in complex bureaucracies does not require evil intentions by individuals. The writings of Hannah Arendt, Zygmunt Bauman, and others who have studied the nature of evil in modern societies show how evil

Fig 4: *Canberra Times* artwork by Geoff Pryor, 13 December 2001

deeds can result from 'average' people just doing their designated jobs as part of the machinery of state.[15]

Officials who consider themselves decent people may have just 'sleepwalked' (to use Mark Lilla's apt word) through their duties. They still may not recognise the moral gravity of what they were involved in. This book might help them better to understand how, although modern bureaucratic systems diffuse and blur responsibility, such systems do not obviate the need for the exercise of individual conscience.[16]

HOW DID ENGAGING IN SIEV X affect me? To this point, authorities have not taken any legal action, I think for several reasons. I have a record of 30 years' loyal and efficient service as an Australian senior diplomat who twice held the rank of ambassador, giving me public credibility that is not easy to undermine. I am asking legitimate questions about the public and covert conduct of government agencies, but I am not defaming individuals. I do not seek to subvert officials or seek improper access to official secrets. My SIEV X campaign is intended to defend the important values of justice and accountability, which have broad public resonance in Australia.

Yet there have been effective sanctions against me, starting in September 2002 with what looked like a concerted effort by the three government senators who took part in the CMI committee's inquiry to discredit (under the protection of Senate privilege) my career achievements and integrity. I successfully challenged these unfounded assertions in the Senate Committee on Privileges.[17] Since that time, my access to mainstream media as a freelance public affairs commentator has diminished as my SIEV X critique has hardened. I have, I believe, been quietly but effectively marginalised from the governance-centred society in Canberra to which I once comfortably belonged.

Governments put whistleblowers under a variety of pressures. Such tactics were employed against Iraq War whistleblowers—the British weapons specialist Dr David Kelly, who committed suicide, and Andrew Wilkie, who resigned from Australia's Office of National Assessments—and recently against Lieutenant Colonel Lance Collins. Wilkie and I came through the most dangerous phase, the time when one is still trying to work through the internal conflict between wanting to retain a belief in the public service institutions to which one's professional career has been devoted and the sober realisation of how these institutions have become vulnerable to improper pressures from above.

My campaign for SIEV X accountability is mostly on behalf of the victims, living and dead. I began as a horrified witness to news of the event. Four months later, I chose to become involved because I saw something was not right. It was then a matter of conscience to start asking questions. No one else was doing it.

But now my efforts are also aimed at helping to defend public accountability in Australia. SIEV X has become part of a bigger challenge. SIEV X is different in kind to the other national cruelties against boat people: the iniquitous temporary protection visa system, the indefinite locking-up of children in detention centres (high-security prisons) for years, the camps in Papua New Guinea and Nauru, and coerced deportation.[18] SIEV X involved 353 deaths, and death is the final irredeemable cruelty. This brings a different kind of response, focused as much on questions of criminal justice as on public decency. SIEV X should not only concern 'bleeding hearts', it should also concern anyone who cares about Australia remaining a society based on law. If something as lethal as the SIEV X sinking can be officially covered up, anything can be.

For all these good reasons of national self-interest, as well as a desire to help achieve closure for the many living victims of SIEV X — the survivors and bereaved families — we must get to the bottom of this scandal. We have to demand truth and accountability about SIEV X from the Australian government.

How the groundwork for SIEV X was laid

The government of Prime Minister John Howard was re-elected late in 1998. Secure at the beginning of his second term, he began to review the issue of border protection: how to keep boat people from the Middle East out of Australia. Howard seems to have identified this as a national-security priority, as well as an electorally advantageous cause, long before the terrorist attacks in the United States on 11 September 2001.

During 1999, the Australian government initiated a range of internal public-service policy reviews to study how border-control mechanisms and deterrents to unauthorised arrivals of boats carrying asylum-seekers could be strengthened. There was concern that the number of asylum-seekers was creeping up because of political instability in Afghanistan, Iraq, and Iran. Most of the asylum-seekers from the Middle East were still trying to enter Europe, but an alternative route seemed to be developing towards Australia.

Howard and his then powerful head of the Department of Prime Minister and Cabinet, Max Moore-Wilton, saw the task as a whole-of-government issue from the beginning — a national security operational matter that also needed a supporting public information strategy. Central to that strategy was to lodge two ideas firmly in the consciousness of national security agencies and the public: that Australia's national sovereignty was being threatened by boat people entering through 'porous' maritime borders, and that people smuggling was a big and rapidly growing international criminal business. These ideas were to be the rationale for enlisting the ADF, the AFP, and even ASIS as protagonists in what had been a low-key civilian border-protection regime run by Coastwatch, an agency of the Customs Department.

Over 2000–01, those two messages—with enthusiastic help from the mainstream media, which saw the news value in them—were driven home. We were all being indoctrinated to fear and hate the people smugglers and to dehumanise their 'human cargo' which, it was claimed, threatened the integrity of our borders.[19]

All successful propaganda campaigns tap into an existing cultural base. The Nazis tapped into layers of anti-semitism in Germany, albeit that Jews had been safe enough before the Nazis came to power. Certainly the fear of uncontrolled arrivals of boat people, and the cultural problems some Australians have in accepting Middle Eastern Muslims, were already there in sections of the populace. Howard was happy to stir up this potent devil's brew. Previous prime ministers—Gough Whitlam, Malcolm Fraser, Bob Hawke, and Paul Keating—had tried to lead Australians away from such visceral fears and prejudices. Howard set out to take the nation back to them.

The Prime Minister's Department was put in charge of new policy making. Jane Halton, then Moore-Wilton's trusted deputy, chaired interdepartmental committees to draw the new policy lines together. She made sure that departmental representatives understood the broader issues at stake and the prime minister's determination to bring about a real change in how boat people were to be dealt with. 'Leave your personal baggage [moral scruples] at the door', was her reported watchword to the more timid or scrupulous.

The policy development was firm and rapid. The Department of Immigration and Multicultural Affairs (DIMA) tightened up the detention-camp regime and temporary protection visa system, worked on a public-information strategy, and prepared (with DFAT) to negotiate possible overseas detention solutions. The AFP duly elevated people smuggling to the proportions of major criminality, and obtained generous new administrative and staff budgets to combat it. People smuggling was to be the AFP's entry into the international big league (this was before terrorism gave the AFP an even greater opportunity for international growth). The AFP and DIMA set up a joint 'people-smuggling strike team' to look at ways of combating the problem at its source in other lands, where people smuggling was seen not as a crime but as an ethical business that helped desperate homeless people to move between countries.

The ADF was told to prepare to take over border protection from Coastwatch and to find legal ways of circumventing sacrosanct 'safety of life at sea' maritime service obligations when these might get in the way of deterrence and repelling unauthorised boats. The national search-and-rescue organisation, which comes under the Australian Maritime Safety Authority (AMSA), was told to review its protocols for rescue at sea; to establish a special regime for SIEVs in trouble that would not require them to be rescued by ADF border-protection elements if that burden could legally be shifted to Indonesia.

Most of these policy-development processes would have taken place out of the public eye and not properly recorded in writing. The most important and sensitive messages would have been conveyed by nuance—meaningful nods, raised eyebrows, etc—and preferably in the corridors rather than in formal committee. Yet enough information has leaked out in the CMI committee and subsequent inquiries to give a sense of what was being set in place.

A hypothetical conversation

At this point I want to use a dramatic device, an imaginary interdepartmental conversation, to encapsulate some of the issues that officials would have grappled with in this period as they were establishing new policies. These policies were fully operational by the time of the 'children overboard' incident and, a few days later, when SIEV X sank. I am not claiming that such a conversation took place, but the following should give a flavour for the kind of considerations that might well have exercised the minds of departmental officers around this time:

> **Department A**: The Prime Minister wants these illegal boat people arriving from Indonesia decisively stopped or sent back. He wants to send a clear signal that people cannot expect to be accepted into Australia if they try to come by this illegal route. How do we achieve this?
>
> **Department B**: Locating and arresting SIEV boats has never been a problem. We have excellent ADF long-distance maritime surveillance capability, for example, through JORN long-distance military radar,[20] and Coastwatch can make efficient interceptions using its small patrol boats. In any case, it is rare that boats try to sneak migrants in illegally. Most suspected illegal immigrants are keen to declare themselves and submit to our refugee-entry processing. We have never tried to push these boats back, say, by using the navy. Overseas experience suggests that passengers might try to disable or sink their boats in front of us rather than return to Indonesia voluntarily. They would count on our international legal and humanitarian obligation to rescue them from sinking boats, under our 'rescue at sea' commitments. And the navy could not stand by and watch people drowning. We cannot tow these boats back to Indonesia either, because the Indonesians would not accept their return. The Indonesian view is that once boats approach our territorial waters, they are our problem.
>
> **Department A**: OK then, how do we stop these boats from leaving Indonesia or reduce their numbers?
>
> **Department C**: That is difficult, too, because Indonesia at national government level is unsympathetic to our concerns on this. In fact, the Indonesians are rather glad to see us having this problem, as payback for our interventionist role in East Timor's independence in 1999. In any case,

Indonesia does not have the police or military resources to monitor hundreds of little harbours and bays to prevent small boats from leaving. And people-moving is not a crime in Indonesia. Small-boat traffic is unregulated, and the small-boat fishing industry is depressed and looking for other income. As long as there is a demand for this trade, and as long as it is reasonably safe, it will happen. People smugglers can earn enough money to bribe poorly paid local police to turn a blind eye to such voyages.

Department A: So what leverage do we have?

Other departments/agencies: Very little now, at national intergovernmental level. But we still have some good contacts with senior people in the Indonesian police, military and intelligence services; people well disposed to Australia and/or open to bribes. Money takes you a long way in Indonesia. Our security agencies could work on these personal contacts to develop good intelligence on people smugglers and their voyages, and also to encourage counterpart Indonesian agencies and individuals to disrupt people-smuggling operations on our behalf.

One could envisage covert deterrent operations carried out by us directly, or preferably by undercover agents, that would support a public information strategy portraying people smuggling as a dangerous area of organised crime, and a risk to passengers' savings and lives. We would need to recruit agents in Indonesia to help us obtain intelligence, and we would need local police co-operation to put people smugglers progressively out of business.

We could not hope to stop all boats from leaving, but through local agents we could over time make the trade more of a problem for people smugglers and their passengers.

Obviously, the more boats that experience engine failure or sink, the more passengers that lose their savings and risk their lives on overloaded unsafe boats, and the more that people smugglers are harassed and put out of business by Indonesian authorities, then the less attractive the trade will become to entrepreneurs and their passengers.

Penetration of the trade would be part of an efficient strategy (as it is in international police operations to disrupt the drug trade). We would seek to finance and shelter 'sting' operations in areas where asylum-seekers concentrate, for instance, West Java and in the Timor/Lombok area. Such operations would be intelligence sources and would also build 'market share' in the people smuggling trade so as to be ready to disrupt and dismantle it at the appropriate time.

We would aim over time to replace autonomous people smugglers by operators under our influence, or under our Indonesian police colleagues' influence.

Department A: These sound like pretty dubious operations that would verge on being illegal, if not actually being illegal.

Departments/agencies: Yes, and so we would need to structure what we were doing carefully, keeping our official contact people in Indonesia at plausibly deniable arm's length from whatever our local agents had been trained to do. The money, training and equipment would necessarily come from us, but we would be wise not to ask exactly what the local agents were doing to disrupt people smuggling—at least, not in any formal reporting sense. Informally, we would try to keep a general handle on what was happening. It would be better for our liaison people not to know certain things. Our general training would cover things like information management in ways that would protect us from any early exposure of Indonesian police or undercover disruption action that might be inconsistent with our operating protocols or with the ADF's obligations on rescue at sea.

A stepped-up ADF border-protection system would only need to receive processed intelligence from Indonesia on boats that were definitely coming into the ADF's interception area. ADF would not need to know about boats that had been prevented, by whatever means, from coming into the area.

Public information would be an important part of the operation—a strong international campaign warning of the dangers of using people smugglers would complement whatever might be being done by our partners to deter, discredit and dismantle the trade. Friendly media contacts could be given preferred Australian embassy briefings to help disseminate the messages we wanted conveyed.

Obviously the less that was publicly known in Australia about such disruption activities the better. It would risk offending legal and humanitarian sensitivities, and it would confuse our effort in Australia to portray people smugglers as ruthless, highly organised criminal syndicates and their passengers as rich queue-jumpers. We would not want to risk public sympathy for the passengers: they would need to remain in the public perception as anonymous and threatening to our security.

Department A: How quickly do you see such a disruption program achieving the desired results?

Other departments/agencies: It's hard to be precise—one or two years. Indonesia is a big country with a lot of small ports and a lot of people wanting to make a bit of money out of moving refugees. We would never be able to stop the odd freelance fishing boat setting out. But once our agents were in place in the main refugee centres, and the word got around that 'our' people smugglers enjoyed reliable police protection and were not being arrested or exposed as others were, they should be able to quickly knock out competition from autonomous people smugglers and build their market share. The asylum-seekers would soon have no other option but to use our people. Thus we would be in a position to close down the trade whenever we wanted—perhaps after one or two dramatic demonstrations of failed voyages to kill off the demand.

WE KNOW from AFP oral and written testimony in the CMI committee (from Commissioner Mick Keelty) and other source documents that by late 2000 the AFP had set up a functioning people-smuggling disruption program in Indonesia.[21] The AFP had signed a people-smuggling protocol with the Indonesian National Police (POLDA). It was an adjunct to an existing bilateral AFP/POLDA agreement against organised transnational crime. The text of this protocol has never been published, but it was probably pretty broad and general. An undisclosed number of AFP informants (including an Australian, Kevin Enniss, who was based in Kupang in West Timor), were reporting to the AFP.[22] Twenty Indonesian police officers had been trained in disruption techniques by the AFP in a special week-long course in Bali during October 2000. The police were organised into five regionally based 'special intelligence unit' (SIU) teams—three in Eastern Indonesia in areas that gave good access to Ashmore Reef, and two in Jakarta and West Java that gave good access to Christmas Island.[23]

Following the 'Tampa crisis' in August 2001, Howard was quick to announce a beefed-up maritime border-protection operation, with the ADF now put in charge. The Norwegian vessel Tampa rescued from a sinking fishing boat 433 refugees, who had to stay put in extreme heat under the control of Australian SAS troops as the freighter anchored off Christmas Island waiting for the refugees to be taken to detention centres elsewhere. The incident was the tripwire for a new system, Operation Relex, that had long been planned and 'gamed'. Operation Relex was a far more ambitious border-protection operation than anything that had gone before. It would use, in a highly visible way, navy and airforce resources which, we were told, would monitor and aggressively patrol international waters north of Christmas Island and Ashmore Reef, to within 24 miles of Indonesia.[24] Authoritatively sourced media articles gave a clear warning of the Australian government's firm intention to deter and repel illegal boats.

Yet Howard took care to temper his message, claiming to set ethical limits on the new operation. Even as he announced stepped-up border protection early in September (just in time for the election), he reassured the public: 'We don't, in this nation, sink boats.'[25]

THE INVESTIGATION OF SIEV X and the AFP disruption program in the CMI committee and subsequently in Estimates committees has been a fascinating battle of minds and wills between four able and determined, but ultimately powerless, opposition senators — Peter Cook (chairman), John Faulkner, Jacinta Collins, and Andrew Bartlett — against senior official witnesses and their protecting ministers intent on revealing as little of the truth as they had to, by taking advantage of various ministerial and legal devices to delay, misconstrue, or simply refuse to answer questions.

Official witnesses' claimed reasons for withholding answers included 'operational' matters (whatever this means), public-interest immunity, protection of sensitive intelligence or other sources, protection of matters of national security or foreign relations, matters that could compromise upcoming or planned legal proceedings against people smugglers, and even the impertinent claim that 'these old matters have already been dealt with'. Sometimes official witnesses took questions or requests on notice then simply forgot to reply, requiring repeated reminders. For the senators, establishing the truth on SIEV X has been like getting blood out of a stone.

Ministers and officials attempted serious misrepresentations and concealment of the truth. Some of these attempts have not yet been challenged by senators; some, after being successfully challenged, were quietly modified or set aside by officials. There was never any sanction or exposure of official transgressions: the CMI committee's report drew a discreet veil over them.

In the end, the effectiveness of Senate committee investigative powers depends on a mutual acceptance by all involved that the rules of the game require truth and integrity from officials representing government agencies whose actions are being questioned. Senators cannot punish officials who lie — they cannot even shame them by saying they do not believe what they are being told, as this would be abusing Senate privilege. If senators point out manifest inconsistencies, officials can fall back on bland 'clarifications' of or 'corrections' to what they have testified.

Finally, as Senator Bartlett gently observed, when the truth is buried under acres of blackout ink in official documents, there is not a great deal senators can do about it.

The incomplete investigation of SIEV X is a dramatic example of the heavy strain now being put on the Senate public accountability system. Yet no serious writer on public administration or Senate powers has tackled the SIEV X case professionally. I hope that after this book is published someone might do so. *Quis custodiet custodes*? Who protects us from the nation's security agencies if their conduct has gone off the rails? We have to remove the 'Do Not Touch' sign that the authorities have hung on this story.

We cannot wait 30 years or more for truth and justice. The survivors and bereaved families at least deserve a chance of closure. And we need to be able to look them in the eye again.

Chapter Two

Embarkation

15–16 October
Abu Quassey and his three assistants recruit around 430 passengers in Bogor-Cisarua area for a boat journey to Christmas Island.

16 October, late evening
Quassey's four-bus convoy departs Bogor-Cisarua escorted by Indonesian police brigadier Agus Safuan.

17 October, early morning
Convoy (after car ferry across Sunda Strait from Merak) arrives in local police chief's hotel, Bandar Lampung, Sumatra, where passengers stay during the day and evening.

18 October, midnight to dawn
Passengers are bussed to nearby Canti Bay and loaded by force onto SIEV X by Quassey and his assistants, helped by 30 armed Indonesian police.

THIS CHAPTER TELLS OF THE FIRST STAGE of the passengers' journey, from their departure by bus from the Bogor–Cisarua area (in Western Java, south of Jakarta) to their embarkation on SIEV X from Canti Bay near Bandar Lampung, south Sumatra.

Sources of evidence

Many named survivors' statements were quoted or cited by Western journalists filing reports in the immediate days after the return of survivors to Jakarta on 22 October, three days after the sinking. Despite their shock, grief, and exhaustion, these survivors as a group were offering accounts of what were still very fresh memories. They had no motive for telling lies to journalists.

The media reports listed below also draw on information from other sources, sometimes named but usually not, that the journalists used to fill out 'background' to the story. It cannot be assumed that such background information was necessarily truthful in content or truthfully sourced.

Nevertheless, the survivor accounts and media reports together comprise a valuable corpus of multi-source evidence. Pending an independent judicial inquiry into the SIEV X disaster with powers to compel truthful official testimonies, these early accounts taken as a whole are the best-quality evidence we have. Most of them were published well before the 2002 work of the Senate CMI committee. Yet very few of them were ever drawn to the committee's attention, except the few items that I came across accidentally in my early inexpert reading of the print media. I tendered them as appendices to my submissions and oral testimony.

The committee attached little if any weight to newspaper reports or survivor accounts. As far as I know, the committee never interviewed SIEV X survivors or journalists who had met them. It relied from beginning to end on the presumed integrity of official testimony.

Much of the remarkably extensive Australian and international media reporting listed below was not known to me until late in 2002. Most of it came from Marg Hutton's internet research after she began in 2002 to search media archives for SIEV X reportage to post on her website, www.sievx.com. Had I known of this material before I testified, some of my evidence to the CMI committee might have been more robust.

The few pieces of evidence that I was aware of at the time gave me enough to question the official record, and that was all I was trying to do. At that stage, I still trusted in the integrity of the public accountability system, once I had raised legitimate questions of potential criminality, to pursue them to a proper conclusion.

A videotape of survivor accounts, made in Bogor by a team of Iraqi–Australian sympathisers on the weekend of 27–28 October 2001, a week after the tragedy, and subsequently translated into English by Keysar Trad, is especially strong primary evidence. The survivors are speaking with one another in a group meeting, in their own language. The Trad translation is on www.sievx.com, and copies of the videotape are available.

The most important retrospective reportage, in terms of focussed questioning and drawing out of new material, was carried out by an Arabic-speaking journalist talking some months later with many survivors living as refugees in several countries. Ghassan Nakhoul's Walkley Award-winning Arabic-language documentary *Five Mysteries of SIEV X* was broadcast by SBS Radio in August 2002.

The media material quoted is referred to by the author's name. All reports, except where noted, are readily accessible on www.sievx.com.[1]

The beginning

Bogor, and nearby Cisarua and Cipanas, once little resort towns in the hills south of Jakarta, offer low-priced villas and guesthouses for Middle Eastern tourists. This meant that asylum-seekers could blend in, living frugally while they negotiated with people smugglers for their voyage to Australia or explored slender resettlement possibilities with the UNHCR and IOM offices in Jakarta.

One of them was a young Iraqi married woman, Sondos Ismail.[2] Accompanied by her mother and her three little daughters, Eman (8), Zhra (6), and Fatimah (5), Sondos was in a Cisarua guesthouse, looking for a smuggler to take them to Christmas Island.

Sondos was only 25 but had already experienced a harsh life. Her father was killed by Saddam's secret police when she was five. When she was 15, her Shia Muslim family had fled from persecution to Iran. At 17 she met and married Ahmed Al-zalime, also an

Iraqi refugee. They were very poor, and eked out a frugal living selling food on the streets of Tehran. They had four children, but one died as a baby for want of food and medical care. Six years later, a brother living in the US sent Ahmed a precious stake of US$3000 to seek a better life for the family in the West. They chose to try for Australia, which they had been assured was a kind and generous country.

Ahmed went first in 1999. He was lucky—he secured a paid safe passage on an Indonesian boat, arriving late in 1999. After a period in detention, he was accepted as a refugee. But under punitive new laws passed in 1999 his temporary protection visa did not allow his family to join him, and he was not allowed to visit them. So they had to use people smugglers to try to be reunited, a move that was a much riskier proposition in 2001 than it had been for Ahmed.

In Tehran, a people smuggler had organised travel for Sondos and her family to Indonesia, via Malaysia. After two months in Kuala Lumpur, they were crammed with 114 others into a small wooden boat for three days, with little food and water. The journey to Indonesia ended when the engine failed off the north coast of Sumatra. Another two-month wait followed in Indonesian immigration detention.

Now Sondos was in Cisarua, looking for a new people-smuggler to take the family on the last sea voyage.[3] She did not have to look far. The Middle Eastern associates of a prominent Egyptian people smuggler, Abu Quassey, approached her.[4]

It is noteworthy that none of the survivor accounts mention negotiating passages with any people-smuggling group other than Quassey's. He seems to have cornered the market in the Bogor area by October 2001.

Quassey's assistants assured Sondos that they would deliver her family to nearby Christmas Island. They promised that Quassey's boat was safe and modern, with three decks, comfortable, well provisioned, and carrying radio and navigation equipment. They offered a cut-price deal: US$500 for her, and the three girls could travel free. Sondos thought this oddly inexpensive, because her husband's passage three years before had cost US$1200. But, being poor, she accepted.

The issue of fares is important to the question of whether greed could have been the main cause of the dangerous overloading of SIEV X. Survivors' fare information varied widely, but the weight of survivor accounts suggests that Quassey and his associates were offering heavily discounted adult travel on this voyage, as low as $500, and free places to some children.[5] This suggests he was keen to fill the boat quickly. Quassey's reported generosity towards women and children passengers may help to explain why, of the 353 who drowned, 146 were children and 142 were women.

Sondos was told to pack quickly because the bus was leaving that night (Tuesday, 16 October). She made a last call to her husband from a phone booth, to tell him the final stage of their journey was under way. He begged her not to risk the sea voyage but she was determined: she had to end her family's misery, the two years apart in a limbo of waiting. The children came on the phone, excited at the prospect of soon seeing their father. Eman told her father as he sat in his bleak Western Sydney flat: 'I want to be with you again, father, I want to see you'.[6] It was the last time Ahmed heard his daughters' voices.

Around Bogor and Cisarua, other women and children made similar calls to their menfolk in Australia. Ali Mahdi Al-Sobie of Sydney can recall his last conversation with his wife and daughters Donia (14), Marwa (12), and Hajar (10):

> They said to me, 'Dad, we are coming to you, meet us. I swear' ... The little one kept saying, 'Pray for us. I swear, Daddy, we will come. It's a matter of a short time'. I said to them, 'My heart is aching. I am very worried. How are you going to cross the sea?' She said, ' What else can we do, Daddy? How long do we have to remain this far apart? Let us come. God will either help us, or take us'. God took them.[7]

The cold cruelty of Australian policies that created such misery is now well known.[8] By October 2001, thousands of Middle

Eastern male asylum-seekers—mostly from Iraq and Afghanistan—had reached Australia by boat. These men were either still in detention camps awaiting final decisions on their refugee status, or they had been granted refugee status and were living in the Australian community on three-year temporary protection visas (as was the situation for the husband of Sondos). In either case, the men could never legally bring their wives and children to Australia.

The families who had fled oppression in Iraq and Afghanistan to nearby countries where they could not safely resettle were finding it legally impossible to come to Australia as refugees. If a family member had already come here as a boat person, Australia for that very reason would exclude them from consideration. Australian policy was that even people accepted by the UNHCR office in Jakarta as refugees would not be considered for entry, because the Department of Immigration was anxious not to strengthen what it called 'pull factors' that might give asylum-seeker family members a greater incentive to go to Indonesia and try to get to Australia as UNHCR-approved refugees.[9]

So even if those who sailed on SIEV X had had their refugee status approved by UNHCR Jakarta, and even if they had close family members living on temporary protection visas in Australia, there was no way they could legally come.[10] These separated families were being forced onto people smugglers' boats because they had no other prospect for their families ever to be reunited. Husbands and fathers in Australia could not say 'wait', because there was nothing to wait for.

IN A COUPLE OF DAYS, associates of Quassey signed up about 430 asylum-seekers around the guesthouses of Bogor-Cisarua. He seemed in a hurry to fill his boat, and his associates had little trouble finding passengers. Some were customers from Quassey's previous failed voyages, and some of those were being offered free places.[11]

Quassey's desire to load his boat quickly with as many passengers as possible seems to have outweighed any desire to maximise his profit. That should have rung alarm bells, but what choice did these people have?

The bus convoy to Bandar Lampung

About midnight on Tuesday, 16 October, four buses with black-curtained windows left Cisarua in convoy. Quassey was in his car at the head, accompanied by a senior Lembang (Bogor area) police officer, Brigadier Agus Safuan. Quite openly, the convoy drove on expressways the 170-odd kilometres to Merak, the port at the head of Sunda Strait. Here the police-watched car ferry took them across from Java to Southern Sumatra, and they drove the 80 kilometres into Bandar Lampung, the chief town. It was now nearly dawn. They went to a heavily guarded guesthouse on the outskirts of Bandar Lampung that belonged to the local police chief. They spent Wednesday resting here. Late on Wednesday night, they were bussed about 15 kilometres to a secluded bay called Canti or Chanti, where their boat awaited them.

It is puzzling now, in view of the claimed uncertainty by official witnesses in the CMI committee as to where and when SIEV X might have embarked, to see how accurately this itinerary was reported in many media stories in the days after the tragedy.[12]

By 23 October, the itinerary was well known to the media. In total, 12 media reports in the first three weeks after the event refer to the boat leaving from Southern Sumatra. Most refer to Bandar Lampung by name, and many refer to 18 October as the departure date. Yet Australian Defence witnesses in the CMI committee were, initially, curiously reluctant to acknowledge this: it came out only in later written evidence.

Also, none of this detailed itinerary information was attributed to any named survivors. So where did it come from? It is highly unlikely that survivors would have had the detailed knowledge of Indonesian geography to report their road journey so precisely. In fact, most of them would have had little idea of where they were. Reporters most likely got this route information from official 'backgrounding'.

There is another puzzle: why did Quassey choose Bandar Lampung in Sumatra, at the far northern end of Sunda Strait, for the boat departure? There were closer embarkation points all along the south coast of Java (for instance, Pelabuhan Ratu and Cilacap) offering much shorter sailing times to Christmas Island, or on the Sunda Strait coast of Java (for instance, Sumur). Why did he add a day's sailing time and 70 nautical miles down the full length of Sunda Strait to the sea journey? Why weren't passengers bussed the short distance from Bogor-Cisarua to the south coast of Java for embarkation?[13]

How was Quassey able to escort a conspicuous four-bus convoy with darkened windows along 250 kilometres of main roads, using an inter-island car ferry, between midnight and dawn, without being challenged by police posts or security patrols on the way?[14]

Was this not the sort of large-scale activity that the AFP later claimed in the CMI committee it had trained Indonesian police people-smuggling disruption teams to monitor and disrupt? It looks very much as though the convoy's unimpeded passage through police checkpoints on the way from Bogor to Bandar Lampung (for instance, at the closely monitored Merak ferry) was programmed and guaranteed.

A similar question arises about the large numbers of police in Bandar Lampung—30, according to most accounts—who guarded the hotel and later helped load the passengers onto the boat.

This supports the proposition that Quassey's venture enjoyed high-level Indonesian police involvement and protection, and that the Indonesian police's interest was not in stopping the Quassey boat and rounding up the passengers, but in facilitating—indeed, as we shall now see, enforcing—their departure on SIEV X.

A forced embarkation at gunpoint

When the passengers arrived at Canti Bay in the pre-dawn hours of Thursday, 18 October, they could barely see the small boat moored out in the dark bay. A police launch ferried them out by torchlight, in batches of twenty-five. Unaccompanied women and children went first; as was customary, they went down into the hold for privacy. Male-led family groups and the unaccompanied men boarded last, to sit on the upper decks.

As more people went out, the boat settled lower in the water. The people were frightened at how tiny and ramshackle it was. The first launch passengers, Sondos included, went below decks passively, but later groups became agitated as they saw the overloading. At this point, Quassey and the uniformed armed police supervising the loading became aggressive. They forced the final groups onto the launches at gunpoint. In some reported cases they threatened or used violence.

There are multiple media reports of the loading by uniformed armed men, detailed in this chapter and endnotes. This did not feature in the first day's media reports based on journalists' meetings with survivors on 23 October, or in Trad's survivor accounts videotaped on 27–28 October. Yet it was widely reported by the media on 24–25 October.

What was written about this is recorded here in detail, because of its evidentiary importance. The survivors' initial reticence may have resulted from official advice not to mention this aspect of the story, for fear of jeopardising their security in Indonesia while awaiting resettlement. However, persistent media questioning broke the story on the second day. UNHCR and IOM were keen on the third day to discount the story. They may have been trying to protect survivors, appreciating how vulnerable they still were.

It is also of interest that the forced loading is not mentioned in any of the Australian intelligence reports of the tragedy (see later), up to and including the embassy cable of 23 October 2001. Was this because the embassy's informants were Indonesian police, who were reluctant to admit this aspect of the operation? Or was the embassy reluctant to report this aspect to Canberra?

Ginny Stein first broke the story, on the ABC's radio programme *PM*, on 24 October:

> When they got there, what they saw was a boat that was very, very, low in the water. They realised it was horribly

overcrowded and some did not want to get on board, but they were forced at gunpoint to do so. On land, people also knew about what was happening. There were about 30 police there and they said that they did not want to go on either. At that stage police, it's claimed, beat them and forced them at gunpoint to get on the boats, and there police were in those boats where they had about 25 people at the time being taken out, and they were forced to get on the vessel ...

The people smuggler was standing there. He was armed with a pistol. He was seen to have beaten two people. I spoke with one of the survivors, and this is what he had to say (translation): 'They had guns, they were preventing anyone leaving. They forced them on to the boat' ...

It was the same story that was told by virtually everyone there today that we spoke to. We spoke to about ten people. They had the same story.

Stein added that she had spoken to others who had survived earlier attempted journeys to Australia. They said police had ordered them on to vessels. There had been a number of cases like this; people did not want to board a boat that looked unsafe, but were herded on at gunpoint and kept on board by force until the vessel sailed.

Stein said in this first report: 'Raymond Hall [head of UNHCR Indonesia office] ... believes it is police at a local level that are involved, that in fact there is a degree of cooperation from Jakarta, but at a local level this is what is going on. He wants a full investigation because he says without that, "we can't really say who is responsible".'

Later that evening, Foreign Minister Alexander Downer said on ABC TV's *Lateline* programme: 'We haven't at this stage been able to verify those allegations. We will be investigating those allegations and talking to the Indonesian authorities about them.' Downer denied that the reports suggested any sort of Indonesian government policy for police involvement with people smugglers.

'Whether there are some people within the police force who may have accepted money to help the people smuggler or not, well, honestly, we just don't know.' Downer said that, given the gravity of the allegations, he supported the UNHCR call for a quick investigation by Indonesian authorities, 'according to their own system'.

Other media then ran similar stories. The Greenlees and Saunders article, 'Forced onto death boat', was *The Australian's* headline story on 25 October:

> Indonesian security personnel forced asylum-seekers at gunpoint to remain on board a dilapidated fishing vessel that later sank … The Indonesian forces, in collaboration with people smugglers, oversaw the boarding of asylum-seekers in a bay in south Sumatra and later intervened when some of the mainly Iraqi passengers had second thoughts about the voyage on the wooden vessel.

Murphy of the *Christian Science Monitor* quotes a named survivor: 'Zayer said he and many others didn't want to get on — but that Mr Kosay [Quassey] had brought 30 armed men, some wearing Indonesian police uniforms, and told them they had no choice.'

The BBC report, 'Indonesian police "aided smugglers"' of 25 October, gives convincing detail from two named survivors:

> Police in Indonesia say they are investigating reports that hundreds of asylum-seekers who drowned when their boat sank off the coast of Java had been forced onto the vessel at gunpoint. Police officers are alleged to have been bribed by people smugglers to coerce migrants who were wary of boarding the 19-metre boat. Officials have said it was overcrowded and unfit to sail. A national police spokesman, Brigadier General Saleh Saaf, said an intelligence team was looking into the allegations. The police have denied the allegations, and other survivors have said no one forced them onto the boat, which was headed for Australia.

> But one survivor, an Iraqi, said on Wednesday that about 30 police officers armed with pistols and automatic weapons forced passengers onto the wooden boat, even though several did not want to go after seeing its poor condition. 'They said they were willing to kill us,' said Achmad Hussein Ali, speaking through a translator. 'The police even beat two refugees with their rifle butts.' He said a police boat then escorted the asylum-seekers' boat out of the port ...
>
> A Jakarta spokesman for the United Nations' refugee agency, Raymond Hall, said the authorities must carry out a 'really serious investigation' into the claims. 'If there was any complicity from the local authorities ... in actually forcing people to get on the vessel that would be a source of ... grave concern', he said.
>
> Another survivor, Ali Ahmmad, a Kurdish refugee from Iraq, said the police were working with three people smugglers who were also armed.

By the next day, the tone of news coverage of the forced loading had changed. Not only Indonesian authorities but also the heads of UNHCR and IOM and unnamed Western diplomats were suddenly keen to discount these disturbing allegations. On 25 October Collins reported (for the Reuters agency) multi-source official denials of the story:

> Indonesia's police chief on Thursday denied a media report that policemen pointed their guns at asylum-seekers who wanted to get off an overcrowded boat bound for Australia that sank last week killing 350 people ... The UN refugee agency and the International Organisation for Migration (IOM) both cautioned that the accusations had not been proven, adding they had come from badly traumatised people ... 'There was nothing like that,' police chief General Bimantoro told reporters, adding police were 'not really convinced' about the testimonies from survivors of last Friday's tragedy.

The [Sydney Morning] Herald quoted survivors who said many thought boarding the rotting Indonesian boat was too dangerous: 'An Egyptian smuggler smashed one migrant over the head with the butt of a gun when he wanted to take his wife and two children off the boat', survivor Kareem Jabar said.[15] 'When most of us saw the boat was too dangerous, we wanted to get off and get our money back,' the Herald quoted 25-year-old Jabar from Iraq as saying. 'Several police in smaller boats pointed their guns at us. The police were protecting the smugglers.'

No survivors interviewed by Reuters earlier this week made accusations against the police. National police spokesman Saleh Saaf told Reuters that a team had been set up to find out what really happened. Defence Minister Matori Abdul Djalil told reporters tough action would be taken if any police involvement was found. 'This information will certainly be discussed and verified. If it did happen, there should be stern action against the officers who are involved in the matter,' he said.

Head of the IOM's liaison office in Indonesia, Richard Danziger, urged caution over the allegations: 'We have to be very cautious as to what the survivors are saying and look at what they've just gone through', he said.

Raymond Hall, regional representative of the UN High Commissioner for Refugees, said [contrary to his interviews the day before] that until now there had never been allegations of migrants being forced on to boats by police. 'There's been no suggestion people have been forced on to boats out of Indonesia ... Criticism of police and immigration so far has been that they have not been doing enough to stop people, and have actually been facilitating the desire of the people themselves.'

The next day, 26 October, Greenlees reported details of further officially expressed scepticism about the survivors' stories of 30 Indonesian police helping Quassey to load the boat by armed force:

> There is a more troubling connection. Analysts of the people-smuggling business say the smugglers have received protection from Indonesian marines in South Sumatra, where Quessai launched his boats. Survivors of last week's shipwreck claim police forced some people who wanted to get off the boat to remain on board at gunpoint. But it is believed the armed men, about eight of them, assisting Quessai with the boarding of the vessel were more likely to have been Indonesian marines. Western diplomats say they are treating the claims that some people were prevented from getting off the fishing boat with scepticism. 'There is a lot of headline grabbing going on — it's a bit outside of what happened,' one diplomat said.

This report by Greenlees is quite startling. Only the day before, he had joined Stein, Murphy, and the BBC in reporting credible multi-source survivor accounts that 30 Indonesian police had used armed force and helped Quassey. Now Greenlees was saying it was down to about eight men, who might have been Indonesian marines. And 'Western diplomats' were reported to be treating the claims with scepticism and saying it could be a case of 'headline grabbing'.

Such manifest attempts to hose down the confronting story of police-coerced loading give rise to serious questions. Who were these Western diplomats? They were probably Australians, as what other Western embassy had the same interest in the story, and which embassy would Greenlees be most likely to approach for information? How did these diplomats know enough about what had happened to be able to express 'scepticism' about the survivor accounts? To what other accounts of the embarkation did they have access? And why were they — along with UNHCR and IOM — so keen to discount these reports?

And who on earth were the 'marines'? They were never heard of again. That same day Aglionby reported:

> 'There were men with guns watching us all the time,' says an Iraqi man named Jordan. Some people say they were in

police uniform, others say they were soldiers. A third group say they were Quessay's thugs. The Indonesian police stressed yesterday that they were not, as an institution, aiding and abetting the people smugglers, but admitted that a few rogue officers might be involved. A team has been sent to Bandar Lampung to investigate.

Probably as a result of the sustained media curiosity—which might never have arisen had Ginny Stein not taken seriously survivors' multi-source stories of coerced loading—the prestigious Jakarta weekly *Tempo* on 8 November reported that police had arrested Quassey on 4 November 2001 in West Java:

National Police intelligence arrested Quassey, after he had long been followed by an operation carried out by the Police together with the Australian Federal Police for quite some time. When arrested, Quassey could not produce his immigration documents ... Quassey, an Egyptian citizen ... is accused of having violated articles 53 and 54 of Law No. 9/1992 regarding Immigration Affairs ... Quassey is the suspected mastermind of a syndicate that has been smuggling people from Middle Eastern countries such as Afghanistan, Iraq and Egypt to Australia via Indonesia as the ultimate place of transit ... Quassey is now being questioned ... 'We can not reveal the results of the questioning as we are concerned that Quassey's partners in this smuggling operation will escape,' Prasetyo [an official spokesman] said.

Apart from Quassey, Lembang Police officer Brig. Agus Safuan was also arrested for allegedly supervising the passage of a group of illegal immigrants to Lampung using four buses from Cisarua, West Java. After arriving in Lampung, these immigrants boarded a leaky boat for the long journey to Australia. Prasetyo declined to comment on the possible involvement of military members as well as police in this people smuggling operation. 'We're questioning Brig. Agus to find out whether he works together with other security forces, including other police officers or those from other institutions', Prasetyo said.

Two things are noteworthy in this *Tempo* report. First, there is the statement that Quassey had long been followed by an operation carried out by Indonesian police and Australian Federal Police. Second, Quassey—though already publicly identified as the leading people-smuggler in the SIEV X case—was not charged with any offence concerning the dangerous overloading by armed force of SIEV X, despite incriminating allegations about him that were consistently made by a large number of survivors. Such alleged offences would certainly have been indictable under the Indonesian criminal code, as they clearly took place on Indonesian territory, in Sumatra. The fact that the passengers were not Indonesian, or that Indonesia has no laws against people smuggling, should have been immaterial. There were numerous charges available, right from the start, under the allegation that Quassey and his associates had gravely endangered the lives of 421 people by forcing them at gunpoint onto an unsafe, overcrowded small boat, which later sank, drowning 353 of them. It is all in the public record of those early days.

Yet nothing was done to Quassey beyond a cosmetic arrest for minor violations of immigration law. After serving a token six-month sentence, he was allowed to return under Egyptian police escort to his native Egypt.

In retrospect, one wonders whether Quassey would have even been arrested had it not been for the intense media coverage that the forced-loading reports attracted, despite concerted Indonesian, UN agency, and Western diplomatic official attempts to suppress that coverage.

Nothing more was heard about Brig. Agus Safuan, and there was never any Indonesian inquiry into the embarkation of SIEV X, as called for by UNHCR head Raymond Hall and by Alexander Downer.

The story of police cooperation with Quassey was strengthened many months later in August 2002, when Nakhoul's radio program

Five Mysteries of SIEV X gave vivid new oral testimonies from two additional survivors, further confirming that the boat was loaded using armed police after the passengers had protested at its dangerous overloading. The program quoted two survivors, Issam Mohammed and Rami Akram:

> **Issam Mohamad Ismail** says: 'The Indonesian police were there. They were carrying automatic guns. They were so comfortable. They were the ones who gave the signals with their torches. Turning on the torch was a signal to send out people. Turning off the torch meant stop … They had weapons we had never seen before. The latest brands … He [the smuggler] pulled out a revolver and said, "'I'll kill you". He [the refugee] replied "kill me". He said, "I will not let you off". There were policemen with the smuggler. They had automatic guns …'
>
> **Rami Akram** says: 'The hotel owner [in Bandar Lampung] was a [police] general. A high-ranking officer.' Rami Akram also says: 'After he was arrested, Quassey called us from prison and said, "Don't think that I am in jail. For me the prison is a kind of rest. When I am out, I will kill you all." He threatened us.'

I have dealt with these various accounts in detail because collectively they offer crucial evidence to support the contention that powerful Indonesian police resources worked with Quassey to load SIEV X. The sequence of events—initial denials of police involvement and violence, implausible official attempts to produce alternative stories, and failure to indict Quassey and his working associates even after the reported events were generally accepted by the media—strengthens my view that high-level Indonesian police were helping and shielding Quassey before, during, and after the sinking. And the role of IOM, UNHCR, and the Australian embassy raises questions.

But let us continue with the narrative.

The boat

There is remarkable precision in early media reporting on the size and unseaworthy condition of SIEV X (reported as a 19-metre wooden fishing boat), and its excessive number of passengers (421), but little of this is attributed to survivors by name. That is because there is no precision on these matters in most primary survivor accounts (See Trad and *Five Mysteries*, ops cit). All that the survivors told the media initially was that the boat was very small, very dilapidated, and flimsy; it leaked almost from the start; it had no safety equipment apart from 60–70 children's life vests; and passengers had been promised a big, safe, three-decker boat. Yet, from the beginning, the media were reporting the size of the vessel and the exact number on board.

Five Mysteries has the most precise description by a named survivor of what the boat looked like to the people who were boarding it: 'Issam Mohamed Ismail went further than his wife to say that the boat was so worn out, even before it had sailed: "The part that was above the water was only half a metre. The boat was not seaworthy. Not even for fishing, let alone for carrying people. It was like a carton."'

Quassey's men lied to passengers that they would be meeting a second, larger boat out in the strait. Survivor number 5, Rokaya Satar, recalls: 'When they came to us and showed us the boat, we were told that this boat was not the one to get us to Australia; it was only a transit boat that would get us to the boat that would bring us to Australia.'

Survivor number 21, Najah Muhsin, says: 'When we were brought to the boat, we were told that we would be transported to the main ship. We found this to be untrue ...'[16]

The following is the chronological record of the main media descriptions of the size and condition of the boat.

Carmody on 23 October reported IOM spokesman Jean-Philippe Chauzy: 'It's safe to assume that the boat—probably an Indonesian fishing boat—was over capacity. Four hundred and twenty-one people on board this type of boat is obviously far too many.'

AAP on 23 October knew the length of the boat: 'Aid and navy officials said shocked survivors had told of 421 men, women and children boarding the 19-metre boat last Thursday at Lampung in Sumatra.'

By 24 October, Murdoch quotes detailed information, claimed to be from a survivor, 19-year-old Iraqi youth Almjib (aka Rami Akram): 'Almjib yesterday told how a 19-metre, rotting and leaking Indonesian fishing boat without a name, sank off Java.' When and how had survivor Almjib measured the boat? He was taken out by launch to a boat moored in the bay in darkness. With more than 400 fellow passengers crammed like sardines on board with him, he would have had no opportunity to measure its length.

Murdoch and others on 24 October reported: 'Up to 70 children were among the more than 350 asylum-seekers who died after the fishing boat, crammed to double its capacity, capsized and sank south-west of Java on Friday afternoon.' Who told Murdoch the capacity of the boat, to enable him to report that it was crammed to double that capacity?

Greenlees on 24 October offered similarly detailed information: 'The Indonesian fishing vessel that took 353 Australia-bound asylum-seekers to their deaths was overloaded with fuel and had more than four times the number of passengers it could safely carry in the heavy seas of Sunda Strait.' Who told Greenlees that the boat was overloaded with fuel and carrying four times the number of passengers it could safely carry? How could passengers have known such things?

The next day, Greenlees and Saunders quote unnamed authorities: 'Survivors of the disaster, interviewed by *The Australian* yesterday, also said the captain of the ship had his own misgivings about the capacity to put to sea with 421 people. Authorities say the 19-metre vessel could safely carry fewer than 100.'

Who were these authorities who already knew so much about the specifications of the boat, and where had their information come from?

Against this background, the third paragraph of the 23 October 2001 Australian embassy cable from Jakarta describes the boat thus: 'The vessel was waiting for them. The dimensions of the vessel were reported as 19.5 metres long with a beam of four metres. A makeshift upperdeck had been added, with the after decks enclosed by chipboard (presumably to enhance seaworthiness).'

So the embassy already knew by the morning of 23 October (it sent the cable at 10:49 that day) the exact dimensions of the boat, and the fact that a makeshift upper deck had been added. The purpose of the upper deck and chipboard enclosure cannot have been to enhance seaworthiness, as the cable bizarrely claims; it must have been to enable over 400 people to be crammed onto a boat designed (as Greenlees twice reports) to carry no more than 100 people—manifestly, at the cost of stability and safety. Anyone with the most basic knowledge of boats or physics would know that putting an extra deck on top of a boat would make it more top-heavy and thus less seaworthy.

Navy people reading this cable in Canberra would have immediately noted the falsity of this statement. Why was it was put there? Was this cable meant to sanitise the story, or was it a coded signal for those in the know that this had been a disruption operation, a sort of macabre in-joke?

This cable offered precise information on the boat, yet it was made public only after insistent requests from senators, eight months after it was first requested and four months after the CMI inquiry had ended. How did the embassy have this knowledge on the morning of 23 October: details of a boat that had already sunk, and at a time when traumatised survivors in Bogor were only just beginning to talk to the media? Such information had to have come from another source.

What this suggests is that the authorities referred to by Greenlees (Australian embassy personnel or people in close contact with them, as the cable and the Greenlees report contained similar information) already knew a great deal from non-survivor sources and passed some of the information on to media people hungry for more detail.

But these authorities did not pass on to the media all they knew: not the precise dimensions of 19.5 metres by four metres but a more vague 19 metres. And they did not pass on the dramatic information about the makeshift upper deck, which might have given rise to unwanted questions. That news did not become public until the cable was released in February 2003.

Where did these authorities get their information? When did the embassy become aware that the Quassey boat, which — as we later learned through the CMI committee and which *Tempo* reported — it had been monitoring for some weeks before the embarkation, had a makeshift upper deck? When was this deck added, and by whom?

The numbers who embarked

It is well documented in the earliest media reports, and again in paragraph 4 of the 23 October 2001 Australian embassy cable, that 421 people went on board the boat and that ten passengers, fearful of the smallness and overcrowding of the vessel, had refused to embark. On paying bribes to police they were allowed to stay behind.[17]

Again, the precision of the information — that 421 people went on board, and that ten did not — gives the game away. How could survivors have known that precisely 421 people had embarked? Who among the survivors from a boat that departed at night, with passengers ferried out to it by torchlight on launches and crammed into the hold and onto two decks, would have had the opportunity or motive to carry out a passenger count? This numerical precision from the beginning, in media reports and in the 23 October embassy cable, is crucial in an evidentiary sense.

Here are the main reports covering the figure of 421 embarking passengers.

The initial 23 October CNN report quotes Chauzy, the IOM media spokesman in Geneva, as saying that the boat had left with 421 people on board. So IOM already knew the exact figure at the earliest stage, even before survivors had begun to talk to the media. Chauzy added that most passengers were Iraqis, and that there were some Algerians, Iranians, and Palestinians. He already knew the nationality breakdown.

Australian Associated Press on 23 October was precise about the numbers, too, and it offered new claimed sources: 'Aid and navy officials said shocked survivors had told of 421 men, women and children boarding the 19-metre boat last Thursday at Lampung in Sumatra.' But who were these officials? Were they Australian, Indonesian, UNHCR, or IOM people? We have never been told.

Murdoch on 24 October gave the same figure: 'It had set out with 421 people on board.'

It is implausible that the primary source for this reported count of passenger numbers could have been the 'shocked survivors'. The only reasonable explanation is that such early precise information came from people with access to the passenger manifest and who knew the circumstances of the boat's embarkation.

From the beginning, possibly before the survivors had got back to Jakarta (see chapter 4), the 'authorities' had access to detailed passenger information—numbers, age, gender, nationality. It is difficult to imagine how such information could have been obtained from any source other than members of Quassey's syndicate or the Indonesian police who worked with them to load the vessel. In other words, this was intelligence information from within the operation. It is strongly indicative that this was a disruption operation, and that the embassy, IOM, and UNHCR had been put into the information loop.

The exact passenger numbers, as well as personal details, could have come from Khaled Daoed's receipt book or Maysam's record book, duly passed on by whoever had access to such data.

The timeline for when the authorities got such detailed passenger information, and from whom, is vital. And it is chilling to think of the subsequent efforts by Australian officials under Senate oath to claim that such information came from survivors, or even from one survivor. Yet such claims were upheld in replies to Senate questioning during 2003 by officials from the Australian Federal Police and the Department of Foreign Affairs and Trade.

Chapter Three

The Voyage

18 October, early morning
Boat leaves from Canti Bay, near Bandar Lampung, with 421 passengers on board.

18 October, mid-morning
Boat disembarks 21–24 Mandaean passengers on an island (assessed to be in the Karakatu group) in Sunda Strait.

18–19 October, midnight (approx)
Boat exits Sunda Strait and enters Indian Ocean on course for Christmas Island.

19 October, 3.00pm
Boat capsizes and sinks after engine and pumps fail, 50–60 nautical miles south of Sunda Strait.

19 October, early evening
Survivors in water recall seeing two or three police-type boats, which shone searchlights on the disaster scene but did not rescue survivors despite their appeals for help.

The boat journey

Just before dawn on Thursday, 18 October, SIEV X slowly motored out of Canti Bay into Sunda Strait. Practically from the beginning of the journey, passengers had to bail water coming in through a large crack in the hull. One of the survivors, Achmad Hussein, said Abu Quassey followed for several hours in a police speedboat to ensure there were no demands by passengers for the boat to return to shore.[1] Soon after Quassey's speedboat left, the overcrowded SIEV X reached an island, which from the timelines cited by survivors appears to be one of the Karakatu group. Here 21 to 24 Mandaean passengers seized their chance, demanding to get off the vessel by transferring to a local fishing boat.[2] This prudent action saved their lives.

The Mandaeans are a minority religious group in Iraq (their religion dates back to John the Baptist). There is an unconfirmed report that they had quietly been warned during the wait at Bandar Lampung by one of Quassey's accomplices, reportedly himself of Mandaean background, that they should try to leave the boat at the earliest safe opportunity. The story suggests that this Quassey accomplice had learned or guessed that the vessel was a death-trap and wanted to warn the people with whom he felt some affinity. What did he tell them exactly, to make them so determined to get off as a group? This could be important evidence. Other Mandaeans—poorer than the group that got off, and without funds to wait for another boat—are said to have stayed on board. There were no reported Mandaean survivors of the sinking.

WITH 397–400 PASSENGERS on board, the top-heavy vessel motored on past the Karakatu islands and slowly down the full length (70 nautical miles) of Sunda Strait. Najah Muhsin (Trad, survivor number 21) described the conditions:

> We felt like sardines, my brother was sick, they put him on the top deck, we were all unwell, the boat moved. I saw a

The Voyage

10-months-old girl: before the accident, she fell from her father's arms into the ocean. People were packed on top of each other, a small ship with people seasick, and women and children afraid and crying.

I have reconstructed a most likely itinerary, using an estimated speed throughout of four knots (four nautical miles per hour). The wooden fishing boat, carrying four times its design load and with a top-heavy additional upper deck, would not have been pushed any faster. This speed also matches the times and places reported for the departure and the sinking.

Admiralty-listed navigation buoys mark the southern entrance of Sunda Strait (where it meets the Indian Ocean), at 6° 30′ south, 105° east.[3] The distance from the Canti Bay area to these buoys is 70 nautical miles. At four knots, this is a sailing time of 17 hours. A prudent captain would have navigated his way down the centre of the strait towards these coordinates, keeping a safe distance from land on either side. Allowing about one hour to let off the Mandaeans in the Karakatu Islands, the boat leaving Canti at 5.30am (just before dawn, according to most accounts) would have passed out of Sunda Strait and entered the Indian Ocean 18 hours later, about midnight on 18–19 October.

Sondos Ismail said the boat did not stop anywhere after letting off the Mandaeans. No other survivor has reported landing or stopping anywhere else. The claim that the boat might have called in elsewhere after leaving Sumatra began in officials' testimony to the CMI committee. It has never been corroborated by any survivor account (or in the embassy cable).

Entering the Indian Ocean about midnight, the vessel would have taken another 15 hours at four knots to sail another 60 nautical miles into the Indian Ocean, to reach by 3.00pm on 19 October the sinking position reported by a DIMA intelligence note on 23 October 2001: 'when approximately 60 NM south of the Sunda Strait, the boat began taking water and finally capsized and sank at about 1500 hours.'[4] This sinking position also accords with the Greenlees report in *The Australian* on 24 October 2001:

'About 80 kilometres from land at 2pm on Friday, the fishing vessel began to take heavy water, listed violently to the side, capsized and sank within an hour.'[5]

Greenlees' cited '80 km from land' was the only geographically precise report available at the time. It accords with the DIMA intelligence note, because the last land that passengers would have seen would have been around Cape Cangkuang, the most westerly point of Java whose promontory extends quite a long way to the south. Eighty kilometres south from its southern tip is close to the sinking location reported in the DIMA intelligence note. This DIMA data was not made public until 11 months later, but it turns out that Greenlees had the sinking location pretty right from the outset (see chapter 5).

Who gave Greenlees this early accurate information? From the beginning, I gave his report credence. A professional journalist would not have invented such a precise statement as '80 kilometres from land'. *The Australian* was so confident of the accuracy of this report that its front page on 24 October 2001 portrayed the route and sinking location in a thumbnail map (see Fig 1, page 5).

The sinking

This section draws heavily on Keysar Trad's translation of survivor accounts made in Bogor on 27–28 October. This videotaped gathering of 22 survivors (men, women, and children together) was primarily a collective unburdening of grief, but it was also an attempt to establish a historical record. Survivors spoke freely in their own language, while memories were still vivid. It is precious information now.

The survivors' voices have the authentic ring of epic tragedy — they speak of pity, terror, and great courage. By the time this videotape was made, survivors had had a week to start absorbing the enormity of what had befallen them. They were ready to talk about it. The record-takers were unobtrusive; they just let the videotape roll. Gradually, the survivors opened up, hesitantly at first, then with a burning clarity and intensity.

These remarkable accounts sing of the strength of the human spirit. The language is religious and poetic, with unselfconscious references to God, to Noah, to Abraham's sacrifice. The survivors are trying to make sense of it all, to come to terms with their inexpressible grief in the context of their shared faith, culture, and communal loss. Despite feelings of emptiness and hopelessness, their stories reflect a heroic determination to stay alive in order to bear witness to the world. The survivors grieve over terrible memories of the death of loved ones before their eyes, yet they draw inspiration from the kindness and comfort of fellow survivors. They look to each other for help.

Reading these accounts, I felt it would be a privilege to know these people — people whom John Howard did not want in Australia.

Supplementing the Trad account are many other accounts of the sinking based on statements to journalists by named survivors.[6] Also, months later, numerous interviews with named survivors were recorded by Nakhoul for Five Mysteries of SIEV X. So there is no shortage of detailed original-source reportage by named survivors of the sinking.

As to the immediate causes of sinking, the elements most often mentioned are heavy seas and rain squalls; engine failure, or the engine being switched off by the captain 'to rest it'; and pump failure, leading to the hold quickly filling up with water through existing cracks or new holes in the hull. All these elements combined rapidly to produce an increasing rocking motion as the vessel filled, leading quickly to it capsizing and sinking. It left only some planks, a huge fuel slick, and initially up to 120 people struggling in the water.

On the fuel slick, the summary minutes for 23 October 2001 of the People Smuggling Task Force in the Prime Minister's Department say, remarkably, '7000 litres of fuel escaped when the boat sank'. How could Australian authorities obtain such a precise figure? Perhaps they subtracted the estimated fuel use, after 130 nautical miles at four knots, from a known fuel load when the boat left Bandar Lampung. But where could the authorities have got this kind of information? Perhaps the 7000 litres was an estimate by the crew of a surveillance aircraft based on visual inspection of an oil slick. It's just one more of the haunting unexplained details that surround the SIEV X story. This information was not in the Jakarta embassy cable: it came from somewhere else.

Greenlees wrote on 23 October that the boat listed sharply and began to capsize at 3.00pm on Friday, 19 October. To this detail he added, in a 24 October report, that the boat sank within an hour of stopping.

Murdoch on 24 October gave more detail, from 19-year-old survivor Almjib (Rami Akram), who now lives in Melbourne with his mother, Amal Hassan Nasri:

> As bad weather turned into a storm that lashed the boat, the captain continued to steer the asylum seekers in the direction of Christmas Island. But Almjib said the boat started to take more and more water. Eventually the last pump broke down and everybody started bailing water with whatever they could find. 'We were being pounded by huge waves. The boat was full of water and then it suddenly turned on its left side. We all ran to the right side of the boat to try to right it but a huge wave splashed across us and it sank within 30 seconds … Most of the people on board went down with the boat, including the Indonesian captain,' he said. 'Within minutes we counted only 120 people in the water,' he said. 'The rest had already gone.'

Murdoch's accompanying chronology said: 'October 19, 4pm: The boat's engine stops and its captain warns all on board that the boat is taking water. It capsizes about 10 minutes later.'

Ibonweb (the *Indonesian Business* website) reported that the vessel sank due to high seas, and that 'the vessel [became] full of water … the vessel sunk completely after momentarily remaining neutrally buoyant.' The embassy cable of 23 October (in paragraph six) contained the same language.

Saputra offered a survivor's recollection of details of a crucial pump failure:

Khan worried about the boat's condition, but boarded anyway. The survivors said the boat, which set out from Sumatra's Lampung province, began leaking a day into the journey. The vessel's water pump was broken, they said. 'An engineer tried to repair the water pump but failed,' Qiyes said. 'We then tried to get the water out of the boat with dishes, but water kept coming in and weighing the boat down.'

Four international reports (CNN, *Christian Science Monitor, Time,* and the BBC) referred specifically to engine failure. The initial CNN report on 22 October (quoting Chauzy at IOM in Geneva) said: 'The captain radioed that the engine had failed and the boat was sinking.'

Murphy reported engine failure:

> But now, at 3 in the afternoon on Oct. 19, the engine had failed and the tiny boat was left to yaw helplessly in a heaving sea. 'When the boat pitched to the left, I saw women and children losing their grip and falling into the sea. When it pitched to the right, I saw the same thing,' says Mohsen, an Iraqi. 'Then she started to go under.'

Elegant wrote:

> And when the engine suddenly stopped and the wooden fishing boat was rocked back and forth like a toy by the 4-m waves, Rokaya could only grab her daughters' hands and try to avoid being knocked over by the screaming stampede of mothers and children. Then came another, bigger jolt as the boat capsized.

Rokaya Satar, who lost her husband and two daughters, is person No. 5 in the Trad accounts. She told her story of the sinking thus:

> As the engine stopped, my husband went to help fix it, the boat started to rock, one of my daughters started calling out

for her father, he came back, hugged his daughter and returned to try and fix the engine. I was holding onto my daughters when the ship sank ...

The engine stopped working, some went to fix the engine whilst others were taking water out, and a third group [tried] to move left and right to keep the boat balanced in the water. The water came from the left and then the right and the boat capsized. When it did, the women and the children started to come out. I grabbed my daughters, aged five and two. My husband was fixing the engine inside. My daughter was crying, wanting her father. Her father came out to see them before the boat capsized and then went back to fix the engine.

But two survivor accounts tells a different story, of the engine being switched off by the captain. Michael Gordon (one year later) reports a survivor, Faris Kadhem, recalling that the captain decided to turn off the engine 'to give it a little break'.[7] Aglionby reports an account by another survivor, Achmad:

[A]bout 1 pm the captain, a man named Zainuddin, suddenly switched off the engine. 'He said it had to rest for a bit,' Achmad says. 'Then at 2pm the main water pump broke. Two spares were started, but they broke within about 10 minutes.' The ship's hold, into which many women and children were squeezed, started filling with water. This additional weight, combined with the increasingly large waves, made the boat start to rock from side to side. Just after 3.00pm it capsized, and within a few minutes it broke up. Many of the passengers, especially the women and children, had no chance to escape. Some people reckon about 120 survived the capsize, but there were only about 60 life jackets. 'And they were far too small for most of us,' one man says. 'It was as if they were all children's size.' Soon after the boat capsized, the rain started.

Another early report (from AAP, on 23 October) reports a survivor, Bahram Khan, from Jalalabad in Afghanistan: 'The hull sprang a hole. The mechanic could not fix it and the boat sank.'

Aglionby's report (above) of the hull breaking up a few minutes after capsizing suggests a seriously weakened hull structure, and recalls the report by Greenlees of a large crack in the hull from the start of the voyage. Is this evidence of a deliberately weakened hull?

Generally, survivor reports show a consistent picture of compounded safety and stability failures, all happening within minutes: pumps, engines, and hull. Any person familiar with the construction of these boats could have predicted that once the immobilised boat started filling with water and rocking, there was nothing the people on board could have done to stop it sinking. The engine failure, or its switching off, was the catalyst for the capsizing of this top-heavy, grossly overloaded, and weak-hulled boat.

The *Five Mysteries of SIEV X* asked why the boat sank so quickly. It quoted two survivors. One, Sadek Razzak, who lost his wife, and miraculously saved his two-year-old daughter Kawthar, recalled:

> There was a hole in the boat. I don't know how it started. We just saw a hole. It was a small one. There were two pumps. We said to the captain: 'The boat is taking water.' He said: 'No problem. Even if the water pours into the boat, the pumps will be able to empty it.'
>
> Another survivor, Rajaa Ismail, the wife of Issam Mohammed Ismail, recalled that something had broken in the bottom of the boat before it sank: 'It was in the cellar. I was there because, sorry for the word, I was dizzy and vomiting. A small hole opened first and the water started pouring in. The boat lost its balance and started swaying from side to side before it flopped. It broke from the bottom, from the cellar.'

Looking at all of the survivor accounts, my question is not why the boat sank so quickly. Its capsizing was inevitable in the ocean swell once the engine and pumps had failed. This was a 'coffin ship' from the beginning,[8] by virtue of its dangerous structural condition (recall the destabilising additional upper deck and the crack in the hull), its faulty engine and pumps, and its gross passenger overload. Active sabotage was not necessary to sink this boat: once its engines and pumps had failed, physics would do the rest.

I consider briefly now two more extreme possibilities involving active sabotage. First, might a small destructive device have been attached to the hull, activated by some means at a certain point? Recall the above accounts by Sadek Razzak and Rajaa Ismail of small 'holes' suddenly opening up in the hull. There is no evidence at this point for such a deliberate, specific act of sabotage. But the possibility cannot be excluded; especially if those who had sent out this boat had become concerned that the boat was getting too far out into the Indian Ocean towards Christmas Island. Could there have been some kind of fail-safe sinking device in place, ready to be triggered if needed ?

We must also reflect on the two disturbing reports from survivors that captain Zainuddin switched off the engine. He knew that the pumps would stop working, and he must have known how unstable the boat would become as soon as it lost its forward motion and began to fill with water. Was he concerned that the boat was getting too far from Indonesian shores? Had it stayed afloat far longer than planned? Had Zainuddin now been instructed (for example, by radio—see discussion below) to halt the boat, whatever the consequences to human life?

I have wondered for a long time whether SIEV X had in fact been intended to sink during the 18 hours that it spent in the relatively safer and more accessible Sunda Strait. We know now that prior to SIEV X there were many reported cases of sinkings, and engine and pump failures, involving boats close to the Indonesian shoreline, that were organised by Kevin Enniss and probably other disruption agents. Might this also have been the original disruption plan for SIEV X?

The Voyage

If the engine and pumps had failed while the boat was in the calmer waters of Sunda Strait, within sight of Indonesian shores and in hailing distance of frequent local fishing vessels and shipping, the sinking might not have happened so quickly. There might have been less catastrophic loss of life. Most importantly, if it was a disruption exercise, the boat would have sunk in Indonesian territorial waters, well short of Australia's border-protection zone in the Indian Ocean. Was this the reason for the boat's remote embarkation point at the northern end of Sunda Strait? It was later to become clear in CMI committee testimony (see Part Two) that nobody in Canberra seemed to have expected 'the Quassey boat' to clear Sunda Strait and to penetrate the Operation Relex zone. Some official witnesses claimed that it had sunk in or near Sunda Strait.

HERE IS HOW some of the survivors recalled the sinking, as recounted by Trad. Person 9 (name unknown) says:

> When the ship capsized, the 150 children kept floating up looking for air to breathe inside their cabin. More water went in, and they were drowned.

I shudder to think of these terrified children's final minutes — trapped in the darkness of the capsized hold, the buoyancy of their securely tied life-jackets giving them no chance whatever to dive down and out, being pulled underwater by panic-stricken drowning women without lifejackets, with the rising water level cramming them all into the fast-shrinking air pocket above them ...

Person 16 is Hassan Jassem from Basra. He lost his whole family: his wife and his three children, Fatima (five), Batoul (one year eight months), and a baby boy Pe (20 days old). He says:

> My wife and daughters were looking at me and crying as the ship capsized ... True, I lost three children and my wife, but the 150 children are like my own too. Those who perished

with their families have found reprieve. But as for us, we are mere empty shells, our souls went with them.

When water started to overtake the boat, my family and I were in a room inside when we saw the water. Many were seasick. When my daughter saw others seasick she did not take much notice, but would continue to play as if things were normal. This time however, she felt that there was a real danger, so she went to her mother, she was very afraid and horrified. Her mother was crying and reading [the Koran], she placed the Qur'an on her daughter's head to pray for her.

I saw my entire family crying. To this day, I remember the scene, my wife holding the 20-day-old child and crying, not knowing what to do, and the children crying ….

There were two engines, one was not working, I was trying to repair it. It was an old engine, but we repaired it as new. I never imagined that the boat would sink. As I would work on repairing the boat, I was looking at my family.

As the boat began to capsize, they were all looking at me, trying to repair the boat. I am still affected by these final moments (weeping). My wife fell whilst holding the 20-day-old baby.

When the boat capsized, I lost my sanity. I was weeping over my misfortune that I did not die with them. I began searching for them, every time I saw a child, I could not differentiate between it and my children. My wife and children stayed under the boat, they never came out.

I was not wearing a lifejacket, I was hitting at my head and lamenting my loss and praying for my own death. I was dragged under water three times. I do not know what kept pushing me up to stay alive.

Anywhere I placed my arm, a drowned child or woman would emerge and lift my arm and the surviving women would cry more.

(All of Hassan Jassem's family remained under water; none floated to the surface).

Person 20 (Haydar—one of a group of 28 doctors from Khuzistan who had lived in Iran for 11 years, of whom only five remained), recalled the sinking thus:

> There were some children and some women amongst the group. There was a call for the strong able-bodied men to take out the water, they were taking up buckets of water from the boat, the water went into the engines, there was also heavy rain and the boat was sinking.
>
> As the water began to rise inside the boat, people started to go en masse to where there was no water, so the boat would tilt and water would follow them, they kept running for dry deck until the boat started to break apart and capsized.
>
> The bottom level of the boat had women and children, the middle level had families and the top level had men only. No one survived from the bottom level. As the boat capsized, people were trapped with little air. I was inside with the children, there remained a small area where air was trapped. I had a lifejacket and was able to swim to safety, but the others, the children and the women, had no chance.
>
> The captain's room was all in the water. Fish were biting at our bodies. There was a section of the boat with people standing on it and seeing their children dying. One would say, 'Haydar, look, my son Mohammad is dead'. I would say, 'We will follow them soon'. I saw the father looking up and calling to God: 'My God, you took my son, a sacrifice for you, if you would also like more, I submit to you.' He died after this.
>
> I do not know how far their voices in prayer reached. If suicide was permitted, I am certain many would have let go.

Najah Muhsin (listed as survivor 4 and 21) lost her brother (20), sister (20), and her son (18 months). When she first spoke, she simply said (as person 4): 'My son was with my sister, as the boat began sinking I grabbed on to my son, he kept going under the water, I would lift him up over and over then I saw the milk coming out of his nose, and he died.'

Najah spoke at greater length later (as person 21): 'I was travelling with my four brothers, one of them was the 21-year-old Haydar, and my sisters, a 20-year-old and an 18-year-old and my son Karrar, eighteen months old. Only my 18-year-old sister Zena survived ...' After describing the conditions earlier in the voyage, she continued:

> Then a crack appeared in the boat and water started to gush inside and the men could not keep up with the water, trying to throw it outside with buckets. There were about one hundred lifejackets only, people were crying. My brothers came and gave a lifejacket to my sister, we started praying to God: 'O God, You who saved Noah, save us!'
>
> I was inside, my sister was carrying my son, then I took my son from her, then we were in the water and the waves kept washing me and my son, dragging him under and over until the milk started coming out of his nose. The boat broke up within seconds, the waves washed the family members apart.
>
> I saw a woman giving birth in the ocean, I saw my brother being washed away by the waves. I called out to him but saw him crying.
>
> When night came, I saw a group of 22 young men with a 13-year-old girl and a lady who lost her three daughters, lost her son and lost her mother-in-law. My brother did not want to come to Australia, he only wanted to get us to safety and return.
>
> Thirst, hunger and salt water—people had not eaten since Wednesday so that they do not throw up. I clung onto a plank with another lady. All the water around us was contaminated with fuel. The little girl died from exhaustion and the cold, she did not have a lifejacket. From our group of 25, there were only seven left.
>
> Time passed quickly, like a miracle, dawn came at what

felt like 1am. I prayed to God to take my life, I could no longer cope with the pain. We were then rescued by an Indonesian boat.

Person 7 was Issam, travelling with his own family, and other relatives (these were Ali Mahdi Sobie's wife and children). Issam, his wife Rajaa Ismail, and son Houssam were among the survivors —their second son, Ammar, was lost.

I saw my friend Abu Fatima drown along with his wife, two sons and two daughters. I felt choking as women and children clung on to me, I was able to swim because I was wearing a lifejacket. The break-up of the boat separated my family; my son Ammar also drowned. My younger son was rescued by a man by the name of Alaa' who also survived.

As the sun was setting, I heard a voice that I recognised; it was that of my wife. Another passenger who was a good swimmer rescued my wife, and then died himself. My wife and I clung on to a piece of timber and we each were wearing a lifejacket. We were both rescued. We prayed, 'God, if this pleases you, we will not complain, you are the most Compassionate.'

The strong rain continued, as we got tired. I was suggesting to my wife that there is nothing to live for after losing our children. My wife said, 'No, we have to survive'. My wife is a direct descendent of the prophet Muhammad, peace and blessings upon him.

She said to me, 'My great-great-grandfather Hussain said we must hang on. God will keep us alive so that we can tell our story, the world must know'.

The next day, approximately 11am, still clinging to the piece of timber being pushed around by the waves, we were rescued by the fishing boats. Then I saw the other people crying. We were a large family (with uncle's wife and children) now there are only three survivors.

Did the captain of SIEV X radio for help?

This is a great mystery in the public record of the sinking. The two earliest media accounts quoted Jean-Phillippe Chauzy, the spokesman for the International Organisation for Migration in Geneva, as briefing the media. During the night of 22–23 October, the global news network CNN reported Chauzy's advice that 'The captain radioed that the engine had failed and the boat was sinking.' Carmody, on the ABC's *AM* on 23 October, had a live audio quote from Chauzy: 'What we do know is that in the early hours of Friday morning, I think it was four o'clock local time, the captain reported that the boat was having major engine problem and the boat was taking water.'

These two early reports of radio messages from the captain are puzzling for two reasons. First, they were broadcast far too soon after the survivors' return to Jakarta to have plausibly come from survivors. Indeed, no survivor has spoken on the public record about any radio distress-calls from SIEV X. Second, the radio story vanished from the public record immediately after these initial CNN and ABC reports.

Where did Chauzy, working out of the IOM in Europe, get this early information? Had the captain sent out a radio distress-call? And, if so, who received it? To whom was it reported? What other agencies, Indonesian or Australian, monitored and overheard the distress messages, and what was their response? Who told IOM about these radio messages, and when? And why did references to them then disappear so quickly?

Many crucial questions are unanswered, and they go to the heart of the most serious international legal obligations for the safety of life at sea. Whoever may have overheard a radio distress-call was obliged to initiate and record urgent search-and-rescue action. Why wasn't anything done?

It has to be assumed that if the captain did send a radio distress-call, it would have conveyed to listeners the boat's coordinates at the time. This is standard distress-call procedure.

And why, in the ABC report by Carmody, does Chauzy say the

The Voyage 69

radio distress-message was sent in the early hours of the morning, about 4.00am local time on 19 October, when all survivor accounts have the boat sinking about 3.00pm on that day? This is a troubling discrepancy. Perhaps Chauzy had deliberately been given an incorrect time to make it harder to establish later that the boat had got so far out into the Indian Ocean and into the Operation Relex zone. At 4.00am, on my calculations, the boat would have been just on the edge of international waters, about 16 nautical miles south of the Sunda Strait buoys. Maybe the captain radioed to some agency at this time that he had just left Indonesian waters?

Chauzy was a senior IOM media spokesman in Geneva. He must have been working from an authoritative IOM report sent from Indonesia — most probably from Richard Danziger, head of the IOM office in Jakarta. If so, from whom did Danziger get his information about radio messages, and when? Danziger has never commented on this.

There is also an official Australian report of a radio in use on board the boat. The Australian embassy cable of 23 October 2001 said (in paragraph four, describing the early part of the voyage): 'The vessel stopped approximately five kilometres from the point of departure, during which time the crew was in radio contact with Abu Quassey.'

So, according to this cable, the embassy knew at least as early as 23 October 2001 that there had been a radio in use on SIEV X. It is entirely possible that the captain used this radio to send a radio signal when the engine failed, and that this signal was picked up, possibly by Quassey and whoever was working with him — and also possibly by other listening agencies, including the Defence Signal Directorate, the Australian national security agency responsible for electronic interception of signals intelligence. The captain had a small private cabin on the boat, and the radio might have been installed there, out of sight of the passengers.

Marg Hutton and I commented on this in February 2003: 'Note the reference to SIEVX radioing Abu Quassey an hour into the voyage. The fact that the vessel had a radio and that it was known to be used during the voyage indicates that DSD may have picked up its transmission."[9]

Subsequently, Australian Federal Police replies to questioning about radio messages were evasive. In written Senate Estimates replies in March 2003 to questions on notice from Senator Collins on 10 February 2003, the AFP said it had no evidence of any radio communication at the time the vessel was sinking.[10] The AFP said in this same set of answers that the embassy cable reference to a radio on board being used to send a message to Quassey early in the voyage had come from a telephoned conversation with a survivor on the evening of 22 October 2001.

But none of this testimony is corroborated by any survivor's public account after the sinking. Survivors said nothing about any radio distress calls from SIEV X—but it seems that others did.

Mystery ships in the night

Another disturbing element in the story emerged in December 2001 and has continued to build ever since. It was this very story that first engaged my interest in the mystery of SIEV X.

It begins with just one account in the survivor meeting, from survivor 17, later identified by Hutton as Ahmed Hussein, or Ahmad Hussain, an Iraqi about 18 years old. His nephew, Hussein Jawad, and brother, Jawad Hussein, survived; his mother drowned. He said:

> The people on the top deck of the boat, as it was rocking before capsizing, saw two large ships. They thought that they would be rescued. None of them came to the rescue. When night came, the two ships turned floodlights and projectors on the people. One felt as if the light was so close that it was next to him (when the night came). We were very close to Australian waters.
>
> On the second day, the Indonesian fishing boats came. I asked them how they knew that we were here. They said that they had seen our luggage, and this is why they came looking

for survivors. They also told us that they never go this far to fish, because of the sharks and whales in this area.

We asked them about the ships that we saw the day before. They told us that they were Australian border-protection ships. [On the video, cries of support for this statement were heard from other survivors.] These Australian navy ships: has the Australian government given orders not to rescue us? Not even the children?

Vanessa Walker, a journalist with *The Australian*, obtained Trad's transcript. She reported this survivor account in her story on 21 December 2001 about the granting of a temporary protection visa to 12-year-old Zaynab Alrimahi (aka Zaineb Al-Ramahi).[11]

Walker also reported the rebuttal she obtained from the Department of Defence: 'The survivors say two boats, which their rescuers told them were Australian border patrol vessels, shone floodlights on them but did not help. A spokesman for the Defence Department said the closest ship was HMAS Arunta, which was 230 nautical miles south of the spot.'

Meanwhile, SBS radio journalist Ghassan Nakhoul had begun to research the story for *The Five Mysteries of SIEV X*, which went to air (in Arabic) in August 2002. He commented in his *Walkley Magazine* background article ('The human tide'):

> The incident [sinking] was shrouded in mysteries. One of the most puzzling was the story of the boats that came at night and ignored the survivors. There were three mysterious boat lights. Initially, none of the survivors mentioned the mysterious boats to me. The first time the story came to my attention was a month after the incident, when I watched an uncensored videotape featuring the survivors in Jakarta, with a visiting cleric from Sydney.
>
> I contacted the source that had provided the tape. They promised to put me in touch with the survivor who had made the claim. Weeks later, nothing was done. I realised I had stumbled over a piece of information that was supposed

to be edited out. By then it had become difficult to talk to the survivors. They had been moved to other locations in Indonesia and some of them had already been settled as refugees in other countries.

When I tracked them down weeks later I challenged the credibility of their story on the mysterious boats. I asked why they had suppressed it in the first place. They were too scared to mention the boats before. They believed the story might hinder their resettlement, as it would implicate the Australian government.

Here is the transcript from *Five Mysteries* regarding the mystery boats. One of the five named survivors, Amal Hassan Nasri, subsequently came to Australia. The other four went to other countries of refuge.

> **Haidar Ata**: At night, around 7.00 or 8.00, there were three lights. Not just lights, there were three boats.
> **Rajaa Ismail**: The three of them were turning around us. We didn't know how to swim. When I saw the boats' lights, I said to my husband, 'Relief is coming. They will save us. They will help us.' And we started shouting. They couldn't hear us, of course, because of the boats' engine noise. Even if we had a loudspeaker, they wouldn't.
> **Issam Ismail**: When we saw them we suffered more. They reached us. I swear to God, trust in the Almighty God, they got very close. One of them was just next to us.
> **Amal Nasri**: We had whistles in the life jackets that we had been wearing. People started whistling in a way that the boats heard us. And the proof was that one of them started moving. I thought that they were coming our way as their lights were directed at us. It was exactly like you would do while holding a floodlight in the dark to see in front of you.
> **Haidar Ata**: They turned around us two or three times.
> **Rajaa Ismail**: We found that when we moved our legs we would almost reach them. I said to my husband, 'Issam,

Issam, we will reach them. Yes, they have arrived.' But every time we moved our legs and we wanted to reach them, they would take their lights away from us.

Akil Jazzany: Even the lights were directed to us. They were like the lights of a car as they reached you. Like a car's lights. Exactly the same.

Amal Nasri: I tried as much as I could to swim to those boats, but the waves were pulling me back. Sometimes I would get close and the lights would be focused on me.

Akil Jazzany: We felt the boats were coming towards us. They got close and we could hear the sound of the engines.

Amal Nasri: Imagined that I could hear their voices. I heard people speaking. It was a foreign language that I couldn't distinguish. I heard voices, just voices.

Akil Jazzany: We kept on shouting 'Allah the Great ... People over there, save us.' In English, in Arabic, but they never saved us.

Ghassan Nakhoul: To whom did those boats belong? What kind of boats would sail in groups? Did some 'bad Samaritans' reach that spot? Had some eyes been watching the tragedy and ignored it? And what if the refugees were lying? Was it possible for all these people to make up such a lie? When we spoke to the survivors about this mystery, they were scattered over many countries. Some of them were in Sweden, like Issam Mohamad Ismail and his wife Rajaa. Others were in Finland: Haidar Ata. And some were still in Indonesia like Akil Dawood Salman Jazzany and Amal Hassan Nasri [Amal Nasri and her son Rami Akram subsequently were admitted to Australia on temporary protection visas]. In their turn, the survivors asked their saviours [the Indonesian fishing boat that turned up the next day] about the mystery of the lights.

Amal Nasri: Those on the Indonesian boat told us that they would never come to that spot. Only Australian or foreign boats would sail there. They said: 'It's not Indonesian waters. But we have seen luggage floating, so we thought people had drowned. We dared to proceed and we spotted you in the morning. We saw luggage and bodies floating.' I had been myself clinging to the body of a woman so I could remain afloat.

Akil Jazzany: After they rescued us the next day, people on the Indonesian boat told us that they hadn't been there. They said: 'There were Australian ships.'

Ghassan Nakhoul: We have contacted the Australian Ministry of Defence to inquire about the issue. A spokeswoman for that department has told us ... the closest Australian navy ship to the incident was some 150 nautical miles away. It was about a few hours' sailing. The Australian navy did not send a ship because they hadn't had any information about the sinking. And the third answer was: had the navy learned of the incident, they would have certainly sent out boats to check. The Defence spokeswoman has also explained that the navy doesn't need permission from Canberra or from the politicians to interfere when people's lives are in danger. In addition to what the spokeswoman for the Ministry of Defence has told us, an inquiry into the sinking of SIEV X—held on the side of the investigation into the [children] overboard affair—has so far shown that the Australian navy and the spy planes involved in the border protection Operation Relex have failed to spot any sign of the boat or the survivors. Returning to our previous question, has the story of lights been fabricated? The survivors have said that they couldn't distinguish the colour of the ships as it was too dark and the lights were directed to them. However, they have insisted on the credibility of their story.

Rajaa Ismail: Three—I swear to God. We saw the three of them turning around us.

Ghassan Nakhoul's separate interviews with five survivors in three countries constitute strong multi-source evidence of these ships. These five taped accounts offer confirmation of what survivor 17 (Ahmed Hussein) said in the Trad videotape.

Might the mystery boats have secretly rescued captain Zainuddin and his crew in response to a radio message? No crew members, or their bodies, were ever seen again by any survivors. Did the crew all drown, or did they swim away from the main group of survivors as part of a rescue plan?

It is noteworthy (see Nakhoul's comments above) how survivors in their earliest encounters with the media at Bogor kept back this part of the story, perhaps prudently fearing that it might jeopardise their resettlement, which depended on the goodwill of UNHCR and IOM, embassies, and the Indonesian authorities. The story came out accidentally from survivor 17 in the group meeting; Nakhoul reported (see above) subsequent efforts to suppress it; and it was only thanks to Nakhoul's persistent follow-up with resettled refugees in 2002 that it was solidly corroborated. It offers strong circumstantial evidence of disruption-program activity and of the tracking of SIEV X. Indonesian police or military boats don't just miraculously turn up at the scene of a sinking 60 nautical miles out to sea. And why did they not rescue survivors?

How did Australian authorities get photographs of the boat?

In the third part of *Five Mysteries*, two survivors said that soon after the sinking they were shown a set of photographs of suspected illegal entry vessels by Australian and Indonesian police officials, in the presence of an official from the IOM Jakarta office.

As *Five Mysteries*s told the story:

> Ali Hamid was delegated, along with the person he mentioned—Abu Ahmad, whose full name was Karim Jaber Hossein—to represent the survivors, as they were showered with questions, from everywhere, once they had been returned to Indonesia.
>
> The photo mentioned by Ali, currently living in Finland—like Abu Ahmad—was that of their boat. The photo was

taken before the boat had embarked on its ominous trip. That photo was among 20 other photographs in which many boats appeared. The photographs seemed like an aerial survey of the Indonesian coast.'

Ali Hamid said: 'Two Australians. They came to question us about the people smugglers. We gave them the names of all the smugglers. It was an investigation. When we finished, they pulled out photographs and said, "Which one was your boat?" We pointed to our boat and said, "This one."'

The program presenter continued:

Ali Hamid told the program that the Australians were from an official security organisation that he wasn't able to identify. He explained that the Australians were most of the time silent, while an Indonesian official was asking most of the questions. This happened two or three days after the rescue operation, although he couldn't remember where exactly the questioning took place. However, Ali did remember that a female staff from the International Organisation for Migration in Jakarta, known as IOM, was present. She was interpreting for them, as the questioning was in English. Ali remembered the first name of the woman — Maha. She was originally from Sudan, with a Swedish citizenship.

When we contacted Jakarta's IOM we were told that Maha didn't wish to speak with the media. As we pressed for information, it was related to us that Maha remembered that Australian police officers, probably from the Federal Police, had taken part in the investigation that followed the incident. However, she didn't remember that photos had been shown.

An IOM official in Jakarta mentioned to us that the involvement of Australian security officers in investigations that had been taking place with refugees on the movements of people smugglers, were considered as 'routine'.

A spokeswoman for the Federal Police described as 'not unusual' the participation of officers from her department in such investigations. But she declined to reveal the nature of that participation, or its frequency or regularity. When we inquired about the nature of the memorandum of understanding signed between Indonesia and Australia in June to combat transnational crime including people smuggling, the Federal Police spokeswoman told us that the agreement was to facilitate the exchange of information.

As for showing a photo or photos to the survivors, the AFP spokeswoman declined to comment. She said that the Federal Police were currently investigating the SIEV X incident and that any comment on the issue might affect the investigation. She also added that a comment was 'not appropriate'. Thus, the AFP spokeswoman hasn't denied or confirmed the story of the photographs.

Ali Hamid concluded his description of the photograph of the boat he identified as SIEV X, as follows: 'It was still anchored on the Indonesian shore. The photo was taken by satellite. It was from above, by satellite. It looked somehow dark or so. I cannot describe it properly. Before it had sailed. It was still anchored on the Indonesian shore. They had taken photos before we boarded, and before we moved.'

In his *Walkley Magazine* piece, Nakhoul summarised as follows:

> Most intriguing was the story of the boat being photographed before it had sailed on its doomed trip. The photo was shown to representatives of the survivors during questioning by police and immigration officers in Jakarta. The photo was black and white. The survivors had the impression it had been taken via satellite. It was among 20 photos taken in an aerial mapping of the Indonesian shore. Two Australians were present during the questioning. After many inquiries, the Federal Police would neither confirm nor deny the story. I believe that spy planes also produce the

same type of photos. I have wondered since if refugee boats have always been under constant surveillance.

Here again, the record of written testimony in Australian Federal Police Estimates hearings during 2003 runs counter to what these two survivors said on *Five Mysteries*. The AFP confirmed in May 2003 that 'on 23 October 2001, two AFP members accompanied INP and Interpol personnel where the INP interviewed two survivors. The AFP members were observers during this interview'.[12] A subsequent AFP reply in October 2003 to a further Faulkner question on notice about these photographs stated that, in this meeting, 'no photographs were presented [to the two survivors interviewed] in the presence of the two AFP members [named by the AFP as Glen McEwan and Russell Smith]'.[13] Further questions as to which agency supplied the photographs, how were they taken, and what they depicted were not answered by the AFP on grounds of non-applicability.

Yet a December 2003 media report of the Quassey trial in Egypt stated:

> Australian authorities have taken an active interest in the Egyptian trial, providing all the evidence, which included statements from 58 survivors, plus people from three previous ships. The statements claim Abu Quassey forced people on board at gunpoint after they complained about the boat being dangerous. *The evidence also included draft drawings of the ship* and a timeline of the voyage.[14]
> [my italics]

How had the AFP obtained drawings of the ship? Were they drawn from the photograph that survivors told Ghassan they identified in the police interview on 23 October?

Reading the convincing weight of detail in the Nakhoul account, I find it impossible to believe that these two survivors made it all up. I do not have the same confidence in the AFP's written denials.

Marr and Wilkinson's *Dark Victory* gives an even more dramatic account of this meeting.[15] In their account, Ali Hamid's amazement that Australian police had an aerial picture of the boat, before it sailed, turned to anger. 'You knew about our boat,' he said. 'Why didn't you try to find us?'

Chapter Four

Rescue and Return to Jakarta

20 October, between 7.00am and noon
Fishing boat Indah Jaya Makmur picks up 44 survivors at 7° 40´ south, 105° 09´ east, and at noon starts to take them to Jakarta.

21 October
Survivors are transferred at sea to a second fishing boat, Arta Kencana 38.

22 October, 6.00pm
Survivors arrive at North Jakarta Harbor and are taken by UN-chartered bus to hostel at Bogor.

22 October, evening–23 October, morning
Story breaks on CNN and ABC news.

23 October, morning
Media people meet survivors at Bogor hostel.

SURVIVOR ACCOUNTS AGREE that after the boat sank there were 100 to 120 passengers still alive but that, by the next morning, when Indonesian fishing boats began picking people up, there were only forty-five. The Australian embassy cable sent from Jakarta on the morning of 23 October 2001 recounts events after the sinking thus:

> [Paragraph] 6. [Friday 19 October] — at 1500, the vessel began to list heavily to port. Within five minutes, the vessel capsized. It sunk [sic] completely after momentarily remaining neutrally buoyant. Debris soon surfaced after the sinking. The majority of the PIIs [potential illegal immigrants] drowned immediately, with some 120 initial survivors. There was a heavy sea running, and it commenced raining after the sinking. The exact position of vessel at time of sinking is unknown, but it is judged as no further south than 8 degrees south latitude on a direct line from Sunda Strait to Christmas Island.
>
> [Paragraph] 7. Saturday 20 October — the survivors remained in the water for approximately 19 hours, with many of the survivors perishing during that period. At approximately 1000, the remaining survivors were approached by two Indonesian fishing boats. One vessel took on board 44 PIIs (41 adults and three children), with the second boat picking up 5 PIIs. Of these, 4 were already dead and the remaining survivor was a female.

There was no mention in the cable of the ships seen by survivors in the night.

How did the Indonesian fishing boats find survivors?

There are many different versions of the rescue. The earliest reports, for example from CNN, say simply that survivors were picked up on Saturday morning by local fishermen. There was no explanation as to how these 'local' fishermen came to be 60 nautical miles out to sea. Immigration Minister Phillip Ruddock, on Sydney radio station 2SM on 23 October, said: 'The fishermen didn't *stumble across* the survivors until 18 hours after the event.' [my italics]

Ginny Stein (ABC *World Today*, 23 October) was scrupulous in reporting what was known, but she was evidently puzzled:

> **John Highfield**: It was purely local fishermen, not official search-and-rescue organisations from Indonesia, which picked them up?
> **Stein**: Well we are not hearing that it was anything more than fishermen. What has been surprising is so little information has come out about this, considering that the vessel capsized last Friday and it's only late last night we begin to hear anything about this incident. Now we do know that it was fishermen and that they were picked up and taken — in the last 24 hours they were brought to shore.

Murdoch (24 October) reports Almjib (Rami Akram) thus: 'By the time an Indonesian fishing boat found them by chance shortly after dawn last Saturday, there were only 44 survivors, most of them men.'

Apparently on the basis of Almjib's account, Murdoch gives the time of the rescue as 7.00am. We know separately that Faris Kadhem was the first survivor to be picked up.[1] Faris recalls that the boat that rescued him picked up other survivors over the next four or five hours, singly or in small groups. In the 16–21 hours since SIEV X sank at 3.00pm the day before, survivors had drifted apart in the ocean current that was carrying them in a west-southwest direction.

Murdoch, et al ('Despair drove us', 24 October), reported:

> A spokesman for the Indonesian Navy, First Admiral Franky Kayhatu, said Indonesia had no plan to mount a rescue operation in the area where the survivors were picked up. 'The boat sank outside Indonesia's water, near to the Christmas

Island. I haven't got details of the accident, but it's clear that the migrants were saved by fishing boat,' he said.

In a report that turned out to be close to the embassy's cabled account, Greenlees (24 October) wrote:

> There were only 44 survivors—people who clung to wreckage or one of the vessel's 70 life-vests for 19 hours until they were rescued by fishing boats about noon on Saturday ... The 44 survivors, including 33 men, nine women and two children, were picked up by an Indonesian fishing boat and returned to Java. Another fishing boat reportedly pulled four bodies and one survivor from the water.'

Aglionby said:

> More than 12 hours later the captain of a passing fishing boat, *only in the area because he had been blown off course by the storm*, spotted clothes, bags and bodies floating in the sea. He swept the area for a couple of hours and rescued 44 of the passengers. Another man, his face half burnt by the blistering hot sun, was picked up a day later by another fishing boat. No more survivors are expected. [my italics]

Coulthart ('The people smugglers') said: 'until they were rescued *by a passing fishing boat* ...' [my italics]

Trad's survivor 17 [Ahmed Hussein] said:

> On the second day, the Indonesian fishing boats came. I asked them how they knew that we were here. *They said that they had seen our luggage and this is why they came looking for survivors. They also told us that they never go this far to fish because of the sharks and whales in this area.* [my italics]

How do we assess such conflicting accounts? CNN, Stein, Greenlees, Admiral Kayhatu, and the embassy cable don't offer a convincing single explanation as to how these fishing boats arrived on the scene 60 nautical miles out to sea, much further than local fishing boats usually went.

Murdoch said the fishing boat found survivors by chance; Coulthart referred to a passing fishing boat; and Ruddock said the fishermen stumbled across the survivors. Aglionby's more complicated scenario has the captain of a passing fishing boat—in the area only because he had been blown off course by the storm—spotting clothes, bags, and bodies floating in the water. Finally, there is survivor 17's account that the rescuers said they had come looking for survivors, to an area where they usually did not go to fish, because they had seen luggage and debris in the water.

The variety of stories here suggests to me that none of them is true. The truth is probably simpler: fishing boats were instructed to pick up survivors and were given the coordinates but were warned not to reveal these facts to survivors. Motorised fishing boats are not easily blown off course. Floating luggage does not drift far from planks and survivors, as they would all drift in the same ocean current.

The most economical and logical explanation is that the fishing boats were sent to search by the military-type boats, most likely Indonesian police boats or possibly Indonesian Navy vessels, that were seen by survivors during the night. The rescue boats could have been radioed at sea, or they could have been radioed to come from a nearby port in western or southern Java—for example, Sumur or Pelabuhan Ratu.

And how would the military boats have known where to look the night before? There are two possibilities, and either or both may be true. First (see previous chapter), a final radio message sent by the SIEV X captain to Quassey's associates or on a general emergency frequency, that the engines had failed and the boat was in distress, was likely to have included the boat's coordinates as estimated by the captain. These may have become known to Indonesian authorities, either as the expected recipients of the captain's message, by the smugglers passing the message on, or by signals monitoring.

Second, SIEV X might have had a hidden tracking device transmitting the boat's position to an Indonesian receiver. The sinking location would be identified by the coordinates at which such a device ceased to transmit. The device would sink with the boat, and the survivors would know nothing of it.

Both scenarios would explain how the military-type vessels found the location of the sinking and observed the scene as night fell just a few hours after the disaster. These ships would not have wanted to rescue survivors, as it would have been impossible for their commanders to explain to survivors and the media how they just 'happened on the scene'. So they kept moving away as survivors tried to swim or paddle towards them.

The military vessels could have instructed the fishermen to lie, if survivors asked about the ships in the night, that these were Australian naval vessels and that they were already close to Christmas Island (as mentioned by Indonesian Navy Admiral Kayhatu).

The rescue circumstances support two hypotheses: at the maximum, that Quassey was working with senior Indonesian police and/or military forces; at the minimum, that Indonesian authorities were unwilling to reveal how they received radio distress calls and/or tracked the boat, went to witness the scene, and why they did not rescue survivors.

Either hypothesis raises questions about when and how Australian agencies may have learned of SIEV X's distress — through DSD or other radio intercepts of Indonesian signals, and/or through monitoring of any tracking devices supplied by Australia to Indonesian police under the people-smuggling disruption program, or simply through being told by Indonesian police, military, or informants — and what they did with this information, however and whenever it was received.

The multi-source survivor accounts of military ships in the night, and the subsequent implausible circumstances of the rescue by fishing boats, strongly rebut a scenario of a greedy, ruthless people-smuggler being assisted by a few bribed police. If that 'more benign' scenario were true, why would police or military vessels have gone out to look for the boat 38 hours after its departure and when it was already at a great distance from Indonesia? Why would the military vessels have not rescued people, when there were still more than 100 alive? And why would the rescue by fishing boats of 45 survivors the next day have been so carefully stage-managed as to seem accidental?

All this offers convincing evidence of a larger and planned disruption operation—a proposition that is further strengthened by the following analysis of reports of the final stage of the story, the survivors' journey back to Jakarta.

The return to Jakarta, 20–22 October

Survivors initially said little about the return voyage, except that fishing boats took them back to Jakarta. No media reports tackled this part of the story. It was a large black hole. So, during March-June 2002, I tried to research the public record, with help from Geoff Parish, who produced three SBS *Dateline* programs on SIEV X between May and August.[2]

The SBS team confirmed to me survivor recollections (see below) that they were picked up by one fishing boat that had not started to fish, but had nevertheless interrupted its work to take them part of the way back to Jakarta. It transferred them to another boat (owned by the same Chinese owner) that was returning to Jakarta with a full catch of fish. The second boat arrived at the North Jakarta dockside at 6.00pm on Monday, 22 October, where Indonesian police were waiting for it. The survivors refused to get off the boat, frightened at the sight of police uniforms, and probably suspicious that the sinking of their boat had been a police action. They waited on board until a UN official came to the dockside to escort them in a chartered bus back to UNHCR-arranged accommodation in Bogor, where they arrived in the evening. Next morning, they were put on display for the international media.

It is not known which person or agency first broke the story of the disaster to the media. Journalists in Jakarta became aware of an imminent story during the evening of Monday, 22 October, when Jean-Philippe Chauzy, the International Organisation for Migration spokesman, was breaking the story in Geneva to CNN and to ABC radio. A series of embassy emails released later referred to 'stories going around on Monday evening'.[3]

Which agency first told the media in Jakarta? The possibilities include the Indonesian immigration police, IOM, UNHCR, or the Australian embassy.

Public information about the return journey raises many questions. Why were survivors taken on a roundabout, two-day, 300-kilometre voyage by fishing boats to Jakarta? Why weren't they dropped off humanely and economically at the nearest coastal landfall in southern Java? They could by Saturday night have had prompt on-shore medical help and a rapid return by ambulance or bus to Jakarta. Also, the fishing boat could have got back to its work. The fishing-boat captain was not paid by the survivors to take them the long way back by sea back to Jakarta. It is unlikely that Indonesian police or military authorities would have offered money to the captain or the boat's owners, but they could have instructed the captain to take survivors back by sea to Jakarta.

Initially, I did not understand how it was that survivors came to be met at the dockside by immigration police. Clearly, the arrival was anticipated by officials. Later, this was partly illuminated by the embassy cable, which said: '[paragraph] 8. The crew of the first boat (44 PIIs) contacted their Chinese owner for instructions. They were subsequently directed to proceed to Jakarta with the PIIs. The time of arrival in Jakarta was approximately 1800 on Monday 22 October.'

We learn from this several important things. First, the rescue boat had a radio, so a police or military instruction to rescue survivors could have been passed by radio. The fact that the rescuing boat had not started to fish suggests that it might have come from a nearby port. It would take an empty fishing boat, leaving a south Java port towards midnight on Friday and travelling at, say, eight knots, about eight hours to travel 60 miles to the sinking area. According to their accounts, survivors were picked up between

7.00am and noon Saturday. The timeline fits a scenario of a police or military instruction to go out and rescue the survivors.

Second, the cable reported that the boat had contacted its Chinese owner and asked for instructions. A reasonable surmise is that the captain was informing the owner of his official instructions to take survivors back to Jakarta.

A transcript of this radio message to the owner would be important evidence. The Australian embassy evidently knew about the message on 23 October, but no survivor mentioned it then or later. Was this another DSD intercept? Or had anyone from the embassy spoken to the captain or the owner? Again, this is a question of when and from whom the embassy got such detailed information. Did the Chinese owner, after being radioed by his captain on Saturday, 20 October that his fishing boat was commencing the long voyage to Jakarta, tell the immigration police, IOM, or UNHCR? Did he tell the Australian embassy?

It would have made sense for the owner to arrange to transfer the survivors as soon as possible to another of his vessels that was returning to Jakarta with a catch. It would have avoided the loss incurred in a long and profitless trip by the empty first boat.

If those who sent out the Indonesian patrol boats—and the owner of the rescuing fishing boats—knew by Saturday, 20 October that survivors were on their way back by fishing boat to Jakarta, why did the story not break until two days later on Monday evening?

I see this as news management. The rescue plan may have reflected three objectives. First, by putting three full days between the sinking and the return of survivors to Jakarta, it allowed time to prepare a media strategy for a sensational, maximum-impact international news story. Second, a return to Jakarta by fishing boat might have been part of an originally anticipated scenario of the boat sinking much closer to Jakarta, in Sunda Strait. And third, such a rescue plan would avoid troublesome questions that might have arisen if the survivors had been landed on the south coast of Java. The media might have then wanted to know how far the boat had got towards Christmas Island, and why Australian

Operation Relex authorities had not detected it and gone to its help.

The rescue and return went far too smoothly for a civil disaster in Indonesia. There wasn't the usual chaotic aftermath of a disaster. The bus was ready to go to the dock, the hotel in Bogor was ready, and the media were primed. Chauzy in IOM Geneva was briefed by IOM Jakarta to give CNN the international news break, and ABC's *AM* the story in Australia a couple of hours earlier, well timed for morning news programs. It was perfectly managed news, and it might well have worked, if Greenlees had not let out the news of the sinking location — 80 kilometres from Java.

I do not think the Indonesian police or military would have organised such expert news management by themselves. What would have been their interest in briefing the international media? What was the involvement of IOM, UNHCR, and the Australian embassy in preparing for the reception of survivors in Jakarta and in the media management of the whole operation?

Three men — Australian ambassador Ric Smith, IOM head Richard Danziger, and UNHCR head Raymond Hall — might be able to help answer these questions, but they have never spoken publicly on it. All have moved on to other countries and other jobs.

The lack of curiosity by international media about the circumstances of the survivors' return to Jakarta is remarkable. No one reported the name of the boat that brought survivors back to Jakarta, or why it did so. No one reported the transfer of survivors between fishing boats. No one interviewed the captains or crews of the rescue boats. No one but Greenlees had anything to say about where the boat sank. No one looked for the ten people who bribed police in Bandar Lampung to withdraw from the voyage, or for the 21–24 Mandaeans who got off at the Karakatu islands. Initially there was no media coverage of either group.

Indonesia specialists have confirmed to me that local media in Jakarta barely touched the story of the sinking and rescue, and when they did they relied on international news-agency reports. There was no local investigative or feature journalism.[4]

This seemed odd to me — I thought it would have been a big,

dramatic, disaster story in Indonesia. I was told by Indonesia experts that this is normal: human disasters happen often and are not especially newsworthy in Indonesia. But I was also told that Indonesian media shy away from a story when they sense that it may involve some police or military special-operations involvement. My sense is that the latter factor applied here: Indonesian media knew that it was a big international story, but they also sensed its 'special operations' smell. So they played safe by only reproducing international agency reports.

My sense of contrivance, of official control of the survivors' return to Jakarta and Bogor, became stronger the deeper I went into this. I felt that the survivors had become display pieces in a major news-management project. The question is, which agencies were involved, and when?

IOM, UNHCR, and the Australian embassy had one declared agenda item in common—they all wanted to use media interest in the tragedy to dramatise the dangers of people smuggling and to put more international pressure on the Indonesian national government to take effective action to stop it. For months, Australia and the IOM had been pressing the Indonesian government to co-host with Australia in Bali an international conference to counter people smuggling—something the Indonesians had hitherto refused to do. The huge global impact of this tragedy finally gave them the leverage they needed to change Jakarta's mind. Two days later, on 25 October, Indonesian Foreign Minister Hassan Wirayuda abruptly announced that Indonesia would now co-host such a conference with Australia, in Bali in February 2002. And, crucially, Indonesia also announced that 'for humanitarian reasons' its military would no longer oppose the forced tow-back to the edge of Indonesian waters by Australian navy ships of intercepted asylum-seeker boats. That made Operation Relex's job much easier. The Australian Navy now had authority to tow SIEV boats back to Indonesian territorial waters and leave them there. The tragedy of SIEV X made that strategy—previously diplomatically impossible—achievable at last.

The challenge to Australia of people smuggling was by this

means ended, though this fact was not immediately recognised by the media. The sinking of SIEV X finally turned the tide. The people-smuggling industry was closed down; at one stroke, the demand for such voyages was destroyed.

Which agencies—the Australian embassy, IOM, UNHCR—were involved in the news management of the tragedy? How seriously might their professional integrity have been compromised by such involvement?

A crucial breakthrough

SBS *Dateline* achieved a news breakthrough in May 2002. It checked with the Jakarta harbour master's office and discovered a report, dated 3.30pm on 24 October 2001, on the survivors' return.[5] The SBS transcript read:

> Translation of Document received from Harbormaster at Sunda Kelapa Port, North Jakarta RE: Where Survivors of Vessel (later known as SIEV X) were rescued by Fishing Vessel 'Indah Jaya Makmur'
> **Note**: After being rescued by the Indah Jayah Makmur survivors were transferred en route to Jakarta on another vessel, the Arta Kencana 38, to complete the journey.
> **Ref**: from Sunda Kelapa harbour master no …
> **AAA**: This is to inform that on the 23rd October, the Arta Kencana 38–GT83 Licence 1207/BC skippered by Mr Madjid carried 44 immigrants from Iraq and Afghanistan. The immigrants were found at 07 40 00S / 105 09 00E and had previously been on the Indah Jaya Makmur on its way to fishing ground.
> **BBB**: Immigrant data: men 33, women 9, boy 1, girl 1
> All the immigrants are now in the care of Immigration and the UNHCR and have been put up at Wisma Palar Gunung Putri–West Java
> **Distribution**: different departments.

The existence of this report was not mentioned in any early media account, or in the embassy cable. It seems to have been entirely unknown until SBS unearthed it. It conveyed important information: the names of the two boats involved in the rescue and return of the main group of 44 survivors, and—crucially—the coordinates where the survivors were rescued.

Yet during 2002, Senator Hill and Defence witnesses before the CMI committee consistently shrugged off and disparaged this report, even after SBS had sent the text to them. What was in this report that was so unwelcome to the Australian authorities? Was it the names of the rescuing boats—especially the first one, Indah Jaya Makmur, given that its captain might be found and questioned at some stage about what had prompted him to go looking for survivors? Perhaps. But what also made this report unwelcome news for agencies was its exact statement of the rescue coordinates (see following chapter). That data would finally expose the lie that the boat sank in Indonesian waters.

Having discovered the harbour master's report, *Dateline* then located the two fishing boats and met both captains. The *Dateline* crew found the captains to be friendly and helpful.[6] This was confirmed by survivors, who said the boat crews had been kind to them.[7]

In Bogor, survivors remember being interrogated by Western journalists, and by some Westerners who did not introduce themselves as such but whom the survivors felt were officials.[8] The previous chapter noted the *Five Mysteries* account of the police interrogation of Ali Hamid and Abu Ahmad. One purpose of the interrogation was perhaps to assess what judgements the survivors were forming about what had happened. My sense is that interrogators already knew a good deal about what had happened to SIEV X, but they wanted to check how much the survivors had observed or deduced about Quassey's operation.

Other people were also interested in the survivors. Sondos Ismail and others—for example, Rami Akram—recalled being approached by Quassey's associates, or even telephoned by Quassey from his comfortable jail cell, in the months they waited in Bogor for resettlement visas or temporary refuge. The survivors said they were told: 'Do not ever testify against us, because if you do we will find you wherever you are in the world and take revenge on you.'[9]

Who lived and who died on SIEV X?

Information on the survivors has been collated from the media, especially *Five Mysteries*, which is particularly strong on names and places. They were scattered to many countries, and about seven came to Australia on five-year temporary protection visas. They had to wait the longest of all. There is still no complete public list of survivors and where they went. Some were granted refugee entry and went to Sweden, Norway, Finland, and Canada. A list of 45 survivor names supplied to the Senate by the AFP in March 2003 had 27 of them blacked out.[10] Why were so many blacked out?[11]

We know from DIMA emails sent from the embassy on 23 and 24 October that lists of names of passengers and the dead were being compiled by IOM and UNHCR in discussion with survivors.[12] But it is clear now that authorities had from the beginning an undeclared full list of names 'from a confidential source'.

As noted in chapter 1, Senator Ellison's final reply to Senator Brown's request for the list of names of victims was:

> Ongoing enquiries with survivors are providing details which will assist in the identification of victims who died in the sinking. A list was provided to the AFP *from a confidential source after the vessel sank. Provision of any details of that list would compromise that source.* It may also compromise a current ongoing investigation in Indonesia. The list purports to contain some details of passengers, but its veracity has not been tested. The AFP believes it is unlikely that a full and comprehensive list of those who boarded SIEV X or those who subsequently drowned will ever be available. [my italics]

And there, it seems, as far as the Australian government is concerned, the matter of names rests.

From survivor accounts and other contacts, Marg Hutton was able to reconstruct the names of eighty-seven of the 353 dead. If a SIEV X memorial is built, its tablets will be able to record only 87 names. The rest of the names remain buried in Australian confidential files.

Chapter Five

Where the Boat Sank

WHERE SIEV X SANK is still claimed by Australian goverrnment authorities to be unknown, yet since early 2003 there has been irrefutable multi-source evidence of the location. Authorities don't want to admit that it sank some 60 nautical miles south of Sunda Strait inside the Operation Relex border-protection zone, because to do so would highlight the issue of Australia's responsibilities related to safety of life at sea, and would undermine many ministerial statements and official accounts submitted to and accepted by the CMI committee. So they continue to take refuge in a claimed uncertainty that has no basis of fact.

The early media reports based on Chauzy's IOM Geneva briefing were inaccurate or vague. CNN reported that the sinking occurred 'in the Java Sea' (the internal sea north of Java), and the first ABC *AM* report on 23 October said only 'off the island of Java'.

Prime Minister John Howard, on Paul Murray's breakfast show on Perth Radio 6PR on 23 October, was oddly precise:

> We had nothing to do with it, it sank, I repeat, sunk in Indonesian waters, not in Australian waters. It sunk in Indonesian waters and apparently that is our fault. Isn't it interesting, every time something goes wrong and you've got a choice between the Australian government … blaming somebody else overseas, Mr Beazley always blames the Australian government, we're always at fault.

These words, spoken by Howard with great insistence and repeated on subsequent talkback programs on 23 and 24 October, suggested that he had been officially briefed on where the boat sank.[1] His assertion to Murray, 'in Indonesian waters, not in Australian waters', is open to only one reasonable interpretation — that he had been told it sank in Indonesian territorial waters.

Later in the afternoon of 23 October, Immigration Minister Phillip Ruddock gave his answer on Sydney Radio 2SM:

> **Howard Sattler**: Can you actually pinpoint where this boat went down?
> **Ruddock**: I am told it was off West Java … It was, I understand, a number of nautical miles off the coast of West Java.

Ruddock's statement suggests that he had been accurately briefed on the sinking location. We later learned that he had been, by means of the DIMA intelligence note of 23 October 2001, released to the Senate in September 2002, which said that the boat sank approximately 60 nautical miles south of Sunda Strait.[2] The minister's name headed the distribution list for the DIMA note.

Don Greenlees' first piece on the sinking in *The Australian* ('I have lost everything', 23 October) referred to a refugee boat that sank in Sunda Strait. But *Indonesian Business* in its Ibonweb report on 23 October, little noticed at the time, said: 'Unfortunately, the exact position of vessel at the time of sinking is unknown, but it is judged as no further south than eight degrees south latitude on a direct line from Sunda Strait to Christmas

Island.' This sentence runs word for word with the 23 October 2001 Australian embassy cable on the sinking location, released in February 2003 (see paragraph 6).

But most media reports at the time were vague. Ginny Stein on ABC *PM* used the phrase 'off the Indonesian coast'. In 'Despair drove us', on 24 October, Murdoch, et al said: 'the fishing boat … capsized and sank south-west of Java on Friday afternoon.' Murdoch in this article also reported: 'A spokesman for the Indonesian Navy, First Admiral Franky Kayhatu, said, "The boat sank outside Indonesia's water, near to Christmas Island."'

The next day, 24 October, Greenlees reported a precise sinking location in the Indian Ocean, in contrast to his article the day before reporting that the boat sank in Sunda Strait. He wrote: 'About 80km from land at 2pm on Friday, the fishing vessel began to take heavy water, listed violently to the side, capsized and sank within an hour.'

From then on, contemporary media reports said little more about the location. The media emphasis shifted to the coerced loading, Quassey's role, and broader commentaries on the dangers of people smuggling.

The survivors said nothing precise about the rescue location, but several said their fishermen rescuers told them they had left Indonesian waters and had been approaching Christmas Island.[3]

The inconsistency between Howard's and Ruddock's versions was noted (but never developed further) by Murdoch on 24 October:

> It was unclear last night if the boat had sunk in Indonesian waters, as the Prime Minister, John Howard, said yesterday. A spokesman for the Immigration Minister, Philip Ruddock, said there were reports that the boat had sunk close to Java, but he could not confirm if the accident happened in Indonesian or international waters.

Ruddock was putting some distance between himself and Howard, without blatantly contradicting his leader.

The Greenlees and *Indonesian Business* reports were close to the truth, as reported in the DIMA intelligence note, but where did they get their information? It was not from the Indonesian Navy, because Admiral Kayhatu was spinning the same false story some of the fishermen had given to survivors, that the boat had nearly reached Christmas Island.

The Greenlees and *Indonesian Business* reports must have come from informed sources. We know now that the latter report came from sources in the Australian embassy, and the former probably did, too. But the information contradicted Howard's claim that the boat sank in Indonesian waters, so one must assume that both media were briefed by mistake. It would have been preferable from Canberra's point of view to have maintained the geographical vagueness that had been accepted by most of the media in Jakarta.

The position that *Indonesian Business* specified as the southernmost limit of the boat's travel—eight degrees south latitude—is 80 nautical miles south of Java, on the line of travel from Sunda Strait exit coordinates to Christmas Island.[4] This is only a few nautical miles south of the position Greenlees reported on 24 October: 80 kilometres from land, the closest land to the Sunda Strait-Christmas Island line of route being Cape Cangkuang, the westernmost promontory of Java. With the DIMA intelligence note defining a point 60 nautical miles south of Sunda Strait, there were now three reported sinking points, all within 20 nautical miles of one another.

All three points are in the international waters of the Indian Ocean, well beyond Indonesia's 12 nautical miles of territorial waters and its contiguous zone of 24 nautical miles—and inside the Australian Operation Relex zone of surveillance and possible naval interception of SIEVs that extended north from Christmas Island to within 24 nautical miles of the Indonesian coast.

All three points also fall technically within a notional Indonesian search-and-rescue (SAR) zone. This theoretically demarcated zone extended to a boundary line with the Australian SAR zone, a line that runs south of Christmas Island. As Rear

Admiral Marcus Bonser (head of Coastwatch) told the CMI committee in his May 2002 testimony, this Indonesian SAR zone had no operational significance, because Australia had positioned substantial ADF resources in border-protection surveillance between Christmas Island and Java, and Indonesia was not surveilling this area at all.

The decisive fourth piece of information was the Jakarta harbour master's rescue coordinates—07 40 00S/105 09 00E. In May 2002, SBS *Dateline* mapped them, announcing that they define a point '51.5 nautical miles from the Indonesian coastline'. These coordinates fall close to the above-defined DIMA, Greenlees, and *Indonesian Business* points.

In December 2002, I put the rescue coordinates to Matthias Tomczak, professor of oceanography at Flinders University in Adelaide. I asked him, assuming that survivors were in the water for a notional 22 hours, how far and in what direction they might have drifted at that time of year before their rescue. His written response was that the ocean current in that season and location would have moved debris and survivors in a westerly direction along the coast, and gradually farther away from it.[5] He calculated that, in 22 hours, depending on the speed of the current, survivors would have drifted 13–26 nautical miles along the coast and 9–21 nautical miles away from it. Marg Hutton and I mapped these professional estimates. We adjusted Tomczak's drift distances for a shorter 19 hours in the water, which we now concluded was a better average time derived from the survivor accounts. We charted a box representing these limits. The centre of this 'drift box' represented the most probable sinking position based on survivor drift towards the rescue coordinates after the sinking.

The drift box was still close to all the points discussed above— Greenlees at point G, the DIMA intelligence note at DI, *Indonesian Business* at EC, and the Jakarta harbour master's rescue coordinates at JH. All these points were inside international waters and inside the Relex surveillance zone (see Map 1, page 101).

There is a further, important, inference. Recall my reconstructed itinerary and conclusion (on page 56) that SIEV X would have passed out of Sunda Strait and into the Indian Ocean, at point S on map 1, at around midnight on 18–19 October. Even by using the most northerly estimated sinking point, DI, which the boat would have reached at around 2.00pm on 19 October, the map makes clear that SIEV X must have left Indonesia's 12-mile territorial waters and crossed into the northwestern quarter of the Operation Relex surveillance zone in the early morning hours of 19 October. SIEV X was moving in Operation Relex zone waters for at least six daylight hours before it stopped and sank.

Drawing the threads together

Suppose there had never been a Senate inquiry into SIEV X, and no requirement for official witnesses to testify under oath on any of these matters. What would intelligence analysts make of the public material reviewed in this book so far? They would see three independent narratives making up this story that became more intertwined as time went by. As the days passed after the rescue, it became harder for survivors and historians alike to separate the sources of the three narratives, because they all began to blend into the one story.

First there was the original survivor narrative, as reported initially by Western journalists, a few days later in the taped Trad, SBS, and Coulthart records, and several months later in Ghassan Nakhoul's *Five Mysteries*. The survivors might have been silent early in the piece about some aspects of their experience—the forced loading by 30 armed police, mystery ships in the night, and their fear of the police on returning to Jakarta. This suggests they were frightened people, acutely conscious of their vulnerability. But by the time survivors in Europe spoke to Nakhoul they were at a safe distance from Indonesia and had achieved permanent resettlement, so they were much more frank.

The survivors from the beginning told of their dealings with Quassey and his assistants, the gross overcrowding and their well-founded fear of sinking from the outset, the leaking boat with a

Where the Boat Sank

Map 1: This map was drawn professionally by www.sievx.com, using the same template as the Operation Relex surveillance maps that Defence submitted to the CMI committee in July 2002.

The clincher came in February 2003 when the Jakarta embassy cable of 23 October 2001 was released. It officially confirmed what *Indonesian Business* reported on 24 October 2001—that the boat sank at a position 'up to eight degrees latitude south'. This point, which we had first named IB, we then renamed EC, after the embassy cable. Australian authorities have still not admitted that the boat sank in the area shown by the points on this map. Yet there can be no other reasonable conclusion from this multi-source evidence, checked against the ocean-current drift movements.

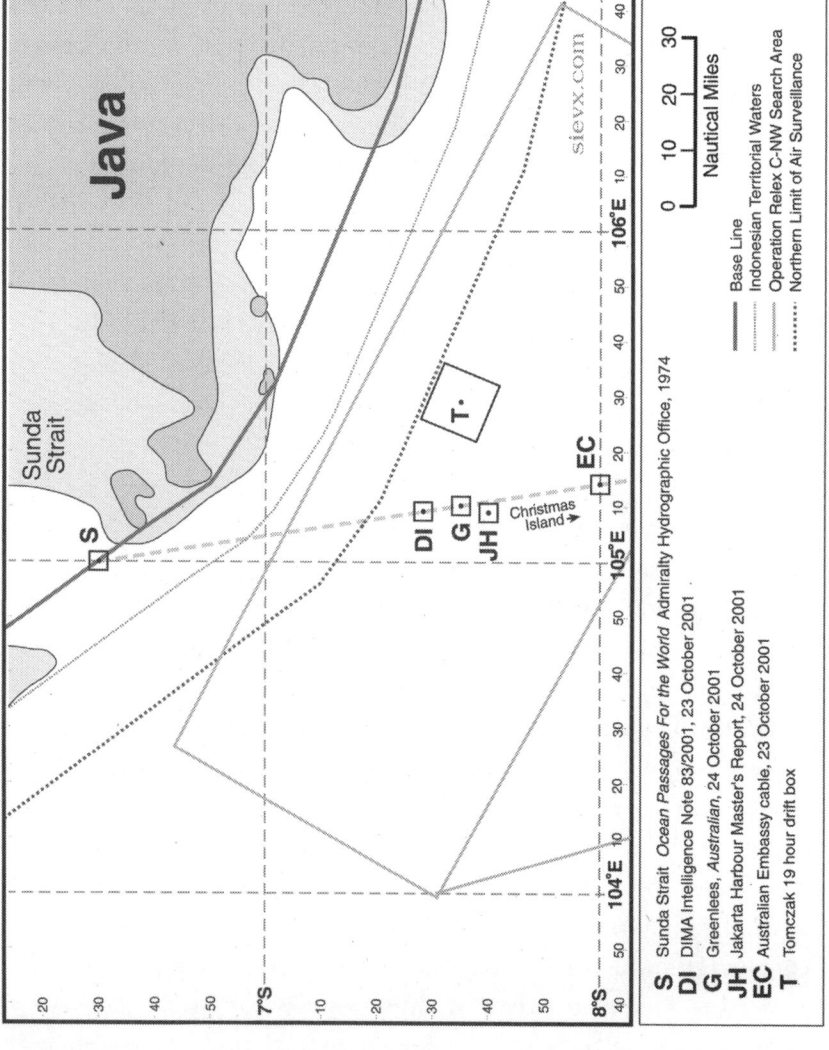

S   Sunda Strait *Ocean Passages For the World* Admiralty Hydrographic Office, 1974
DI   DIMA Intelligence Note 83/2001, 23 October 2001
G   Greenlees, *Australian*, 24 October 2001
JH   Jakarta Harbour Master's Report, 24 October 2001
EC   Australian Embassy cable, 23 October 2001
T   Tomczak 19 hour drift box

long crack in the hull, the final engine and pumps failure, the catastrophic foundering, and the collapse of the hull. By the time of the Trad transcripts, recorded five days after the return, survivors had internalised some of the other two narratives in their attempt to put into context their personal tragedies. For example, survivor 14 recited detailed figures:

> There were 418 passengers on the boat. Only 45 survived. Four are children ... 146 children drowned. There were 150 women, eight (including the young girl) survived. There were 113 men in total, 33 survived. The boat sank at 3:10pm on Friday the 19th of October 2001.

This was clearly not from first-hand recall: he had absorbed data heard afterwards in Bogor.

The second narrative was the selective material or 'backgrounding' provided to the media, and increasingly to survivors — most likely by UNHCR, IOM, and Australian embassy officials. From the beginning, there was an effort to package the public presentation of the story, to give the survivors' accounts the extra touches of believability and news value that come from accurate detail. This narrative also emphasised elements that would encourage the media and the Indonesian government to draw desired policy lessons, and it de-emphasised or omitted features considered unhelpful to the intended message.

All the media reports contained examples of this narrative — some more than others. The media reports were seasoned with 'facts' about the organisation of the people-smuggling trade in Indonesia; the range of fares usually paid; the kinds of risks passengers commonly ran due to gross overcrowding of boats, structural frailty, and the lack of safety equipment; the responsibility of the Indonesian government for this human tragedy that happened in Indonesian waters; and the need for Indonesia urgently to deal with the people-smuggling problem through greater international diplomatic cooperation and tougher law enforcement. These messages came through loud and clear in most media reporting — they did not come from survivors.

As part of this narrative, and to bolster its authenticity, the media were given a few selected facts and figures that could not plausibly have been known to the survivors: the 19-metre length of the boat; the exact number of people (421) on board and their nationality, gender, and age; the bus convoy's itinerary; and the place (Canti Bay, near Bandar Lampung, in south Sumatra) where the boat was loaded.

The third narrative was made up of material that was not supposed to get out, but 'leaked'. Early examples are the first reports from IOM Geneva to CNN and the ABC of the captain's radio distress-calls, the precise reports of the sinking location by Greenlees and *Indonesian Business*, and Ruddock's first well-informed statement on the location. And from the survivors, after the first day back in Bogor, there were multi-source reports of a large-scale, well-resourced operation involving coerced loading by Quassey and 30 armed Indonesian police. These reports were quickly discounted or minimised by the Indonesian police and others (the UNHCR, IOM, and 'diplomatic sources'). All official agencies went into immediate damage control.

Then, a few days later with the Arabic-speaking video team (Trad transcripts), one survivor broke another preferred silence, revealing the military ships in the night that came, saw them, but then failed to rescue them.

In 2002, survivors scattered around the world confirmed to Nakhoul the ships-in-the-night story, and told him in convincing detail about Australian and Indonesian police interlocutors jointly showing them aerial photographs of Quassey's boat, and how Quassey and his associates had continued to threaten them afterwards. They now freely admitted their despairing realisation that there was no use denouncing Quassey and his associates because they all had Indonesian police protection, and perhaps even UN agency protection.

Also in 2002, another unintended narrative element emerged: the Jakarta harbour master's report, with its documented rescue location coordinates, the names of rescuing and transfer boats, and the proof of the itinerary of the survivors' maritime return to Jakarta.

When the embassy cable was finally released in February 2003, it confirmed the sinking location and also revealed the recently fitted makeshift upper deck and the radio message from the rescuing boats to the Chinese owner.

Looking at the timelines of the official backgrounding (second) narrative, we clearly see an official system well prepared for the tragedy and not at all taken by surprise when survivors arrived back in Jakarta. This was a seamless news-management operation from the beginning.

The issues of Australian government credibility that emerged during and after the CMI inquiry makes these questions about contradictions and anomalies in the early public narratives all the more pertinent. Even in the situation before the Senate inquiry began, we see something like a stage set that has failed to sustain the illusion of reality. We can see the machinery, the waiting actors in the wings, and the prompters.

Part Two

The Investigation

Chapter Six

A Presumption of Regularity

When Tony Kevin first came to me with this material, I must confess that I was reasonably sceptical ... essentially as a journalist, I'm a 'presumption of regularity' person. I believe that most public servants like their jobs, believe that they're acting in the public interest, and would not consciously assist in or connive in something that was clearly morally wrong, let alone criminal.

— Jack Waterford, senior editor, *Canberra Times,* speaking at a public forum on SIEV X at the Australian National University, Canberra, 18 October 2003 [full text on tonykevin.com]

WHEN SIEV X SANK, my first thought was that John Howard was enjoying the devil's own luck. This terrible event, the worst in a series of pre-election border-protection dramas, locked in the view among mainstream voters that the people-smuggling trade had become a serious threat to national security and that only John Howard was able to deal firmly and wisely with it. Labor under Kim Beazley had no credible policy alternative to offer.

First, there had been the 'Tampa affair' (26–31 August).[1] A few days later came the government's announcement of a robust new military border-protection operation to detect, intercept, and repel suspected illegal entry vessels—the long-planned Operation Relex, which was ready to swing into action.

Howard announced on 2 September that he had authorised 'saturation surveillance' of international waters between Australia and Indonesia.[2] He said: 'We don't, in this nation, sink boats ... But we're certainly talking about acts which are designed to deter and encourage deterrence, and also to enhance the fact that we are quite properly endeavouring to discourage people from setting out in the first place.' Howard refused to say how he would deal with vessels carrying asylum-seekers, except that the Australian Defence Force would act lawfully and decently.[3]

Megan Saunders reported, based on a briefing from the Immigration Minister, Philip Ruddock, that the navy and airforce would patrol international waters as close as 30 nautical miles from Java, in an attempt to deter asylum-seeker boats from setting out.[4] Ruddock said: 'We intend to ensure every boat is approached. You might well find people who are concerned that when they are still very close to home, they might be more willing to turn back.'

Saunders also reported an Immigration spokesman saying: 'Maybe the show of force out there might make people think twice. To see a frigate bearing down on you and suggesting that maybe you might like to turn around does have a certain psychological effect.'

Brendan Pearson and Paul Cleary noted that 98.5 per cent of asylum-seeker vessels were already being detected and peacefully arrested before they reached Australian waters.[5] They speculated on what would change under this new enhanced surveillance: 'Does the answer lie in changes to the application of the Border Protection Act 1999, which lays down the "rules of engagement" for Australian authorities? Government sources were not responding on that point.'

After Tampa, only three boats came in September, and were intercepted at Ashmore Reef (SIEVs 1–3, on 3, 10, and 12 September). The passengers were removed in navy ships to detention centres in the Pacific.

There was a long time interval—24 days—during which no boats came. On 1 October, it was reported that the government had halved the original Operation Relex deployment of five navy vessels and four PC3 Orion surveillance aircraft that were used in detecting people smugglers to Australia's north.[6] The report said: 'Operation Reflex [sic] is now understood to involve two frigates and two Orions.' Defence Minister Peter Reith stated that sufficient capability was being maintained.

The election was called on 5 October 2001. Almost immediately came a rush of boats, and the 'children overboard' drama of SIEV 4. Photographs published on 8 October of asylum-seeker children in the water being rescued by the crew of HMAS Adelaide were claimed by government ministers to depict children who had been thrown overboard by their parents as a way of morally blackmailing the authorities to allow them into Australia. We knew little else about this interception. Many Australians agreed with the ministers' chorus that we did not want people like that in Australia.

On 23 October came news of the SIEV X tragedy, which seemed to validate all the warnings by the Foreign Minister, Alexander Downer, and the Immigration Minister, Philip Ruddock, that people smugglers were greedy, ruthless, and life-threatening criminals who loaded too many people onto dangerous, leaky boats, and that lives would eventually be lost.[7] Even the brief wave of public sympathy for Sondos Ismail over the loss of her three little daughters (for a moment, an asylum-seeker family was allowed a human face) did not dispel the general public view that this sinking was the fault of people smugglers, and maybe of their reckless customers as well. It seemed to make it more important than ever that the government prevent these boats from coming.

Howard quickly distanced Australia from the tragedy, repeating endlessly on talkback radio on 23 and 24 October that the boat had sunk in Indonesian waters and was not Australia's responsibility.

On 25 October came the apparent solution: news of a more cooperative Indonesian government response to the problem. Australian naval ships were now being allowed by Jakarta to tow boats back to Indonesian territorial waters. (We learned later that the first towback—SIEV 5—was completed on 19 October, the day SIEV X sank). Also, Indonesia agreed at last to co-host a people-smuggling conference. And that seemed to be that. Labor went on to lose the election it had been confident of winning.

In his victory interview on ABC television on 10 November, John Howard told Kerry O'Brien:

> Well, the pipeline—that is, people leaving countries and going to Indonesia and Malaysia—our advice is that it has already slowed. We had advice last week to the effect that the flow of people to Malaysia has virtually stopped ... It's a bit hard to know how quickly the people who have accumulated in Indonesia are going to try and come here. Obviously the more difficult we make it, the less likely they are to come, in the near future.

Hardly any SIEVs arrived after the election. Somehow, the pipeline tap had been turned off.

ON 7 NOVEMBER, a senior Naval Reserve commander, consultant psychiatrist Dr Duncan Wallace, disembarked from HMAS Arunta in Darwin at his own request, after 30 days' service on that vessel engaged on border-protection duties. He sent a prepared public statement to leading newspapers, saying that what was happening in seas north of Australia at the hands of the ADF was 'morally wrong and despicable'. Wallace wrote: 'I participated in the boarding, attempted removal and actual forced removal of suspected illegal immigrant vessels to Indonesia ... Nearly everyone I spoke to that was involved in these operations knew that what they were doing was wrong.'

He wrote that the ADF always performed with skill and professionalism, but 'they should not be asked to perform these reprehensible duties'.[8] Wallace's outspoken protest was little noticed at the time, and he never publicly returned to it.

As became known in December 2001, HMAS Arunta had been the closest Australian Navy vessel to SIEV X when it sank. Did Wallace's protest stem only from taking part in HMAS Arunta's harsh interceptions of three asylum-seeker boats from 19 October onwards, or might there have been something more to it?

EARLY IN 2002 I chanced on a newspaper report of the arrival in December 2001 of Zaynab Almirahi, a 12-year-old orphaned girl who was one of the few children to survive the SIEV X sinking. Two sentences caught my eye: 'The survivors say two boats, which their rescuers told them were Australian border patrol vessels, shone floodlights on them but did not help. A spokesman for the Defence Department said the closest ship was HMAS Arunta, which was 230 nautical miles south of the spot.'[9]

This piqued my curiosity. The reporter who filed the story, Vanessa Walker, told me that this information had come from a videotape of survivors' accounts, recorded in Bogor in the days after the sinking and later translated into English by Keysar Trad, community affairs spokesman at the Lakemba Mosque, Sydney.

Trad, at my request, e-mailed me his transcript. I was profoundly affected by it, and also had an immediate intuition that something was wrong. I checked my scanty news clippings on the sinking, and was struck by the precise report in *The Australian* by Don Greenlees on 24 October 2001, and by the accompanying thumbnail map, showing that the boat had sunk 80 kilometres south of the western tip of Java, in an area of the Indian Ocean that I knew was being intensively patrolled by the ADF.[10] I had not yet focused on Howard's claim that the boat sank in Indonesian waters.

But the final sentences of the Greenlees report did not make any sense: 'Australian authorities had been monitoring the departure of the boat people from Indonesia. Unaware of the tragedy at sea on Saturday, search-and-rescue officials in Australia issued an overdue notice on Monday morning.'

If Australian authorities had monitored the boat's departure, and if Australian search-and-rescue officials knew by Monday morning that it was overdue, how could it be that they were unaware of the tragedy? Had Australian border-protection operations not been intensively surveilling the area of the Indian Ocean where, according to Greenlees and the map, the boat had sunk? Why hadn't they tracked this boat and turned it back, according to the announced Operation Relex doctrine of intercepting as close as 30 nautical miles off Java? And where had Australian search-and-rescue officials got their information about the overdue boat?

The Defence response to Walker was that the nearest naval vessel, HMAS Arunta, was 230 nautical miles south of the sinking. But that would have put it well south of Christmas Island. What was the vessel doing down there, when it was supposed to be on station, ready to intercept illegal boats as close to Java as 30 miles?

Where did the military ships come from—those reported by survivor number 17 as surveying the disaster scene without attempting a rescue? And how had Indonesian fishermen known where to look for survivors?

This was how my questioning about SIEV X began. There was no Defence whistleblower tipping me off, I knew practically nothing yet about what had happened, but I recognised that various parts of the public story did not fit together.

I assumed that the ADF would share my interest in uncovering the full truth, and if the border-protection system had known about the plight of these people it would have tried to help them. I did not then conceive of a possibility of systemic negligence by the Australian border-protection system of its safety-of-life-at-sea responsibilities to asylum-seekers.

I did not believe then—and I still do not—that the mystery ships reported by survivor 17 were Australian naval vessels. I guessed they might belong to the Indonesian police or military.

Initially I held to Jack Waterford's presumption of regularity. There had to be reasonable explanations for the ADF's failure to go to the aid of SIEV X—maybe some errors in handling information, or even a human rogue element in the system that had neglected a proper duty of care. If the latter were the case, the system would want to expose any such rogue element.

Over the next two months I sent three documents to the CMI committee: a letter on 18 February 2002 to the then Labor Party leader Simon Crean, copied to Senate opposition leaders and the clerk of the Senate; my first submission to the committee on 4 March; and a follow-up submission on 11 April.[11] Each document reflected a progressive hardening of my concerns. I was then invited to testify in person on 1 May.

AN UNDERSTANDING of the Australian Senate investigative and accountability system is crucial to this book. The Senate and its committees are important elements in the checks and balances that sustain our democratic system of government.[12] As long as opposition parties constitute a majority in the Senate (a result which is usually produced by its system of proportional representation), the upper house and its committees are the strongest independent watchdogs we have — apart from the courts — over the conduct of executive government.

Senate investigative committees (Estimates and other standing committees, and ad hoc select committees on particular issues) have considerable reserve powers to summon witnesses and compel testimony, under threat of imprisonment for refusing to testify. But they normally do not exercise such powers, relying on established conventions with government ministers and senior officials that are based on mutual courtesy and a voluntary approach.

All witnesses appearing before Senate committees have the protection of privilege. Witnesses testify under oath, and committees assume that they are telling the truth until proven otherwise. If it becomes apparent that a witness has not told the full truth, subsequent 'corrections', 'amplifications', or 'clarifications' are usually taken to be in good faith and duly accepted into the record.

In one sense, Senate committees are united in the pursuit of truth in relation to abuses of government or administrative powers. Certainly this is so if a committee is investigating suspected personal corruption or misconduct by a particular minister or official. Committees usually enjoy a professional camaraderie, and employ humour to relieve the more boring parts of working sessions.

But Senate committees also have a politically adversarial character. Opposition senators try to extract admissions from officials giving evidence that they hope may disadvantage or embarrass the government. Ministers, assisted by government committee members, may try to shepherd witnesses and head off damaging admissions. As a result, officials do not enjoy appearing before Senate committees, especially on politically contentious matters. While under oath they may be pushed and pulled between government and opposition senators seeking agreement to a particular view of events or policies. These committees can at times get pretty rough on witnesses.

Officials have some protection: they may decline to answer questions on matters of government policy or matters that are operationally confidential. The committee may in the latter case go into private session, but opposition members don't like this because it constrains what they can say publicly afterwards. Officials faced with a curly question may stall by asking for time to research a written reply. They may decline to produce a requested document, or parts of it, on the grounds that it is confidential, or is related to ongoing operational matters. There are many ways in which officials can avoid or delay giving Senate committees the information they seek, provided the officials know they have the support and protection of their ministers.

In recent years, Senate committees have become more adversarial, as executive government has increasingly demanded total commitment by senior officials to the defence of sensitive government operations. The once-gentle committee system has become sharper, more edgy. Nowhere was this more clear than in the CMI committee—the Select Committee into a Certain Maritime Incident—which investigated the 'children overboard' claims and the sinking of SIEV X. The investigative failures of that committee continue to echo through the Senate.[13]

When an investigation is over, a committee agrees to the form of its report (although minority reports are frequently included) and tables it in the Senate. Because committee numbers reflect Senate numbers, majority reports are always approved. The parliamentary convention since 1983 has been that the government must respond to reports within three months. Non-compliance lists are regularly published.

The CMI committee strained these conventions to the limit. Interrogation of witnesses was unprecedentedly long and intensive, often from both sides.[14] The atmosphere was tense, often angry. At one point, on 5 April 2002, the committee nearly broke down.[15] Unusually, the integrity of two witnesses—Jane Halton and me—was later denounced under Senate privilege.[16] The government did not bother to respond to the committee's report.[17] In December 2003, Alexander Downer publicly mocked the four Senate motions concerning SIEV X as 'just a political stunt'.[18]

In all these ways, the history of the CMI committee and of subsequent Senate questioning about SIEV X and the people-smuggling disruption program signifies a low point in government and executive respect for the Senate committee accountability system. This in itself suggests the extent to which this particular Senate committee inquiry got under the skin of the Howard government.

THE CMI COMMITTEE had a broader political context that needs to be outlined. It was set up by Labor in February 2002 with the avowed aim of exposing the government's 'children overboard' lies, which had helped in the November 2001 election victory. The incident had been fixed in the nation's consciousness by the widespread reproduction of e-mailed navy photographs from 8 October 2001, which showed the rescue of women and children by crew members of HMAS Adelaide from the water after their disabled vessel (SIEV 4) had sunk suddenly after having been towed in circles by Adelaide for 22 hours. Canberra had ordered that passengers be kept on board the unseaworthy vessel during this tow.

The CMI committee's chairman, Senator Peter Cook, said on the day the committee's report was tabled:

> The asylum seekers themselves ... are innocent of the charge that was made [that they had thrown their children overboard in efforts to blackmail Australian authorities] ... The truth is that they did not—they never did those things—and there is no evidence anywhere in this inquiry to suggest that they were other than caring and responsible parents. Somebody has got to say that these people have been defamed.[19]

Early in the CMI committee's inquiry the government had decided to widen the field of inquiry by opening up the hitherto largely secret record of 12 SIEV interceptions by Operation Relex that took place in September–December 2001. On 5 April, Rear Admiral Geoffrey Smith, RAN, who commanded Operation Relex, tabled 12 interception chronologies, RAN data on vessel deployment, and an accompanying summary 'matrix' of data. This material was intended to substantiate government claims that, in general, asylum-seekers on the 12 boats had been reckless with their families' safety and that, therefore, the 'children overboard' claim was generically true, even if not proven so in the particular case of SIEV 4.

The tactic backfired. The committee's examination of large quantities of oral and written evidence from RAN personnel concerning the 12 interceptions—despite an array of supportive general judgements offered by testifying RAN admirals—did not throw up any cases of irresponsible parental behaviour by asylum-seekers. Certainly there was evidence of their extreme distress at being told they could not apply for refugee processing in Australia and were required to return to Indonesia. However, the worst things found to have happened to children on the 12 SIEVs during interceptions were instances of children being held up on deck by adults, possibly in response to aggressive navy interception tactics, as if to signal, 'Be careful—we have children on board'; and one case of a child wearing a lifejacket being held over the side and dropped (not thrown) from a SIEV when a cooking stove caught fire as the boat was being held under RAN guard in the Ashmore Reef lagoon.

One view of this evidence was given by the Chief of Navy, Vice Admiral David Shackleton, on 25 March, the first day of hearings:

> The point is that this has been very difficult. The people who are engaged in the SIEVs—that is, the people themselves—are in difficult circumstances. The point is that they are trying to get to Australia. It has been the navy's job to stop them doing this.[20]

Harsher views were put by Smith, as well as by Rear Admiral Chris Ritchie, Commander Australian Theatre, RAN, in a Senate Estimates committee a few weeks earlier:

> Nobody has spoken about the context here: what are we looking at and what are we seeing? What we are seeing is a group of people who are offering violence to themselves. That is the normal way they go about business. These are a group of people who are prepared to break up the boat which they are on, to use glass, wood or whatever as weapons to threaten people in boarding parties. We are seeing people who jump, or somehow or other get into the water, in order to place themselves in a situation where they believe that they have created a safety of life at sea incident, and that that will entitle them to some different treatment under our immigration laws. What we have is a group of young sailors inexperienced in doing this sort of work. It is nasty business; it is not something that you would wish people to have to do every day, but it is their business, and they do it, and they do it well.[21]

Under close questioning on the 12 SIEV interceptions, other perspectives came into focus (though the asylum-seekers were never given an opportunity to speak for themselves). Senators began to see a picture of harsh navy tactics of forcing and tricking people on SIEVs back to Indonesia, callousness about asylum-seekers' welfare and human dignity, and possibly neglect of the navy's moral and legal obligations for these people's safety of life at sea. Evidence in the CMI inquiry established that the navy had been under government orders to go to the limits of law and decency to try to make these people turn back.

Asylum claims under the UN refugee convention by people on SIEVs carried no weight as far as Operation Relex was concerned. Smith made this clear on 11 April, under questioning from Senator Andrew Bartlett:

> Our mission was clear—that is, to intercept and then to carry out whatever direction we were given subsequent to that. The status of these people was irrelevant to us.[22]

These confrontations at sea would have been traumatic for both sides. It is a cruel thing for Australians to order boatloads of distraught, weeping men, women, and children, who are asking for refuge, to go away. Human nature being what it is, some of those required to give such orders will blame their victims. Oral testimony and documents supplied to the CMI committee contain examples of a barely concealed resentment and dislike for the asylum-seekers. Such testimony offers a context for Duncan Wallace's disembarkation from HMAS Arunta and his media release.

It was also clear that some in the ADF found their new border-protection task deeply disturbing, both as military professionals and human beings. They saw the work the navy was now being ordered to do as brutalising. On 12 April, Admiral Chris Barrie, then chief of the ADF, made this revealing comment:

> We are very fortunate that our people have a very good mix of downright courage, resourcefulness and compassion ... I have a worry that if you leave people in these operational situations for too long, some of those elements start to disappear—the compassion starts to disappear or they become hard-nosed.[23]

The pressures encouraging callous, safety-negligent Operation

Relex practices came primarily from the harsh new rules of interception of SIEVs that had been developed in government policy committees from 2000 onwards. Senator Jacinta Collins noted in her additional comments to the CMI committee's report:

> In the months prior to the government's introduction of its new border-protection regime, some senior defence officers were privately raising serious concerns at a new direction and culture developing within the Department of Prime Minister and Cabinet. Defence representatives in the government's interagency consultations were made to feel like 'bleeding hearts' in comparison to a hard-line stance developing out of the Prime Minister's department.[24]

An ADF in-house magazine from this period contains a story, whose ethical implications are disturbing, about a confiscated SIEV being towed out to sea by a navy vessel, then sunk by cannon fire as target practice—to cheers and merriment all round.

Another factor was the micro-management from shore of interceptions. For example, Commander Banks of HMAS Adelaide testified that during the interception of SIEV 4 he understood himself to be under guidance from his immediate commanding officer, Darwin-based Brigadier Mike Silverstone, commander, Northern Command, RAN, not to be 'suckered' by the people on SIEV 4 into a safety-of-life-at-sea situation.[25] Silverstone maintained regular telephone contact with Banks during the whole SIEV 4 interception.

The opening up of such areas of evidence was made possible by a government move in March to add a fourth CMI committee term of reference covering 'operational procedures observed by the RAN and by relevant Commonwealth agencies to ensure the safety of asylum seekers on vessels entering or attempting to enter Australian waters'.

Labor's Senator John Faulkner later ironically congratulated government senators, in the Senate debate on 23 October 2002 on the tabled CMI committee's report:

I would like to thank Senators [Brett] Mason and [George] Brandis for their helpful suggestion to extend the terms of reference of the committee—one of the greatest 'own goals' in Australian politics. Without this extension we could not have explored the knowledge that Australian authorities had about the vessel SIEV X and we could not have explored the government's people-smuggling disruption program.

THE 'CHILDREN OVERBOARD' AFFAIR bears importantly on SIEV X in the way it reveals the pressures on the ADF during October 2001 and in the history of the CMI inquiry. Four days after HMAS Adelaide's failure to make SIEV 4 return to Indonesia, there was discussion of 'disruption activity, and scope for beefing up', in a high-level policy committee in the Prime Minister's Department (a committee known as the People-Smuggling Taskforce, or PST).[26] The boat now known as SIEV X sank one week later.

During the testimony heard by the CMI committee in March and April, opposition senators discovered just how cavalier the interceptions of SIEV 4 and other SIEVs had been about the safety of asylum-seekers. This inclined the senators to take my questions about SIEV X more seriously. The more they pursued the questions, and the more that official witnesses misled them about SIEV X, the more their concerns were reinforced.

Senator Faulkner's initial role in the CMI committee was to nail down how the government's 'children overboard' misrepresentations had been initiated and thereafter protected. Faulkner was to be entirely successful in this (see the committee's report 'Findings of Fact', pages xxiii–xxiv). Two other committee members— Andrew Bartlett, who was elected leader of the Democrats during the inquiry, and Labor's Jacinta Collins—worked to expose humanitarian shortcomings in the conduct of Operation Relex. They painstakingly extracted ADF testimony on what, to me, was the most important fact in the children overboard story: Commander Banks of HMAS Adelaide had been illegally ordered to keep 223 people (167 adults and 56 children), in a life-threatening situation on their unseaworthy, rescued boat under a directionless tow for 22 hours; and his final order to rescue them from the sea, in the moments when their boat was foundering, entailed a grave risk of drownings, for which he as the rescuing ship's captain would have been responsible. Yet, if he had defied his rescue and towing orders, his career would have been in ruins. His conflict of obligations comes out clearly in the CMI committee's evidence.[27] Reading the full official testimony is harrowing; the CMI report does not adequately encompass it.

There were prevarications and disputations in testimony to the CMI committee. How does one define an unseaworthy boat—when it sinks, or when it is half-sunk? Doesn't the Australian Navy always put safety of life at sea ahead of all else? Doesn't the ship's commander carry the responsibility of deciding when to take people off a rescued boat? Are not commanders trained to make those decisions properly?

At the end of the SIEV 4 testimony, two things were clear: Commander Banks had been under intense pressure of illegal orders and explicit or implied expectations from his chain of command; and he and his officers would have carried the entire moral burden and legal liability if people had drowned as a result of those orders and command expectations. It is not a reassuring picture for the navy. The issue has since been brushed aside, due to the public focus on the lesser issue of the misrepresented rescue photographs and their political cover-up in Canberra.

At the end of the CMI committee's inquiry, Senator Collins laid the blame squarely at the door of the Prime Minister's Department, and Jane Halton's chairing of the People-Smuggling Taskforce. Although Collins commended the 'absolute integrity of the ADF' (as did all the Labor senators in the committee), she said in the Senate:

> I would like to reflect on the management of the People-Smuggling Taskforce and of course its manager, Ms Jane Halton. Ms Halton was involved in a policy that was playing chicken with people's lives ... In respect of SIEV4, at 7.51

... the boarding party 'request to move children and women off'. But at 10.09 ... they are still on the ship, and we have the recommendation to 'put people in the water' on the double. At 10.36, the ship is 'contacting parliament on the crisis'. We have people in the water and we are contacting parliament on the crisis, according to this log. Finally, at 11.00 ... which is 51 minutes after these people were put in the water—HMAS Adelaide's RHIBs [rubber dinghies] were instructed to bring children on board the Adelaide. How can it be that the discussions that were going through the taskforce and through PM&C [Prime Minister and Cabinet] in relation to how to manage these asylum seekers allowed people to be put in the water for 50 minutes?[28]

I am less generous than Senator Collins in exonerating the ADF in these SIEV 4 events. The concerns over safety of life at sea in the SIEV 4 story—which so dominated questioning from Collins and Bartlett—were given a highly sanitised summation in the committee's report. The dilemma faced by Commander Banks was discussed fairly sympathetically, but was presented in the context of a 'moral risk' of 'personal consequences' rather than in one of a commander improperly burdened with illegal orders.[29]

In the end, the CMI committee's report fudged the issue of safety of life at sea in SIEV interceptions, offering an agreed view that, 'at the general operational level ... more should be done to embed SOLAS [safety of life at sea] obligations in the planning, orders and directives of ADF operations'.[30] The committee pronounced itself impressed by the RAN's serious commitment to safety, but it nonetheless expressed 'a degree of concern about the extent to which this imperative figured in the mission tasking of other arms of the government architecture supporting Operation Relex'. It is not hard to extract the real meaning of these bland euphemisms.

The committee urged that 'international and legal safety obligations should be given prominence in all mission tasking orders for ADF operations', especially 'in law-enforcement operations involving non-combatants'. Such concerns were faintly echoed in the final recommendation of this chapter of the report:

> The committee recommends that operational orders and mission tasking statements for all ADF operations, including those involving whole of government approaches, explicitly incorporate relevant international and domestic obligations.[31]

However, even this almost content-free recommendation was apparently accidentally omitted from the list of numbered recommendations that went into the executive summary of the report. In the end, the report contained no recommendations on safety-of-life-at-sea issues or on SIEV X. So much for the additional CMI committee term of reference, suggested by government senators.

THE CMI COMMITTEE'S proceedings, as recorded in Hansard and asssociated documentary evidence, offer many examples of an Australian Defence Force organisational culture that, by September 2001, was ready to carry out orders contrary to maritime safety obligations. I have noted the aggressive interception and boarding techniques that HMAS Adelaide employed with SIEV 4. A few hours later, SIEV 4 was ordered north, after navy crew had carried out temporary steering repairs and donated a bushwalker's hand compass.

The defining moment of choice came a few hours later, after Commander Banks had (properly, and apparently by his own independent decision) returned to rescue the by then clearly unseaworthy SIEV 4 on 7 October. At this moment of rescue—the beginning of the 'second phase' of the interception of SIEV 4— Banks had the legal duty to take the passengers on board his ship for their safety, and to tow their crippled boat the short distance to Christmas Island, the nearest port. Instead he was ordered to tow the boat in a circular path, remaining in international waters until the government had decided what to do, with the people kept on board their unsafe boat. That was the point at which the ADF should have said no to the government. It had the entire law on safety of life at sea on its side. Yet for 22 hours the ADF acquiesced without protest in life-threatening and illegal government orders.

The blame cannot all be laid at the door of ministers, or senior civilian bureaucrats like Halton: the ADF had itself been culturally conditioned by now to think of asylum-seekers as a threat to the security of Australia.[32] In the CMI committee in 2002, ADF admirals were still trying to justify the need for illegal 'border protection' procedures, even while such practices were being exposed on an ABC *Four Corners* program.[33] Many in the ADF had come to see asylum-seekers as the enemy.

I have asked myself since April 2002 how might such a mindset have affected the way in which Operation Relex would respond to uncertain intelligence about the possible risk to life of people on the latest 'Quassey boat', reported as having departed, small and overcrowded, with 400 people on board? Might an indifference to the lives of boat people have by that time become so ingrained in the system that nobody would really much care about a boat that failed to arrive?

THERE WAS an earlier event with a potentially important policy connection to SIEV X—Palapa, the asylum-seeker boat whose mostly Afghani passengers were saved from death by MV Tampa on 26 August.[34] Palapa was a grossly overloaded, ill-equipped, unseaworthy small fishing boat carrying 438 people (a similar number to those on SIEV X; no other SIEV carried such large numbers) that broke down at dawn on 24 August, about 60 miles north-west of Christmas Island. Its overtaxed engine had worked loose on its mountings and fallen off, causing the gears to shear. It was irreparable.

There are haunting similarities to the SIEV X story. Palapa sailed at 4.00am on 23 August from a little port, Pantau, near Pelabuhan Ratu on the south-west coast of Java. *Dark Victory* reports that one vessel set out from the same port a month earlier and allegedly got lost in rough seas.[35] Finally, it turned back and headed north, running aground a couple of days later on a beach at Bandar Lampung, at the northern end of Sunda Strait. A glance at a map shows how improbable this location is: how could this boat have stayed 'lost' all the way up Sunda Strait?

Was this earlier voyage a disruption project? Had this group of passengers always been intended to get 'lost' and finish up at Bandar Lampung?

As on SIEV X, a flimsy temporary upper deck had been fitted to Palapa in order to cram more people on board. The passengers were taken to Pantau in an overnight convoy from the Jakarta area. There were at least six buses. Indonesian soldiers and police officers helped to escort the convoy and load the boat.

Dark Victory does not name the Palapa people-smuggler, but two articles by Don Greenlees name him as Abdul (aka Achmad) Pakistani or Achmad Punjabi.[36] The first article (1 September 2001, days after the Tampa affair) describes him as 'the main man' in Jakarta's people-smuggling trade. He was said to have organised the Palapa voyage—the largest to date—in partnership with up to three other unnamed smugglers. The second article on 27 April 2002 reported that he had returned to Pakistan to marry, and may have left the business. Like Abu Quassey, he seems to have been well known but strangely immune from arrest. Was Quassey one of his partners? Was Abdul Pakistani a disruption agent?

On 26 August, Australia had known 'for days' that this boat was on its way, and on 25 August DIMA knew it had been 'on its way for almost 24 hours'.[37] (This is consistent with later evidence in the CMI committee that Australian intelligence knew about most boat sailings.) A Coastwatch civilian aircraft then found Palapa 'dead in the water' at 10.00am on 25 August. However, this apparently simple fact begs a question. How could the boat have been located so readily by a small Coastwatch aircraft, with limited flying hours, unless it knew where to look? Operation Relex did not yet exist: border protection was still under the Coastwatch-directed interception and processing system known as Operation Cranberry. We can only speculate about what means were used to locate Palapa. Cranberry presumably had access to intelligence from Indonesia about Palapa's departure time and place, and it could have worked out a 'window' in which to locate it. If there had been Jindalee Operational Radar Network (JORN) radar tracking of Palapa, or a tracking device fitted to the boat, it would have been even easier to find.

The pilot radioed to Coastwatch his observation that the boat's roof was jammed with men, women, and children waving their life jackets and shouting for help. Coastwatch informed DIMA, the Australian Maritime Safety Authority (AMSA), and the Department of Prime Minister and Cabinet. They did not judge it to be a distress situation. The same Coastwatch plane returned that afternoon and made a video, later shown in the Perth trial of the Indonesian crew. Again, people were signalling frantically. Coastwatch reported to agencies that the vessel seemed to be in distress. That evening, AMSA informed the Indonesian rescue authority, BASARNAS, whose nominal zone of search-and-rescue responsibility extends to south of Christmas Island, that a vessel required assistance in its zone.

All that day, 25 August, no Australian action was taken to send a boat from Christmas Island, only 60 nautical miles away, to help these people in distress. That night there was a violent storm, and Palapa nearly sank. Had it sunk, it would have become an earlier version of the SIEV X mass-drowning tragedy. Coastwatch, AMSA, the Prime Minister's Department, and DIMA would have faced questions as to whether they had been criminally negligent in not initiating rescue action the day before, while there was still time. Next morning, the same Coastwatch aircraft returned. This time, the people had painted 'HELP' and 'SOS' on the cabin roof with black engine oil. Australian authorities finally acknowledged a distress signal requiring a response, and alerted shipping. The nearest merchant ship, MV Tampa, responded. The rest is history.

IN THE DAYS following the Tampa crisis, AMSA (overseen by the Department of Transport) experienced an unusual degree of personal contact with senior officers of the Prime Minister's Department (Max Moore-Wilton and Jane Halton). The department was pressing Transport and AMSA to review their procedures on rescue at sea in respect of people-smuggling vessels in distress. Senators Faulkner and Kirk have probed this area closely in the CMI and subsequent committees, but PM&C, Transport, and AMSA have revealed little.[38] The documents they provided on request are replete with blackout ink.

Alhough the head of AMSA, Clive Davidson, assured the committee that the responsibility of all search-and-rescue agencies is to respond comprehensively and completely to every search-and-rescue event, this was manifestly not done in the Palapa case.[39] Nor does it explain the apparent pressure on AMSA to draft a new protocol to govern search-and-rescue procedures for people-smuggling vessels.

Could this be one of the keys to why, about seven weeks later, Operation Relex, with all its resources, failed to detect SIEV X sinking in its surveillance zone? Was it by then understood that if SIEVs were thought to be at risk of sinking on the high seas, but still a long way from Christmas Island or Ashmore Reef, they should not be searched for?

Once Operation Relex was running, Australia could no longer claim that SIEVs which needed rescue in the Indonesian search-and-rescue zone extending to the south of Christmas Island and Ashmore Reef were an Indonesian responsibility. The nearest ship was legally obliged to go to the rescue, and Australia had naval vessels and RAAF aircraft intensively surveilling the area. Operation Relex personnel should have known before anyone else if a SIEV got into distress or sank in its operational waters. This point was firmly made in testimony by Rear Admiral Marcus Bonser, head of Coastwatch, on 22 May:

> The surveillance that has been put in place is quite comprehensive and covers a broad area, and it is intended to pick up the boats as they pass through the area ... The whole general area is being covered by what is probably the most comprehensive surveillance that I have seen in some 30 years of service.[40]

COMPLIANCE ISSUES related to the safety of life at sea run like a thread through the whole fabric of the SIEV X story. Ever since European colonisation, Australia has depended on a universal maritime code to help anyone in danger of drowning at sea. Safe communication with the mother country depended on it. Sometimes this principle is taken to great lengths: substantial resources are expended to rescue yacht crews who get into trouble even thousands of miles from Australia. Yet, under pressure of Operation Relex, decisions may have been made in government and ADF offices, or on ships and in aircraft, which violated Australia's rescue obligations.

In September 2002, two dark-skinned men — one an Australian citizen, one Samoan — were rescued from a small dinghy by a local fishing boat about 30 miles off the coast of south Queensland.[41] They had drifted without radio contact for 12 days after their boat foundered 80 miles out from the Gold Coast en route to Noumea. The men claimed after their rescue that many ships had passed them by, ignoring their flares and signals for help. One came as close as 50–100 metres, stopped for several minutes to observe them, then moved away. One of the men said to an ABC news team filming their return, as their faces were being ineffectually shielded from the camera by police hands: 'When you see a ship turn away from you, and we were in such dire need of help … I just couldn't believe a ship would turn away from us like that.'

Was the shipping industry aware of new Australian confidential advice to merchant shipping, after the Tampa rescue, that suspected illegal immigrants in distress should be left for border-protection authorities to deal with? Does this incident offer clues to a new, undeclared sea-rescue regime, the effect of which is to deny to suspected boat people in distress the normal right of maritime rescue?

Chapter Seven

The Thirteenth SIEV

'Is there any other point to which you would wish to draw my attention?'
'To the curious incident of the dog in the night-time.'
'The dog did nothing in the night-time.'
'That was the curious incident,' remarked Sherlock Holmes.

—'Silver Blaze', *The Memoirs of Sherlock Holmes*, Sir Arthur Conan Doyle, 1894

How often have I said to you that when you have eliminated the impossible, whatever remains, however improbable, must be the truth?

—Sherlock Holmes, *The Sign of Four*, Sir Arthur Conan Doyle, 1890

ONCE THE CMI COMMITTEE accepted my (still confidential) first submission, I set about stimulating media interest. My early attempts to publish in *The Australian* failed. However, on 25 March, *The Age* ran my first opinion piece.[1] The same day, the *Canberra Times* ran my first magazine-length feature (2500 words).[2] These two articles had a considerable effect in Canberra official circles.

The first sentence of the *Canberra Times* story introduced the SIEV X name: 'The sinking 80km south of Java of an unnamed asylum-seeker vessel bound for Christmas Island—let's call it SIEV X for convenience—about 2pm on Friday, October 19, became world news on Tuesday, October 23.'

I coined this term because it was short and convenient, and because it would usefully link my questions about this boat to the 12 suspected illegal entry vessels that had been tracked and intercepted by Operation Relex. The signifier 'X' indicated that this was an unknown, thirteenth SIEV. The name caught on, and has been in general currency since.

A NEW ELEMENT entered the story. A feature on Channel Nine's *Sunday* program on 17 February, 'The Australian People Smuggler', made serious allegations about an Australian individual. These allegations became headline news. In parliament on 18 February, government ministers, without commenting on specifics of the case, said it was normal Australian police practice to use informants from inside criminal industries.[3] Justice minister Chris Ellison asked the AFP to review and report on the allegations. The next day, in Senate Estimates on 19 February, AFP Commissioner Keelty testified that Kevin Enniss had been one of an undisclosed number of paid AFP informants on people smuggling in Indonesia.[4] He said the AFP's informant relationship with Enniss had run from August 2000 to September 2001, and that information thus obtained on people smuggling had saved the nation $22.5 million by preventing 451 asylum-seekers from coming to Australia. Keelty said, 'We knew he was engaged in people smuggling because he was telling us what was going on.' A supplementary written AFP reply following Keelty's 19 February testimony (to Senator Ludwig, QON 84) said:

> At the commencement of the AFP's relationship with Mr Enniss the AFP was aware that Mr Enniss moved in a circle of friends and associates who were either closely linked to persons, or were themselves involved, in people smuggling.

From February to September 2002, issues of legality and propriety in the AFP–Enniss relationship were bitterly contested between Channel Nine and the AFP, and between Labor and government senators. There are many uncertainties, and sorting out the truth is well-nigh impossible without public access to AFP files. Enniss insisted that he was only acting out a people-smuggler role in order to do his job as a police informant, a claim publicly endorsed six months later by the AFP.

The *Sunday* program contained allegations by Enniss's two Australian former business partners. A press story on 4 March by Lindsay Murdoch, ('I'm just a good spy, says our man in Timor')[5] gives Enniss's position: after a business disagreement, these partners lodged complaints, which included fraud, misconduct, and stealing, to Indonesian authorities. Local police arrested him in June 1999. The case was never heard, and he was released from Kupang jail in December 1999. According to DFAT Senate testimony, the Australian embassy gave consular help to Enniss and his family during this period.[6]

The Murdoch article presented Enniss in a favourable light, as a man who did good work for Australia and was anxious to clear his name. Murdoch writes that, soon after Enniss's release from jail in December 1999, he telephoned Australian police in Jakarta, and that, according to senior police in Australia and Indonesia, Enniss 'ran a secret intelligence network with Indonesian police that stopped hundreds of asylum seekers reaching Australia during 2000 and last year' [2001]. Murdoch quotes Enniss:

> How could people think I was anything else [than a people smuggler]? This is what I did for a living. It was my job to know everything that was happening in people smuggling: when the boats were going, who arranged them, who was on them. Sure, many people thought I was a people smuggler and I never tried to make them think otherwise. But I am not a people smuggler, nor have I ever been one.

Murdoch reports Enniss as a man with encyclopaedic knowledge of people smuggling in Indonesia, holding computer files on more than 600 people involved in such activities there, 'from the heads of six major syndicates to local fixers and boat crews'. Murdoch quotes Enniss as saying:

> The Australian police are handicapped by always having to deal with the Indonesians through official channels. The bureaucracy made it hard for them. But the police in Kupang were genuine in wanting to stop boats going to Australia and to arrest the smugglers. I was able to work with them unofficially every day. We effectively closed down their operation.

On 24 August, the AFP released two public statements, 'AFP investigation into alleged people smuggler completed' and 'Summary: Kevin John Enniss's role as an informant', which supported Enniss's claim to have been acting out the role of a people smuggler:

> Put simply, Enniss assumed an identity designed to convince asylum seekers to deal through him so he could report back to Indonesian authorities who could then interdict those asylum seekers. What *Sunday* observed, and was reported by others who were not aware of Enniss' formally sanctioned role, was Enniss acting out his cover story.

The public controversy continued. A second *Sunday* program on 1 September 2002, 'The Federal Police and People Smugglers', made further serious allegations about Enniss. Faulkner now called for a full independent judicial inquiry into AFP operations in Indonesia. Ellison rejected this call.[7] Then, on 26 September, Keelty personally authorised a strongly worded AFP media release, 'Senator Faulkner has got it wrong'. Inter alia, it said:

> Kevin Enniss has been formally interviewed since the Nine Network's *Sunday* program alleged his involvement in the

sabotaging of vessels. He emphatically denied any such involvement.

A mystery remains. There are numerous refugee accounts that, during 1999–2001, many boats were springing leaks, experiencing engine failure or stove fires, and sinking soon after embarkation, while still in Indonesian waters or close to Indonesian land.[8] These many failed voyages would have certainly exemplified public messages that Australian ministers Ruddock and Downer were emphasising at the time—that people-smuggling voyages were dangerous, and that they put passengers' lives at grave risk. But might any AFP informants have conceivably been involved in such life-threatening disruption activity? Would the AFP have conceivably known if they were? We do not know.

On 23–25 September, Senator Faulkner made three impassioned adjournment speeches in the Senate (see pages 222–24 in this book), deeply critical of the Australian government's people-smuggling disruption program in Indonesia. The issue climaxed in the Senate on 26 September, when Question Time, a Take Note of Answers motion, and a Personal Explanation by Faulkner gave rise to hours of angry debate. Faulkner's main themes were the lack of accountability in the disruption program, the risks to human life thereby, and the need for a full powers' judicial inquiry into these matters: all propositions rejected by the government. He used the Enniss case as an example of his concerns.

Faulkner, in his individual comments in the final Senate Report into a Certain Maritime Incident, issued on 23 October 2002 (see pages 455–56 of the published report), restated his concerns about the disruption program and about inconsistencies in AFP accounts of its relations with Kevin Enniss. He renewed his call for a full powers' judicial inquiry into the disruption program. There the matter rests.

SIEV X CAME UP TWICE in the first CMI committee public hearing on 25 March.[9] Without naming me in Hansard, Senator Brett

Mason questioned Rear Admiral Shackleton on my 18 February letter to Simon Crean, which was how I learned that Crean had forwarded it to Defence Minister Robert Hill. Committee chairman Senator Peter Cook helpfully named me, noting that people referred to under parliamentary privilege would have the right of reply under privilege to any allegations made. He said there was a probable case for me to appear and give evidence. This was the first indication that I might be invited to testify in the committee, and that my credibility was already in question.

Senator Bartlett asked Shackleton whether he was aware of the concern raised by a survivor that there may have been Australian vessels in the vicinity that did nothing.[10] Shackleton replied that, after checking available information, there was nothing to indicate that any Australian ship was closer than about 230 nautical miles.

The committee next encountered SIEV X on the third, fourth, and fifth days of hearings (4, 5, and 11 April), with Rear Admiral Smith's testimony.

Senator Bartlett first established the general SIEV interception procedure. On 4 April, Smith said 'there is intelligence that sits behind' information that SIEVs were on their way.[11] On the basis of such information, Operation Relex made assessments on 'windows' when these vessels might appear. Normally, Relex would have a fair chance of knowing when a SIEV of significant size was departing and from where.

> We were relying upon a whole series of activities to give us the information that we needed ... We certainly had some information that boats might be being prepared in different parts of the archipelago ... We pretty much knew where things were going.

Bartlett asked whether Operation Relex normally would know how many people were on SIEVs.[12] Smith said this would be information drawn from intelligence that Relex was provided with. If Relex had information that a vessel was being prepared, there would probably be a rough idea of the numbers. He said Relex never had a strong idea of when boats would sail, but would be prepared in any eventuality.

On 4 April, Bartlett asked about the boat that sank: why was the nearest navy vessel so far away? Smith replied:

> We had some information that a boat might have been being prepared in the vicinity of Sunda Strait but we had no real fixed information as to when it was going to sail. Indeed, the first time that the navy knew that this vessel had sailed was when we were advised through the search-and-rescue organisation in Canberra that this vessel may have foundered in the vicinity of Sunda Strait. At that time our nearest ship was about 150 miles away.

Smith said navy ships did not patrol up close to Indonesia, but stayed back nearer Christmas Island's 24-mile contiguous zone, ready to board SIEVs as they approached that line. The next day, questioned about aerial surveillance, Smith confirmed that RAAF P3 Orion flights reported to Operation Relex.

> The air surveillance was being conducted up near the Indonesian archipelago as close as 30-odd miles and south from there. The ships, however, were positioned … to maximise our chances of interception. So the whole layered surveillance operation was operating more deeply than previously, but the ships more often than not—and it varied from day to day—were closer to Australian territory.

Bartlett then asked whether the surveillance aircraft that were close to the Indonesian coast were not aware of the departure of the vessel that sank. Smith replied: 'At no time under the auspices of Operation Relex were we aware of the sailing of that vessel until we were told that it had in fact foundered.'[13]

SIEV X came up a third time on 11 April, in the final minutes of Smith's testimony. Senator Cook asked Smith about 'the Kevin hypothesis'. Smith said:

> We had no knowledge of the boat having sailed. The first that we were aware that this vessel had sailed from Indonesia was when we were contacted by the search-and-rescue organisation here in Canberra, on 22 October, when they advised us that this vessel was overdue and it was feared it had foundered in the Sunda Strait area. None of our surveillance that we had operating—aircraft or ships—had detected this vessel.

Bartlett asked: 'How did Search and Rescue know it was overdue if they did not know it had left?' Smith replied:

> They had advice from Coastwatch Canberra to say that the vessel believed to have sailed on or at the 19th for Christmas Island was overdue. Where they got that information from is a bit sensitive I think; it is intelligence.[14]

Smith's three days of testimony, including the new information he supplied on 11 April, produced the following picture:

- The nearest navy vessel, HMAS Arunta, was 150 nautical miles away.
- Relex had some information that a boat might have been being prepared in the vicinity of Sunda Strait.
- Relex had no fixed information as to when it was going to sail.
- Air surveillance was conducted as close as 30-odd nautical miles from Indonesia, but no one saw the boat.
- Relex's first knowledge that this vessel had sailed was on 22 October when the search-and-rescue organisation advised that this vessel was overdue and feared foundered in the Sunda Strait area.
- Search and rescue had advice from Coastwatch Canberra to say that the vessel believed to have sailed on or at the 19th for Christmas Island was overdue.
- Where they got that information from is sensitive intelligence.
- Had Relex known it was happening, whether in Indonesian

territorial or international waters, it would have gone to the rescue.

There were, however, gaps in this testimony, and inconsistencies arising from it:

- How did Coastwatch learn about what it passed on to search-and-rescue authorities on 22 October—that SIEV X had sailed on or at 19 October for Christmas Island and was assessed as overdue, believed foundered? And why hadn't this intelligence on SIEV X's sailing gone to Relex at the same time as it went to Coastwatch?
- What specific intelligence on SIEV X did Coastwatch receive? When did Coastwatch receive it? Should this information have triggered air surveillance—under the safety-of-life-at-sea convention—of the area of Indian Ocean adjacent to Sunda Strait, from where SIEV X was reported to have sailed?
- Why wasn't Relex told to surveil the area by air, and to locate this approaching boat? Why wasn't the normal practice followed?

The issue by now was gaining public traction. When two letters expressing concern appeared in the *Canberra Times*, Smith sent this letter in response:

> In this case, the first that Navy knew that this vessel had sailed was when advised through the search and rescue organisation in Canberra on October 22 that this vessel might have foundered in the vicinity of Sunda Strait. At that time our nearest ship was about 150 miles away.[15]

I wrote another *Canberra Times* commentary. 'Truth missing in murky waters', setting out my latest analysis of the sinking of SIEV X, and the survivors' rescue and return to Jakarta.[16] I suggested that the analysis lent weight to the following hypotheses:

- This boat's sinking was not accidental. It resulted from deliberate prior actions intended to render it likely to sink early into its voyage to Christmas Island.
- The rescue of 44 survivors on 20 October and their transshipment to Jakarta, arriving there on 22 October, was also a managed process, aimed at making survivors accessible to media in order to maximise the international news impact of the disaster.
- The shock of this tragedy was a turning point. It quickly halted the flow of suspected illegal entry vessels to Australia, and it prompted the Indonesian government to cooperate with the Australian government to oppose people-smuggling.

I then suggested:

> Questions about information flows within the Australian SIEV detection and interception system must be resolved, before we can be sure that no Australian authority failed to respond in a timely way to a known or suspected SOLAS [safety of life at sea] situation, when there might still have been time for the RAN to save lives.

On the basis of my analysis of Smith's three days of testimony, I wrote:

> The only logical conclusion is that somewhere in the Australian information chain it was known, possibly as early as October 18 or 19, that this boat had left but had not, or was not going to get, very far before foundering ... It is crucial to know what precise intelligence came down from Australia's various police and/or intelligence sources in Indonesia regarding this vessel's departure, when it was sent, which agencies in Australia received it, and when they received it. It is possible that neither Coastwatch nor [the search and rescue organisation] received relevant information until well after the October 19 sinking. In this case, the

burden of question falls on the source intelligence agency: was information about this boat's overloaded and unseaworthy state omitted or delayed, information that could have saved many lives? ... It is possible that timely and complete intelligence reports came down from Australian informants in Indonesia, but that further action was blocked by their own parent organisation in Canberra, or by some higher information-processing agency in Canberra: perhaps the interdepartmental committee chaired by the Department of the Prime Minister and Cabinet, perhaps Strategic Command, perhaps an even higher authority.

I was going out on a limb. In the absence yet of firm evidence, I was trying to shake something out of the system. I concluded:

On the basis of research so far, I cannot be confident that [safety of life at sea] obligations were properly met at all possible stages in SIEV detection and interception. If true, this is a very serious hypothesis and it needs to be investigated seriously ... Unlike the more murky question of what was done in Indonesia, the [CMI] committee has powers to interrogate and thereby throw the light of truth on what happened at the Australian end. Exposing the full truth on this aspect could in time help to illuminate the larger story from Indonesia.

I still had no idea how much credibility my initial letter and two submissions, and my three newspaper articles on SIEV X, might have with members of the CMI committee. Bartlett and Cook seemed interested in SIEV X, but was anyone else? Senator George Brandis had already labelled 'the Kevin hypothesis' as 'absolute rubbish'.[17] Did opposition senators on the committee see the validity of the questions raised by Smith's SIEV X testimony?

Many months later, I learned informally that my concerns had some foundation. At that stage, in April 2002, there was still much scepticism in the committee—not just on the government side—about my SIEV X questions. Basically, the questions were being pursued more as a courtesy to me as a former ambassador, rather than in any real expectation of uncovering anything serious. 'Probably another Defence stuff-up' was still the general Labor opposition expectation at that time, right up until the dramatic testimony by Rear Admiral Marcus Bonser of Coastwatch on 22 May—testimony that was to change everything.

Smith gave other significant testimony.[18] He said that whatever came out of the inter-departmental committee process on SIEVs [the PST chaired by Jane Halton] was understood by Operation Relex as a 'government direction'. This committee met regularly to make decisions as to the next step in particular SIEV operations. If reports were received of a SIEV on its way to Australia, this committee would leave it to the navy to decide on the detail of interception tactics.

Smith noted that the places where SIEV boats had embarked from were blacked out from the Defence data matrix because that information was 'drawn from intelligence'.[19] I wondered why it was so important not to reveal where boats sailed from. Other witnesses (Banks, Shackleton) had similarly declined to say where boats sailed from.

On 16 April, Jane Halton testified for the first time. Briefly questioned about SIEV X, she was vague and dismissive:

> I have certainly read some things in the newspapers in the last little while about our state of knowledge of particular vessels which, I have to say to you, from where I sat, is absolutely not correct.[20]

AT THIS STAGE, the lid seemed to be still firmly on SIEV X. I looked forward with trepidation to my testimony, now scheduled for 1 May. I knew I would face tough questioning. I had little to go on, apart from my instinct, the gaps and inconsistencies in Smith's statements, and my still rudimentary research.

I prepared my ground as thoroughly as possible. My second submission to the CMI committee, on 11 April, covered every avenue of possible questioning. I was suggesting to the committee senators: 'Here is a full checklist of questions to which you might like to seek answers.' It was an unusual position for a Senate committee witness to take, but I had gone too far to turn back now. My submission suggested that the committee try to explore the intelligence on boat departures. Against the background of Smith's evidence as to the success of general procedures for SIEV detection and interception, was it not strange that SIEV X had not been detected?

I noted the possibility (after Smith's denial that any Australian navy vessel was near the sinking) that an Indonesia-based boat or boats might have inspected the scene and reported the sinking coordinates, so that fishing boats might go to the area later to pick up a few survivors.

I noted that Australian search-and-rescue authorities apparently had learned of the possible sinking before survivors reached Jakarta on the evening of Monday, 22 October. In order to be able to put out a 'boat overdue' notice on 22 October, those authorities must have had prior information about when this boat set out for Christmas Island, and from where. Making assumptions about the overloaded boat's speed and the distance from Bandar Lampung to Christmas Island, the issuing of the overdue notice on 22 October suggested to me that Australian authorities expected it to arrive at Christmas Island by 21–22 October, on the basis of a departure on 18–19 October. Where did Australian search-and-rescue authorities get such departure information, and when?

I wrote that I had not been able to obtain any information from Australian search-and-rescue authorities about the overdue notice. I urged the CMI committee to try to obtain from AMSA an account of its knowledge and activity in this matter.

I suggested it was reasonable to assume, on the basis of Smith's testimony and other indications—for example, recent reports and parliamentary evidence concerning the activities of AFP informant Kevin Enniss—that, at a time soon after the boat's departure in the early morning of 18 October, a police or intelligence report might have been sent to Australia saying this boat had left from Bandar Lampung. Such a report might also have contained information about the number of passengers, the armed men that had forced them to board, and the boat's grossly overloaded and unsafe condition (that is, the long crack in the hull reported by Greenlees). I suggested it was important for the committee to establish the full timing and contents of any such intelligence. I added:

> Some 30 hours after embarkation, the boat sank. It seems to me improbable that a police or intelligence report would not have been sent during this long period of time: unless a deliberate decision had been made to delay its despatch to Australia, or to delay its on-forwarding by the initial recipient within Australia to other authorities, e.g., AMSA/AUSSAR [safety, search and rescue], Operation Relex.

I wrote that it would seem important to establish the facts about when such a police or intelligence report concerning the departure of this boat had reached the relevant Australian authorities, and concluded this section:

> I am assuming that there would have to have been such a police or intelligence report for the Australian authorities to have issued the overdue notice on Monday 22 October, and for the Australian search and rescue authorities to have informed Rear Admiral Smith and Operation Relex that the boat had foundered.

I next addressed the possibility that Australian RAAF Orion and/or Coastwatch aircraft may have tracked the movement of this boat, and noted its disappearance from its observed course or observed wreckage and survivors:

> I do not know whether a police or intelligence report [of departure] would have reached relevant operational authorities in Australia in time to mount such aerial surveillance. I do know that from the time such a report was received, it could have been quickly acted upon. Surveillance aircraft

could have been sent out to monitor a relatively narrow strip of sea along the boat's reported course from Bandar Lampung [in Sunda Strait] towards Christmas Island, based on its known departure time and a range of assumptions of how far it might have got at its estimated speed.

I concluded here that it would be desirable for the committee to try to establish clearly whether Australian surveillance aircraft had made any observations as outlined above and, if so, the action that was taken.

If Operation Relex did not know about the sinking until it was too late for navy ships to reach the scene, did any other parts of the Australian system know and, if so, did they delay passing on this information to Operation Relex and the navy? Though I did not say so, I was thinking of possible covert means of obtaining information—for example, Defence Signals Directorate (DSD) interceptions of radio messages, or satellite surveillance.

I then raised another possibility:

> Assuming there was no aerial surveillance that would have allowed Australian authorities to have sent a message to Indonesian authorities giving map coordinates where the sinking took place or where wreckage might be found, it would still have been possible for an Indonesian authority or agency to have independently, that is, without Australian assistance, tracked the asylum-seeker boat from behind. An Indonesian ship could have followed the boat's course using out-of-sight observation technology (as the Adelaide used with SIEV 4). Or the asylum-seeker boat, or a crew member, might have carried a tracking device. So it is quite plausible that an Indonesian ship may have relatively easily found and inspected the scene of the sinking during the night of 19–20 October, without assistance or briefing from Australian authorities. Having observed wreckage and survivors in the water, such an Indonesian ship might have sent back messages that might have been received or intercepted

by Australian signals intelligence. Such an intercept might have been the basis for the first Australian information that the asylum-seeker boat had sunk.

I summarised the information I had at the time about the people's journey, sinking, rescue, and return — information that led me to suspect that the sinking was a managed event rather than an accidental one. I said that this information lent weight to my hypothesis that the boat may have been intended to sink, thereby creating a major loss of life and a major deterrent signal against people-smuggling from Indonesia to Australia:

> For that to work, it was necessary not simply that the boat disappear without trace, leaving a mystery — but that some survivors be found and transferred to Jakarta where they would be accessible to international media, so that a major concrete international news story would be generated. I believe that this major human tragedy in waters near Indonesia, which came under the spotlight of world media attention, forced Indonesia's hand, by making people-smuggling in these waters an Indonesian problem also.

My submission was essentially an ambit claim. In retrospect, it is remarkable how close to the truth much of it turned out to be. It must have been hard for the authorities to believe that I did not have a whistleblower providing me with inside information. Yet that is the truth.

IN MY TESTIMONY in the CMI committee on 1 May, I did not make accusations that I could not yet prove. I was asking the committee to explore the inconsistencies and gaps I had identified in the official evidence to date. I was also trying to convince the senators of the high probability that the boat had sunk in international waters and in the Operation Relex zone. I was more successful in the first objective than the second. These extracts give the flavour of a challenging two hours:

> **Faulkner**: I want to be clear on this. You are not suggesting any direct or indirect Australian involvement, or possible Australian involvement, in what you describe as the probable sabotage, are you?
> **Kevin**: I am not going to go beyond what I have said in my submissions on that. I have said that it is conceivable and I have said that the possibility has to be taken into account, but clearly one has to begin to get some hard evidence.
> **Faulkner**: But you do not have any hard evidence.
> **Kevin**: The route into that sort of evidence, I believe, is finding out why this SIEV boat's embarkation for Australia was not normally handled in the Australian information and command system of Operation Relex. Once we know why that happened, we will have a basis on which to investigate further these very serious matters.
> **Faulkner**: Yes, but you do not have any evidence of this, do you? You do not have any evidence of any possible Australian involvement.
> **Kevin**: If I had that kind of evidence, I would be putting it in the hands of the police.
> **Faulkner**: Yes. So you do not have any, do you?
> **Kevin**: No.[21]

After lunch came questioning from Mason—seeking, as he put it, to 'deconstruct the conspiracy and all facets to it'. By the time he had repeated the word 'conspiracy' (a word I was careful not to use myself) five times in two minutes of questioning, I was alerted.

> **Mason**: Sure, but it does not establish a conspiracy, does it?
> **Kevin**: I am not trying to establish a conspiracy; I am trying to establish the facts.

The most difficult moments came towards the end, with Brandis.

Brandis: ... torture this testimony from Admiral Smith as you will, it does not seem to support the proposition that you advanced in your statement this morning that it is clear that there was some official Australian foreknowledge of the circumstances that led to the deaths. There is an innuendo, wouldn't you accept, in what you said this morning of some Australian culpability or responsibility for those deaths? That is the innuendo you make. You do not come out and say that; you are willing to wound but afraid to strike. But that is the innuendo, isn't it?

Kevin: I do not want to wound anybody and I did not come here to make innuendos. I came here to point out inconsistencies in the public record.

Brandis: Do you or do you not say that there was any level of Australian culpability in those deaths?

Kevin: I say that it is for your committee to find out.

Brandis: What do you say?

Kevin: I say it is for your committee to find out.

Brandis: You have raised the issue and then said, 'I believe that the public record as it now stands would cast a serious slur on the honour and competency of our navy and the ADF generally'. You, with respect, sir, have cast the slur. Do you or don't you say that there was some Australian culpability for these deaths?

Kevin: With respect, sir, I say that your committee has the power to call official witnesses under oath to find out the truth on these disturbing discrepancies in the public record ...

Brandis: So you do not make that allegation.

Kevin: Senator, I am not here to make allegations; I am here to bring to your committee's attention to discrepancies in the public record of what Australia knew about this boat and what it did with the information. A system of intelligence, surveillance and interception that worked very well in the case of every other SIEV boat that was coming down in this period failed to work in this case and 350 people died.

Brandis: Do I understand you to be telling me that you do not allege any Australian culpability in these deaths?
Kevin: I am not here to allege; I am here to bring discrepancies on the public record regarding the Australian system of information and command to your attention, for your committee to do what you wish to do with it.
Brandis: Perhaps Senator Faulkner, Senator Mason and I are all stupid, but it is not apparent to us that there are such discrepancies in the public record.
Faulkner: I wish you would not include me in that group.
Brandis: In any event, Mr Kevin, you do not suggest there is a culpability. Is that what I take from your evidence? At the end of the day, you do not make an allegation to that effect.
Kevin: Senator, I am not in a position to say whether there is culpability or not. It is for your committee to find this out.
Brandis: And it is for you, is it, to leave the slur on the honour and competency of the navy and the ADF on the basis of no evidence at all?
Kevin: No, it is for me to say that this public record shows that the information and the command chain was not working as it should have been in this very important case and 353 people died.

I did not convince the committee on the sinking location. All I had to go on then was the article by Don Greenlees on 24 October 2000 and the map in *The Australian*, which government Senator Alan Ferguson dismissed as just a newspaper report, and my rough estimates of times and speeds based on survivor accounts. That I was right did not become clear until later, when three items of corroborating evidence came before the committee: the Jakarta harbor master's rescue coordinates, the People Smuggling Taskforce minute of 23 October 2001, and the immigration department's intelligence note of 23 October 2001. The fourth piece of evidence, the Jakarta embassy cable of 23 October 2001, arrived four months after the committee had concluded its work.

Chapter Eight

Accidental Whistleblowers

REAR ADMIRAL SMITH'S TESTIMONY seemed to exonerate Defence, but it left new questions about the conduct of Coastwatch and the Australian Maritime Safety Authority. Clive Davidson, chief executive officer of AMSA, testified on 1 May. He said AMSA was first advised by Coastwatch at 2.40pm on 22 October that:

> it had had advice from a number of sources that a vessel carrying an unknown number of people had left Indonesia on 19 October, whereas it appears that the actual date of sailing, as later reported, was 18 October. The vessel was reported to be transiting the Sunda Strait and heading for Christmas Island. Coastwatch calculated by then that it was overdue.[1]

Davidson said AMSA did not initiate any search-and-rescue action, because there was no information that the boat might be sunk or in distress. AMSA informed its Indonesian counterpart, BASARNAS, that the boat was overdue, had not arrived, and there was concern for its safety. It did not follow up when it received no response; it was quite normal for BASARNAS not to reply to such AMSA messages.

In explaining AMSA's apparently very limited concern on 22 October for SIEV X's safety, Davidson said:

> The nature of the number of people on board the vessel was unknown, the departure point was unknown ... The information we had at the time was that a number of sources were reporting that a vessel carrying an unknown number of potential illegal immigrants departed the west coast of Java on 19 Friday, transiting the Sunda Strait and heading for Christmas Island. That was the sum total of our information ... There was complete uncertainty about whether the vessel existed at all ... We were advised from Coastwatch that there were a number of sources of information that were advising that the vessel was departing on or about the 19th [October] and that it was overdue by their calculations.[2]

Davidson emphasised that AMSA had not received any information from Coastwatch to indicate that the vessel was in distress, or that it had foundered.[3] That was why AMSA had not put out a call to all shipping in the area.

It became clear to the CMI committee three weeks later, in testimony by the head of Coastwatch, Admiral Marcus Bonser, on 22 May, that Coastwatch knew far more about SIEV X than it told AMSA—and at least two days earlier. AMSA was brought in at a late stage, on 22 October, when Coastwatch and the People Smuggling Taskforce finally concluded that SIEV X was a missing overdue boat (the record is unclear as to which agency reached this conclusion first). Until then, Coastwatch and the Australian Defence Force had not told AMSA anything about SIEV X, and even then AMSA was not told that 400 people were believed to be on board a small, overloaded boat—a remarkable example of apparent indifference by the PST, Operation Relex, and

Coastwatch to their safety-of-life-at-sea obligations.

A senior DFAT official, Dr Geoff Raby, also testified on 1 May.[4] Asked whether Foreign Minister Alexander Downer had been briefed in any way by the department about SIEV X, Raby replied: 'I would have to take that on notice, I think. The sit rep [situation report] seems to be the only brief that we provided on that.'

He added a little later:

> there was a lot of cable traffic. When you ask, 'was the minister briefed', he would have been receiving reports from Jakarta, and the embassy was very assiduous in following this up. There is a lot more on an issue like this than just the sit rep.

The subsequent DFAT answer in June 2002 to a follow-up question on notice by Senator Cook, asking whether Mr Downer had received any briefing on the drowning of asylum-seekers from SIEV X, was simply, 'No'.[5]

Cook also asked Raby:

> Have there been any discussions about trying to tie down the actual circumstances of SIEV X; where it may have foundered; how many people were involved?

Raby replied:

> The post [embassy] in Jakarta has been very active in trying to establish all the facts and circumstances, and that is a big post with defence, police and others attached to it.

Downer and Raby were named recipients of the Jakarta embassy reporting-cable of 23 October 2001 that dealt in detail with the very information sought by Cook. Raby had ample opportunity here, in his oral testimony, and in the above question he took on notice, to inform the committee of the existence of that cable. He did not do so. Raby did not lie. He said there was a lot of cable traffic, and perhaps he understood the question about 'briefing' not to include this reporting cable, sent to many high-level recipients including the prime minister and Raby's own minister. He was not asked in so many words whether the embassy had sent a cable reporting the sinking.

BEFORE HIS TESTIMONY on 22 May, Rear Admiral Marcus Bonser, the head of Coastwatch, asked Defence three times to amend Smith's testimony that the first time Operation Relex knew about SIEV X was on 22 October 2001.[6] Bonser knew this was wrong. First, he phoned Smith's office staff on 16 April 2002. Then, on 22 April, Bonser told Rear Admiral Raydon Gates, who was heading the CDF/Secretary taskforce that was coordinating Defence briefing for the committee, that he believed there were inconsistencies.[7] Bonser recalled that Gates said he would speak to Smith. Finally, on 10 May, Bonser advised the navy chief (Shackleton), who directed, 'If there is any ambiguity, it needs to be cleared up'.

Smith then contacted Bonser on 16 May to say he was writing to the committee. He sent his letter of clarification (not seen by Bonser) the next day.[8] It was received by the committee's secretariat on 21 May, and had an unusual subsequent history. The committee decided at first to release it, along with other letters of additional evidence. Then it decided to recall the document and rescind the decision to release it, subject to its being properly cleared.[9] However, the press gallery already had copies. The letter was never properly cleared for public release and was not included in the committee's documents, but it went into wide circulation, and is considered by default to be published. It was frequently footnoted in the CMI committee's report, and is publicly archived on the *Sydney Morning Herald* Webdiary and sievx.com.

This letter was simply absorbed into Smith's testimony. Defence's first attempted cover-up—blown by Bonser—was politely ignored in the CMI committee's report.

Smith's clarification letter detailed six reports that Operation

Relex received on SIEV X—which he referred to as 'the Abu Qussey vessel' [sic]—between 14 and 22 October 2001. Coastwatch initially reported on 14 October, 'based on intelligence analysis in the daily Civil Maritime Surveillance Program Operation Summary (OPSUM)'—OPSUMs were a regular series of intelligence summaries prepared by Coastwatch—that the vessel had been delayed and remained a potential departure from Pelabuhan Ratu on the south coast of Java. The OPSUM of 18 October reported that the boat had departed the previous day from Pelabuhan Ratu, and it could 'possibly' arrive at Christmas Island on 18 or 19 October. The OPSUM of 19 October reported the vessel as having departed.

The next OPSUM, on 20 October, reported that the vessel had 'allegedly' departed, still on 19 October, but now from a different place: Sumur (in the Sunda Strait on the west coast of Java). The vessel was now described *'allegedly as small and with 400 passengers on board with some passengers not embarking because the vessel was overcrowded'* (my italics). The OPSUM on 21 October 2001 repeated such advice. The 22 October OPSUM advised that the vessel was now considered overdue. Coastwatch assessed that the 'delay could be due to the poor condition of the boat and the large numbers on board, or the use of an alternative route to avoid detection'. This report maintained the advice that the boat allegedly had departed from Sumur early on 19 October. Finally, the Rescue coordination Centre (in AMSA) reported the vessel as overdue on 22 October 2001. The vessel was reported as 'not yet arrived and concerns have been expressed for its safety'.

Smith's letter continued:

> On 19 October 2001 when the Abu Qussey vessel departed Indonesia and foundered in the Sunda Strait, air surveillance assets and navy surface units were conducting layered surveillance operations and responding to SIEVs close to Christmas Island and Ashmore Island. While the intelligence reports regarding the Abu Qussey vessel were from Coastwatch assessments and normally reliable sources,

they provided only an assessment of 'alleged' departures and 'possible' arrival windows. No specific confirmation of departure was ever received. Without confirmation and only reporting of alleged departures there was nothing in the Coastwatch reports that caused me to change the strategy of intercepting SIEVs anywhere else but close to Australian territory.

Finally, and to ensure categorically that there is no misunderstanding, my headquarters did not receive any information (intelligence or otherwise) that could lead to a definitive assessment that the vessel had departed Indonesia. The only time this headquarters received confirmation that the vessel had departed Indonesia was when Coastwatch concerns for the overdue vessel were raised on 22 October 2001, followed by media reports that the vessel had sunk. My answer at CMI [Hansard page] 461—'Indeed the first time that the navy knew this vessel 'had' sailed was when we were advised through the search and rescue organisation in Canberra that this vessel may have founded [sic] in the vicinity of Sunda Strait' therefore remains accurate.

SMITH'S LETTER was the beginning of the second phase of the Defence cover-up. Because of Bonser's determination to set the record straight, Defence could no longer claim that it had known nothing about this boat before 22 October. The new strategy was to admit to detailed intelligence reporting from 14 October onwards, but to claim that this reporting was all so imprecise and variable that Defence could not take any action on safety of life at sea. It was a thin argument, and Smith (who was about to retire) was left to carry the main burden. But it is reasonable to assume that his letter was worked over and cleared by the Gates taskforce (see endnote 7). Admirals do not research and write such letters themselves.

Reflecting on these OPSUM reports, I note that there are two ways of hiding a military target: conceal it by camouflage or lose it among a number of decoys.

First there were three OPSUM reports that the Quassey boat was about to depart (14 October) or had departed (18, 19 October) from a port on Java's south coast, Pelabuhan Ratu. Then there were three more OPSUMs (20, 21, 22 October), claiming it had departed on 19 October from Sumur, a port on Java's west coast in the Sunda Strait. All six OPSUMs were misinformation in the sense of wrongly reporting this boat's departures for Christmas Island, because the boat actually departed from Bandar Lampung in southern Sumatra, on 18 October. It is possible that these OPSUMs were true in the sense that the Quassey boat may have been moving around the coast without passengers from Pelabuhan Ratu to Bandar Lampung. In that case, where had the boat originally come from? Had it perhaps come from eastern Indonesia, where Enniss had been working as an AFP informant and people smuggler?

The Australian authorities have never revealed the registered name of SIEV X, where it was registered, or who owned it. I believe they have this information, and that it is pertinent to the real story of the sinking.

Let us assume here that Coastwatch and Defence believed the six OPSUMs were true at the time they were received. Somehow, streams of misleading information on this particular boat's departure for Christmas Island were being fed into raw Australian Federal Police intelligence reports from Indonesia—reports on which (as Bonser would soon testify) the OPSUMs were based.

Smith's original testimony on 4 and 5 April, before SIEV X became an issue, had been that intelligence reporting on SIEV departures was usually quite accurate. During the course of the committee's inquiry, that claim was reversed. From June onwards, official witnesses began to stress the imprecision of intelligence on SIEV departures. Finally, Jane Halton testified on 30 July that 'only one in 10' reported incoming boats ever arrived.

The reports on which the six OPSUMs were based are not confirmed by any survivor evidence that Quassey tried to embark the SIEV X passengers from a port other than Bandar Lampung in Sumatra on 18 October. Surviving passengers do not report any proposed, then cancelled, bus journeys from Bogor to Pelabuhan

Ratu or to Sumur.[10] They were told once only to pack on 16 October in Bogor for a bus departure that night.

Maybe Quassey or his collaborators were moving his empty boat around, westwards, to Bandar Lampung; but, as far as the passengers were concerned, nothing happened until they set off from Bogor by bus at midnight on 16–17 October. Were the six intelligence reports decoys, designed to anaesthetise Operation Relex into ceasing to take seriously reports about Quassey boat departures? What attempts were made by the AFP to authenticate them at the time, or to find out afterwards why they had been so misleading about departure locations and times?

Had someone been crying 'wolf' so well that, by the time the wolf really came, no one involved on the ADF side of border protection paid much attention any more? And were such effects foreseen by those who put out so many confusing reports about 'the Abu Qussey vessel' in the weeks and days preceding the sinking of SIEV X? Such questions cannot be answered until we see the raw material, the still-secret intelligence reporting sent down from Indonesia by the AFP and DIMA in this period.

Another important point in Smith's letter was its revelation that the Coastwatch OPSUM on 20 October reported that the vessel was then being described 'allegedly as small and with 400 passengers on board with some passengers not embarking because the vessel was overcrowded'.[11] We now know (see Part One) that each of these four elements of intelligence—'small', 'overcrowded', '400 onboard', and 'some passengers not embarking'—was true.

Where did these facts come from, that the OPSUM reported on 20 October? Did the same intelligence source that supplied them also supply the false information about the departure from Sumur, or did the two batches of information come from different sources? It is hard to believe that a source who gave the AFP these four accurate details (especially the last, very precise point about some passengers not boarding) about a SIEV departure did not also accurately report when and where the boat had embarked its passengers. Such a source would have had to be either within or closely observing the Quassey group, which embarked SIEV X in precisely these circumstances in Bandar Lampung on 18 October (see chapter 2). So why wasn't the AFP given the correct departure time and place? These questions go to the heart of the matter, and it was the detailed OPSUM account in Smith's letter of clarification that exposed them.

Coastwatch, Defence, and AFP did not refer willingly again to this accurate information about departure circumstances during their testimony to the CMI committee. Bonser would not confirm the 400 figure or the refusal of some passengers to embark, in reply to questioning from Collins.[12] Neither the Defence review of intelligence on SIEV X (see chapter 10) nor Keelty's AFP evidence (see chapter 11) made any reference to SIEV X being known on 20 October to be a small boat carrying 400 passengers, or that some passengers had refused to embark because of overcrowding. The 400 figure only re-emerges in CMI committee evidence in the PST minutes and in the DIMA intelligence note for 22 October 2001, that were sent to the committee on 6 June and 30 August 2002 respectively.

It is also significant in terms of search-and-rescue obligations that the AFP, Coastwatch, and Defence already knew these four facts on 20 October 2001. Those facts, combined with what was already known to Australian authorities about Quassey's poor previous safety record, should have screamed 'safety of life at sea'.

On the issue of the sinking location, Smith's letter of clarification hardened his April claim in evidence that the boat sank 'in the vicinity of Sunda Strait'. His letter now referred three times, without qualification, to the vessel sinking 'in the Sunda Strait'. Yet Smith, as commander of Operation Relex, must have been briefed on the embassy cable and DIMA note of 23 October 2001 that the boat sank at a point up to 8° south latitude (according to the cable), or 60 nautical miles south of Sunda Strait (according to the DIMA note). Again, one assumes that the Smith letter was drafted in, or checked with, the Defence taskforce. Thus a new false claim was being launched here by the Defence authorities.

Accidental Whistleblowers 157

NOW WE TURN to the Bonser testimony.[13] Bonser made it clear that, apart from an intermediary role in preparing OPSUMs and conveying advice on safety-of-life-at-sea events to the Australian search-and-rescue authority, Coastwatch had no operational border-protection role in the Christmas and Ashmore Island areas. From 2 September 2001, border-protection management of these areas passed to the ADF's Operation Relex.

Bonser revealed, in his 22 May testimony and his additional written evidence on 17 June, important new information that was to expose more aspects of the cover-up.[14] In summary:

- SIEV X sank 'somewhere between the Sunda Strait and perhaps up to 80 nautical miles south of it'.
- There had been numerous reports about Abu Quassey and SIEV X, starting in August 2001. The Smith clarification had revealed only the six OPSUM reports, starting on 14 October. But Bonser revealed two more important facts: these OPSUM reports came from the AFP in Indonesia, and there had been a series of earlier DIMA intelligence reports on Quassey and this boat going back to August 2001.[15]
- Coastwatch had received advice by telephone (unusual in itself) from the AFP on 20 October about the departure of the boat, 'reportedly small and overcrowded', on the previous day, and again from the AFP on 22 October that the boat was now potentially overdue. In his 17 June letter, Bonser added that in the AFP phone call to Coastwatch on 20 October, 'the AFP officer providing the advice also offered a personal opinion that the vessel may be subject to increased risk due to the numbers reportedly on board'. He added that Coastwatch immediately telephoned this report to Australian Theatre Joint Intelligence Centre [ASTJIC] and to Headquarters Northern Command [NORCOM, in Darwin], at 0950 and 1000 respectively.
- His letter also noted that 'Coastwatch received a cable from DFAT, dated 23 October 2001, which contained a

reconstruction of events as they were recounted in Indonesia following the rescue'.

Bonser's opening statement noted the extent of early but inaccurate (apparently DIMA-based) intelligence information about Quassey:

> Coastwatch originally received information as early as August 2001 that Abu Quassey was allegedly in the process of arranging a boat departure of illegal immigrants, probably to Christmas Island. In the ensuing period, Coastwatch received information that the vessel was expected to depart, or had departed, Indonesia on four different dates in August, anywhere within a seven-day block in September and on five separate dates in October.[16]

Bonser said that, on Saturday, 20 October 2001:

> Coastwatch received telephone advice from the AFP that a vessel was reported to have departed from the west coast of Java the previous day. The information included advice that the vessel was reportedly small and overcrowded. The full detail of the advice is classified. This information was passed by telephone from Coastwatch to the Australian Theatre Joint Intelligence Centre [ASTJIC] and to Headquarters Northern Command [NORCOM].

He said that ASTJIC included this information in a classified intelligence report (known as INTSUM) issued to Defence operational authorities on 20 October 2001. Bonser said that, on 22 October:

> AFP provided further advice to Coastwatch that corroborated the previous advice about the departure of the vessel and that, by now, the vessel should have arrived in Australian waters. Coastwatch agreed that the vessel was

potentially overdue, although it noted this was not unusual and might be due to a range of factors, including diversions.

He said that, by 22 October, SIEV X met the criteria for an overdue vessel, based on the additional information received from the AFP on that day. Coastwatch then contacted the search-and-rescue authorities. He said the same AFP information on SIEV departures would usually be sent 'in parallel' to Operation Relex and to Coastwatch.[17] Thus, Relex did not need to await Coastwatch advice on SIEVs.

Bonser confirmed that the first report of sinking came from ASTJIC on 23 October, and later that day CNN reported the sinking and rescue of survivors.[18] However, he later corrected this in his statement of clarification of 17 June, saying that the ASTJIC report included advice of 45 survivors, and that Coastwatch had also received a DFAT cable dated 23 October 2001. This was how the CMI committee became aware of the crucial embassy cable. It spent the next eight months trying to see it.

Bonser was then asked about the sinking location.[19] His answer became headline news:

> I can only go off what I have seen in media reports that indicate it was somewhere between the Sunda Strait and perhaps 80 miles south of Sunda Strait, or 80 miles south of Java.

He confirmed that this area included areas under Operation Relex surveillance, using ships with helicopters, and aircraft.

Bonser's '80 miles south of Sunda Strait' estimate corresponds closely to the advice in the embassy cable, of which he had been a named addressee, that the boat sank at a point up to 8° south latitude. He could properly attribute this information to media reports, as the latitude had already appeared in the *Indonesian Business* report on 23 October 2001, based on the embassy's briefing. I did not know of this media report then, but no doubt it was on official files.

At the time Bonser testified, the official version was that the boat had sunk 'in Indonesian waters' (Howard), or 'in or near Sunda Strait' (Hill, supported by Smith).

As I write this book, the official position is still as it was set out in the July 2002 Defence review, that 'Defence can only speculate on where SIEV X sank'.[20] That claim, initially accepted by the CMI committee and written into its report (paragraph 8.5), now has no public credibility.. A Senate motion that was proposed by Senator Bob Brown on 15 October 2003 refers to SIEV X as the boat that 'sank 100 kilometres south of Indonesia, in international waters that were being closely monitored by Australian air and naval forces'.[21]

Bonser was closely quizzed on how the AFP intelligence might have changed between the reports of 20 and 22 October 2001, in order to have convinced Coastwatch by 22 October that the boat was overdue. Bartlett put his finger on the central logical problem.[22] What changed in the AFP's reporting between 20 and 22 October, given that the AFP already had reported on 20 October that the boat had left in a dangerously overloaded state? Here are key parts of the transcript (emphasis added):

> **Bonser**: That was based on *separate information* that we received on 22 October that corroborated the original advice of a possible departure, and *confirmed for us that this vessel had most probably departed*. On the basis of that we were able to assess that it was, indeed, overdue ...
> **Bartlett**: So that information came through AFP as well?
> **Bonser**: Yes, it did—on 22 October.

Cook and Collins later returned to the same unanswered question.[23]

> **Cook**: But the intelligence sources would not know that it was overdue, would they, from events on land?
> **Bonser**: I beg your indulgence; I think that goes to the nature of the information, and matters in the national

Accidental Whistleblowers

interest. It ought to be discussed in cabinet ...

Collins: So it was additional intelligence?

Bonser: It was additional information that confirmed for us that a boat had most probably departed and, on the basis of that, was therefore overdue.

Collins: You are now telling us that there is additional intelligence that you received on the 22nd confirming the departure.

Bonser: We cannot predict what the intelligence will be. We only know when it arrives that it exists ...

Cook: My question was about, really, how an intelligence report — which is not surveillance but, I assume, some on-land intelligence capability — would know that a boat at sea was overdue.

Faulkner: That is right.

Bonser: My answer remains the same.

The significance of these Delphic replies became more apparent on 11 July, when AFP Commissioner Mick Keelty refused absolutely to reveal what was in AFP reports on 20 and 22 October. That crucial information is undisclosed to this day.

Bartlett asked a scathing question on why the AFP report on 22 October, if it confirmed a departure, had not triggered a search-and-rescue operation by Operation Relex:

> Just going back one last time to 22 October, Rear Admiral Bonser, you advised search and rescue that the vessel was overdue because SIEV X met the criteria that you had confirmation of departure dates and it was known to be overdue. According to Admiral Smith's information, you notified via an OPSUM to Admiral Smith that the vessel was overdue possibly due to poor condition of the boat and the large numbers on board ... But it does not seem that search and rescue or anybody else actually requested anybody to do anything about it, to go and look for it ... And they did not seem to do so with the Relex people either. You

have said before that, as far as you are aware, there has been no report or even any form of informal investigation into this situation. This was a circumstance where admittedly it was probably in international waters and closer to Indonesia than here, but we have been involved in fairly extensive efforts to rescue a single yachtsman or yachtswoman a huge number of kilometres from the Australian coast. We have had a few fishermen drown at sea and had coronial inquests and Senate inquiries when there were three or so. We have had massive inquiries when we have had two or three people die on the Sydney to Hobart yacht race. All of those circumstances have their own specifics and I am not trying to say they are all the same thing, but we have an incident in which 353 people drown and nobody has even made a general comment about whether there is some way we can perhaps stop this happening again or whether there is anything we can do better.[24]

Bonser did not respond. There may be an answer to this accusatory question, but not one that could have been given publicly. Possibly by 20 October, and almost certainly by 22 October, Coastwatch and Operation Relex already knew from highly classified intelligence that the boat had sunk on 19 October and survivors had been rescued on 20 October. It would have been too late for Operation Relex to conduct a search on or after 20 October.

That may be why Bonser was keen to have the CMI committee move into closed session: he proposed this four times. He may have wanted to clear the name of Coastwatch, Operation Relex, and AMSA, but he could not do so in open session without breaking his service oath to protect classified information.

It is possible that secret intelligence on 20 and 22 October contained advice—whether from the AFP or other intelligence sources (such as ASIS or DSD), and possibly originating with the Indonesian police disruption-teams or with AFP undercover operatives working with Quassey—that the boat had sunk and that 45 survivors were already on their way back to Jakarta. After all, the sinking had happened on 19 October and the rescue on 20 October, and the whole public history (as set out in Part One of this book) suggests Indonesian police involvement with Quassey and the organisation of the rescue.

The Australian Federal Police, the Australian Defence Force, and Coastwatch—and Keelty, Smith, and Bonser as individuals testifying under oath—were trapped in the need, as they saw it, to safeguard the intelligence secrets of Australian border-protection authorities ... and they still are.

Chapter Nine

Opening Pandora's Box

SIEV X, to my knowledge, never ever came within our search area, and we did not change our search area specifically to look for SIEV X.
— Rear Admiral Chris Ritchie, Commander Australian Theatre, RAN, in Senate Defence Estimates, 4 June 2002

The case for a wide-ranging inquiry into what Australian authorities knew and did about the SIEV X is now unanswerable.
— Editorial, *Canberra Times*, 17 June 2002

ON 9 MAY 2002, I addressed my first public meeting on SIEV X, organised by the Canberra Refugee Action Committee. Kirsten Lawson of the *Canberra Times* wrote the next day:

> The Howard government was misleading the public about the location where 353 asylum-seekers drowned in October

last year so it could deflect blame for the tragedy, former diplomat Tony Kevin suggested last night. Original reports placed the sinking 80km from land, well into the Indian Ocean in international waters and at the edge of Australia's aerial surveillance for the naval blockade. But Defence Minister Robert Hill said in March[1] that all indications were the boat sank in the Sunda Strait between Java and Sumatra. Mr Kevin said a Sunda Strait location made it easier for the government to wash its hands of the affair ...

Mr Kevin said he suspected the navy had more reliable information about where the boat sank and it should be made public. 'I believe that these 353 people died because somebody wanted to send a strong political message that people smuggling had to stop,' he said. 'I don't know who that person or persons might be ...'[2]

On 22 May, SBS *Dateline* ran its first television current-affairs program on SIEV X, 'Cover Up or Stuff Up?'[3] The program brought the story vividly to life, dramatically interweaving video footage of Senate proceedings with interviews with Sondos Ismail and me. I still cannot watch it without feeling a shiver down my spine.

The program revealed crucial new documented evidence:

> *Dateline* has obtained a set of coordinates from the harbour master here at Sunda Kelapa port in north Jakarta. The coordinates are from this document [Indonesian document shown on screen], detailing the rescue by Indonesian fishing boats and showing the point where the survivors were picked up. The position is very similar to Tony Kevin's calculations of where the boat went down. Expert advice provided to *Dateline* says the coordinates are 51.5 nautical miles from the Indonesian coastline. If the coordinates are correct, then the vessel sank in international waters well beyond the Sunda Strait and within the surveillance area of Operation Relex.

The program concluded with footage from Bonser's testimony before the CMI committee that same day, and text from Smith's letter of clarification. Presenter Geoff Parish said: 'Be it confusion, conspiracy or cover-up, it looks increasingly like Tony Kevin's concerns are well founded.'

The story at last had media 'legs'. On 28 May, Margo Kingston's *Sydney Morning Herald* 'Webdiary'—an influential barometer of public issues—took up the cause of SIEV X with a hard-hitting opening commentary.[4] Kingston introduced me to her readership thus:

> A bloke called Tony Kevin has opened another Pandora's Box at the inquiry into 'a certain maritime incident' ... Kevin is one of those pesky, obsessive, inquiring types—a career diplomat who fell out with his department after a stint as Australia's ambassador to Cambodia.

She recounted the committee's history to date, and summed up:

> By the end of Bonser's evidence, the inquiry's chief prosecutor, John Faulkner, had switched his priorities. His primary focus is now on the mystery of SIEV X ... This inquiry is unique. Its utterly focused, forensic approach competes with a public service and a government determined to volunteer nothing. It could conceivably take years to get to the bottom of what happened when John Howard so dramatically swung his boat-people policy after the Tampa and implemented it with utter ferocity throughout the election campaign. The public service and the defence force, under intense practical and political pressure, are players in what has become a compelling political thriller. Many books will be written in years to come about the detail and the implications of this saga—for government, for our defence force, for our public service, and for our citizens.

Marg Hutton, a trained research historian, took up the SIEV X issue on her personal website on 1 June.[5] Two weeks later she opened a new website dedicated to SIEV X, www.sievx.com.[6] Hutton understood even before I did that SIEV X was going to become a long-running, major political story. Her goal was to set up a professional online research archive of all Hansard and documentary evidence and public commentary. Her website evolved over the next year, gradually shedding non-essential functions and narrowing down to focus on the archive, with occasional authoritative analysis of developments.

SIEV X could not have been sustained as a public issue without Hutton's website. It quickly became an indispensable reference and a highly regarded participant in the story. It will be a vital resource for any future judicial inquiry.

In 2003, her site came under nightly covert monitoring by a specialist IT security firm 90East.[7] This work was commissioned by the Australian Federal Police. One wonders why they bothered, as the site draws entirely on the public record and has never been seditious or defamatory. After Hutton, working with the IT news editor on *The Australian*, Kate Mackenzie, exposed the AFP's nightly trawl, it stopped.

BY THE END OF MAY, the SIEV X story was running wild. On 24 May, the *Australian Financial Review* ran a first analysis from me.[8] On 1 June, Phillip Adams wrote a blistering critique in *The Australian*.[9] Then, on 3 June, the *Canberra Times* ran its first editorial, 'Probe needed on drownings', that made the first public call for an independent inquiry:

> The lack of action [to search for the boat after the intelligence reports of early departure] seems puzzling. Even in more relaxed times, Australian maritime authorities maintain close surveillance over ship movements in the area, marrying patrols by Orions and coastguard authorities with

navy patrols, intelligence from the Australian Federal Police and other operatives in Indonesia, and signals intelligence. There are processes for coordinating the information gathering, and the response. These processes were in overdrive, especially in relation to refugee boats, during September and October. Somehow, however, this boat slipped, as it were, through the radar.

Was this negligence, incompetence or is the unthinkable possible that someone in Australia turned a blind eye to the fate of the boat, thinking that it might help 'send a message' to deter further potential boat people?

... as fresh evidence has emerged through the children-overboard inquiry, it has become clear that an independent inquiry, with access to all of the facts, is essential.[10]

The next day, 4 June, Kingston wrote a powerful commentary in the *Sydney Morning Herald*, 'Mass drowning case could sink navy's reputation', which concluded:

> Bonser's evidence and Smith's letter have ignited inquiry interest. The Australian Federal Police and Admiral Gates will give evidence on June 21. Labor's Senate leader, John Faulkner, told the *Herald* that SIEV X was now his top inquiry priority.
>
> What is going on in the navy? Has its core ethos mutated under the political stresses of Operation Relex? Has it got something terrible to hide, or is it so incompetent that it needs a shake-up much bigger than a change of leaders at the top? Stay tuned.[11]

That same day in Senate Defence Estimates, Faulkner closely questioned Rear Admiral Chris Ritchie, who stressed that Operation Relex's surveillance of its search area 'was continuous and ongoing and was not dependent in particular upon any particular piece of intelligence information'. Regardless of what particular intelligence reports might say about boat departures, routine RAAF aerial surveillance continued over the whole area, and navy ships waited for SIEV boats to come down through 'funnels' approaching Christmas Island and Ashmore Island.[12]

Ritchie said: 'SIEV X, to my knowledge, never ever came within our search area, and we did not change our search area specifically to look for SIEV X.' He said the specific AFP intelligence report on 20 October that SIEV X had departed with more than 400 people on board did not trigger any special action from the navy.[13]

Ritchie said there had been no RAAF or RAN surveillance photographs taken of SIEV X in transit anywhere, and he had not seen and was not aware of any other surveillance photographs of SIEV X. 'I say that because it could well be that some of the intelligence sources have taken photographs of it.'[14]

Ritchie confirmed what media people already knew, that a taskforce led by Rear Admiral Raydon Gates had been set up to review SIEV X intelligence material. Senator Hill told the committee more on this the next day: 'my office, on my behalf, tasked CDF/Secretary taskforce to seek the formal advice. They did this to ensure that an answer that I had previously given to Mr Crean was accurate and complete. That brief is being finalised and I expect to get it in the next few days.'[15]

This shows that the Gates taskforce was set up some time after Hill's response on 26 March to Crean's letter of enquiry, and that it was tasked to confirm the advice in Hill's letter to Crean that the refugee vessel sank in the vicinity of Sunda Strait.[16] The Defence taskforce was, from the outset, writing to a ministerial brief.

HERE WE CAN fast-forward. In May 2003, Marg Hutton, published her authoritative research paper 'SIEV X & the DFAT cable: the Conspiracy of Silence',[17] which dissected exactly how the Defence intelligence review, that Hill finally sent to the CMI committee on 4 July 2002, had influenced the final committee's report.[18] Her paper detailed how the Defence taskforce manipulated and misrepresented the official sources of information available to it, in order to produce an apparently authoritative but untrue conclusion that 'Defence can only speculate as to where the vessel foundered'.

Hutton's important conclusions were:

> Rather than pointing out to the CMI committee that it appeared that Hill's information was inaccurate and incomplete, the review falsely concluded it was unable to say where SIEV X sank ... In order to reach this false conclusion, the Defence review had to denigrate, misrepresent and conceal key evidence ...[19]
>
> As well as denigrating and traducing this public evidence, the review also continued to conceal other evidence such as the key DFAT cable that pointed to a sinking location in international waters. It is clear that the DFAT cable was part of the Defence holdings reviewed by Gates ...
>
> Through such sleight of hand, the Gates review was able to conclude that SIEV X could have sunk anywhere. The deliberate misinformation and obfuscation in the Gates review finally removes any doubt as to whether the withholding of the 23 October 2001 DFAT cable from the CMI inquiry was deliberate. The Gates review was intended to be the final word by Defence on its knowledge of SIEV X. Gates had the role of providing reassurance to the committee that Defence evidence had been open and honest. Instead the Gates review manifests a contempt for the prerogatives of the Senate committee.

ON 6 JUNE 2002, the committee received documents from the Prime Minister's Department that were seriously to upset the government's efforts to contain the issue: a running set of 'minutes' (or 'meeting notes') of Jane Halton's People Smuggling Taskforce (PST) covering the period from 27 August to 9 November 2001.[20] The committee chair had twice in May requested the department to provide these minutes. They arrived heavily blacked out, but still containing much evidence relevant to SIEV X. The key extracts were:

Opening Pandora's Box

12 October
- Discussion of disruption activity and scope for beefing up.

18 October
The meeting discussed:
Further Prospective Arrivals:
- Intelligence re 2 boats with total 600 PUAs [potential unauthorised arrivals] expected at Christmas, with one possibly arriving today, a further 3 boats with total 600 expected at Ashmore, with earliest arriving Monday [22 October]. Some risk of vessels in poor condition and rescue at sea.
- No confirmed sightings by Coastwatch, but multisource information with high confidence level ...

19 October
Current State of Play:
- ... Next boat to CI [Christmas Island] could be 250 [people] ... [Author's note: SIEV 6, the first of the two boats noted by PST on 18 October as 'expected at Christmas', had just been intercepted by HMAS Arunta. It had 227 people on board. The next expected boat was SIEV X.]

20 October
Current State of Play:
... Further Arrivals
- Second boat expected at Christmas tomorrow. If arrives, assessment to be made whether possible to return larger vessel. Arunta to relieve possible overcrowding ...

21 October
- Check Defence P3 is maintaining surveillance over Christmas Island.

22 October
Status Report:
... SIEV 8 [Author's note: which we now know was SIEV X]
- Not spotted yet, missing, grossly overloaded, no jetsam spotted, no reports from relatives.

23 October

Current State of Play:

... Indonesia ...

• Detailed report from 19 yo Afghani male survivor—reports sunk vessel departed 0130 hours 18/10 with 421 on board, including 70 children. Stopped near Karakatu group of Islands at 0900 where 24 left vessel. 397 still onboard. At 1400 on 19/10 vessel was taking water out of sight of land. Sank very quickly but resurfaced. About 120 people on surface. 7000 litres of fuel escaped? Seas rough. Only 70 lifejackets—none worked—19-20 hours in water from 1500 on Friday 19/10 till rescued by two fishing vessels around 1100 on Saturday 20/10. One fishing vessel rescued 44 people; another rescued 5—4 deceased and one survivor. 41 adults and 3 children survived, 353 drowned. Survivors taken to Jakarta—being cared for by IOM at Bogor outside Jakarta. Vessel likely to have been in international waters south of Java.

The next PST meeting notes, on 25 October, show no text on SIEV 8 or the sunken boat, but include three substantial, blacked-out sections (including three blacked-out headings of about the right length to possibly be 'SIEV 8'.

The next PST meeting notes, on 29 October, have a section on a different boat called 'SIEV 8'—a boat of Vietnamese origin intercepted northwest of Tiwi (Bathurst) Island on 27 October. The identifier number '8' had simply been re-assigned to the next arriving boat. Thus, there would be no gap in the numerical series of Relex interceptions. This reassignment was done just one week after SIEV X sank.

Looked at simply as text, these minutes point clearly to specific PST knowledge of a SIEV, expected at Christmas Island in the days of 18–22 October, that can only be SIEV X. Yet over the next two months official witnesses (from the Department of Prime Minister and Cabinet and the Department of Immigration and Multicultural and Indigenous Affairs in particular) offered in evidence much explanatory comment to try to cast doubt on such inferences.

Why had PM&C provided so much information relevant to SIEV X, when so much other text in PST minutes was blacked out? I think the fact that so many departments' representatives attended these meetings, and possibly took their own notes, meant that it would have been impossible credibly to black out all references to this boat. The sinking had to be seen to have been discussed in PST on the day it became public, and some relevant entries in earlier meetings retained, otherwise the PST minutes would have had no credibility and there might have been leaks. I believe that PM&C made some fine judgements about how much to risk revealing. It would be a first priority for a judicial inquiry to see all the text of the blacked-out PST notes.

It is obvious that the discussion on 23 October in PST (at 3.15pm) was based on the 23 October Jakarta embassy cable that had arrived that morning. Numbers and other factual information in the PST minute closely match those in the cable. We know this cable was addressed to every department represented at the table. Presumably, most if not all attendees had access to it.

There are a few omissions and additions. Some of the detail in the cable is left out of this summary: the boat's dimensions and added upper deck, the reported radio contacts with Abu Quassey, and the fact that the boat sank somewhere between Sunda Strait and up to eight degrees south latitude. And there are statements in the PST note that are not in the cable as finally published: the claim that this detailed report came from a 19-year-old Afghan survivor (this may have been in the initial blacked-out section of the cable, which DFAT later testified dealt with information sources), and that 7000 litres of fuel may have escaped during the sinking.

Looking at the PST minutes as a chronological series, obvious questions arise. The now famous PST discussion on 12 October of the scope for 'beefing up disruption activity' comes just days after the failed attempt by HMAS Adelaide to repel SIEV 4 on 6–8 October, and after dramatic written advice from PM&C to the prime minister at the height of this crisis:

> A strong signal that the people smugglers have succeeded in transporting a group to Australia could have *disastrous consequences*. There are in the order of 2500 potential unauthorised arrivals in the pipeline in Indonesia awaiting transport, therefore *this should be avoided at all costs*.[21] [my italics]

In these mid-October days, a new Operation Relex strategy was being set in place for coerced towbacks of SIEVs by the navy to Indonesian territorial waters. Was beefing up of disruption activity in Indonesia seen as a necessary 'softening-up' of Indonesian authorities as a means of persuading them to accept that new strategy? What did the phrase 'beefing up of disruption activity' signify to some of those around the PST table on that day? Innocuous explanations were later to be offered by every departmental witness (from the AFP, DIMIA, and PM&C) asked this question.

On 22 October comes the ominous entry, 'SIEV 8: Not spotted yet, missing, grossly overloaded, no jetsam spotted, no reports from relatives'. Does this note tell us that the 22 October PST meeting already had some sense that SIEV X (then being designated SIEV 8) had sunk or was in danger of sinking?

PM&C and DIMIA were soon to deny this (see chapter 12). But isn't this the only reasonable interpretation of such a starkly written notation of five disturbing points of discussion? I spent much of my public-service career attending and taking notes at such interdepartmental meetings. I am sure that, had this meeting been of the view that SIEV X had probably never left or that it had returned to Indonesia, this PST summary note would have added a reassuring closing annotation such as 'probably returned or never left'. A note-taker would not have left an important concluded discussion up in the air. My strong sense is that these notes accurately reflect a worried discussion that came to no comfortable conclusion.

It is likely that by then there was some highly classified intelligence, known to some around the table, that the boat definitely or probably had sunk (see chapter 8). Remember, this was three days after the sinking, and the survivors were almost back in Jakarta. Some people at that meeting, even if they were not direct readers of such intelligence, may already have had a whiff of the truth.[22]

THERE IS NO MENTION in the notes on PST meetings on 20, 21, or 22 October of the AFP's report and telephoned comment to Coastwatch on 20 October expressing fears for the safety of the overloaded SIEV X with more than 400 on board, or of the AFP's 22 October follow-up report to Coastwatch confirming the departure of SIEV X (as testified by Bonser and Smith). According to later DIMIA and PM&C testimony (see chapter 12), the PST meeting on 22 October did not discuss these reports.

Such information breakdowns in PST are extraordinary and inexplicable. The CMI committee report addressed the question of these communication breakdowns on 20–22 October 2001 involving Coastwatch, AFP, DIMA, PM&C, and the PST. It came to no satisfactory answers.[23] Any judicial inquiry would need to go far more deeply into this. Why had the AFP and Coastwatch bypassed the usual intelligence-sharing system involving DIMA and PM&C? Yes, it was proper for Coastwatch to urgently phone this AFP intelligence through to ASTJIC, but why did not Coastwatch make immediate follow-up calls to put DIMA and PM&C in the information loop? And why can no witness recall any discussion of the AFP reports in PST meetings of 20, 21, or 22 October? Something very odd is happening here.

These PST minutes (or, as they were later renamed by PM&C and Defence after 21 June, 'notes') were PM&C internal typed notes, in some cases reconstructed later by PM&C from rough meeting notes. They were not cleared with or even circulated to other departments.

The unremarked corollary is that some other departments' representatives would no doubt have made similar meeting notes of their own, for record purposes and to help them brief their departments afterwards. One would have liked the CMI committee to ask to see any meeting notes held by all other participating departments, as a check on the PM&C notes, but this was not done—reliance was placed on PM&C testimony, assisted on some points by DIMIA testimony, to explain the context for these PM&C meeting notes. A judicial inquiry would want to cast the net wider. If notes on these PST meetings are still in departmental files, they should be accessible. At any rate, there would be personal memories.

THE REFERENCE TO SIEV 8 in the PST notes for 22 October evoked an almost obsessive anxiety from Defence to have it expunged. The initial PM&C covering letter to the CMI committee, forwarding the minutes on 6 June 2002, stated that 'reference to SIEV 8 in the PST minutes of 22 October is incorrect. SIEV 8 arrived on 28 October 2001 off Bathurst Island carrying 31 Vietnamese'.

PM&C sent a follow-up letter on 21 June to the committee, restating the advice in its letter of 6 June, and adding, 'to further clarify, the SIEV referred to at this point in the notes is the vessel now known as SIEV X'.[24]

That was obviously true from the whole context of the committee's questioning of the PST minutes' reference to SIEV 8. Yet Defence three times tried to deny this. On 21 June, Gates wrote to the committee, saying:

> the PST minutes ... of 22 October 2001 inaccurately represent SIEV X as SIEV 8 ... I am concerned that the fact that the select committee has not addressed the error in the minutes has and will continue to cause serious damage to the reputation of the Australian Defence Organisation.[25]

Hill then weighed in heavily on the same issue with a letter to the committee on 25 June:

Both letters [from PM&C to the CMI, on 6 and 21 June] clearly state that the reference to 'SIEV 8' at the meeting of 22 October 2001 is incorrect. You would be aware that Defence does not allocate SIEV numbers to boats that have not been identified. In fact the title SIEV X was only allocated after Defence became aware that the boat had sunk. The error in the PM&C documents, however, has allowed some to incorrectly allege that Defence was aware of the location of SIEV X when it sank ... Given the incorrect media reporting to date, I believe that the committee, in fairness to the reputation of the ADF, should make a clarifying statement when it next sits to ensure that these unfounded allegations do not go unchallenged.[26]

Finally, in his letter forwarding the Gates review to the committee on 4 July, Hill again complained, citing a reference in a *Sydney Morning Herald* article by Margo Kingston on 2 July that, 'The task force is so confident it later gives SIEV X a name — SIEV 8'. Hill requested a correction in the CMI committee and hoped that Kingston would 'report it accurately in future'.

Obviously, this was a door that Gates and Hill very much wanted firmly closed. In the end, the committee's report obligingly footnoted: 'It should be noted that these notes mis-attribute SIEV X as SIEV 8.'[27] In other words, the committee 'accepted' Defence's emphatic claims that SIEV 8 was not SIEV X. Yet it is obvious that, in the PST notes for 22 October, SIEV 8 was the boat we now know as SIEV X.

Why were Hill and Gates so anxious to correct this claimed 'error' in the PST notes? Was it to head off any possible future requests to Defence to produce all information regarding any Operation Relex data holdings in the period 18–23 October 2001 for 'SIEV 8'? Did they already know that such material existed? I believe it would be necessary for any judicial inquiry to explore all contemporary ADF and Defence records, not just to 'the Qussey boat' but also to 'SIEV 8'. There might be some surprises in store, if the data have not already been destroyed.

KINGSTON'S VIEWS on the PST minutes and on the Gates review team appeared under the headline 'Moments of truth at death boat inquiry' in the *Sydney Morning Herald* on 14 June 2002:

> The [PST] minutes are the first proof that the [PST] task force was told about SIEV X, and contradict evidence by the taskforce head, Jane Halton [on 16 April 2002], that it received no information on the boat's departure. The minutes also contradict evidence by the incoming chief of the navy, Admiral Chris Ritchie, that the mystery boat, dubbed SIEV X by the Senate's children overboard inquiry, 'was not a SIEV (suspected illegal entry vessel) as far as we were concerned'.[28]
>
> The Defence Minister, Robert Hill, moved yesterday to stop a witness, Raydon Gates, giving evidence on the matter. Admiral Gates was due to give evidence next Friday on his review of all intelligence reports received by the navy before SIEV X sank.[29]

On 17 June came a second, very strong, *Canberra Times* SIEV X editorial, 'Judge should inquire into drownings':

> The case for a wide-ranging inquiry into what Australian authorities knew and did about the SIEV-10 [sic] is now unanswerable. Evidence has emerged that the Prime Minister's people-smuggling taskforce knew a lot more at the time than it had been claiming. Heavily censored minutes of the taskforce given to a Senate committee last week appear to contradict evidence earlier given by bureaucratic witnesses that the taskforce was not aware of the boat. They also undermine statements made by the Prime Minister about where the boat was thought to have sunk, and raise questions about whether it had been the subject of any searches by the Australian intelligence and surveillance apparatus. By no means yet does the evidence demonstrate the unthinkable, that Australian authorities stood by and

allowed a grossly overloaded vessel to sink. But what is now known means that this possibility must now be seriously examined in an independent forum, as must an alternative, also very unpleasant: that gross negligence led to 353 drownings ...

The Senate committee investigating the children-overboard affair has done a good job in dragging from generally reluctant witnesses some of the facts. These have contradicted almost everything which was initially said about the disaster. The committee itself entered this part of its investigation gingerly, after a former Australian diplomat, Tony Kevin, raised plausible questions about what had happened. Like Mr Kevin, the committee was unwilling at first to think the unthinkable, but as fresh evidence has emerged, has been forced to contemplate it. No doubt it has been spurred on in part by the obstruction of the government, the most recent manifestation of which has been its refusal to allow a senior naval officer to give evidence of his review of the intelligence on the matter ... why Senator Hill is seeking to buy time is not clear.

The Senate inquiry is also hamstrung by a lack of access to sensitive intelligence information, and, on the record so far in this inquiry, there can be no certainty that some of the material is being withheld only on national security grounds. Another curious aspect of the affair is that it is clear that many officials must be aware that the community is being misled. The taskforce, for example, contained representatives from a host of agencies involved in gathering intelligence about the movements of boat people, conducting surveillance, planning interceptions and aggressive deterrence, as well as the reception of those who got through the net. Given the minutes which have been tabled, they can hardly have failed to recognise that a formal statement that the taskforce had no knowledge of the boat was less than frank. At the least, they are compromised by their silence. That so many agencies are involved, and that statements by ministers and senior defence officers are in question, emphasises the need for an independent inquiry. It should be by a judge with unlimited rights to see security material, rather than an internal whitewash. The truth may be unpleasant for some, but, until it is known, it casts a slur not only on our border protection mechanisms, but on all Australians.[30]

The government information system was now off balance, and throwing out poorly coordinated answers. In an interview on Channel Nine's *Sunday* programme with Laurie Oakes on 16 June, Hill said:

> We don't know exactly where it sank. What we do is that we didn't have a capability to assist it because we didn't know where it was.

But three days later, on 19 June in the Senate, questioned by Senator Bartlett, Hill gave a different answer:

> I have referred to it as in the Sunda Strait; [the Prime Minister] referred to it as in Indonesian waters. The best evidence is that both of those answers are still correct.

On the same day, Secretary of Defence Allan Hawke was telling the National Press Club: 'The fact is that nobody knows where the boat sank.'[31]

On 20 June, Prime Minister John Howard was publicly questioned on the CMI committee's inquiry into SIEV X for the first time, by a terrier-like Margo Kingston at a multi-subject press conference.[32] He stonewalled and finally took refuge in indignant patriotism:

> Q. Do you now accept that the boat most likely sank in international waters?
> A. Well, there remains conflicting evidence about that ...

Q. Can I ask what you are doing to assure yourselves that Australian authorities did everything they could to rescue those people?

A. Well, I am satisfied from what the navy has said that every effort was made by them and I will put on record the fact that I think this attempt being made to besmirch the name of the Royal Australian Navy in relation to this incident is appalling, and I think the way in which an attempt has been made to suggest that the navy sort of stood by and allowed people to die is appalling ... I am perfectly satisfied that the navy behaved honourably, decently, and expeditiously. ...

Q. Mr Howard, on the same issue, given that we did have in place the most extensive surveillance cordon we've ever had in position in that area, are you surprised that we didn't see this boat coming, didn't know it had sunk, didn't know where it was ...?

A. No I'm not surprised of that particularly given that all the information was that it sank in an area near the Sunda Strait, and the Sunda Strait as I understand it passes between Java and Sumatra. And the information I had was that it was in the Indonesian search and rescue zone.

Q. But the information that the People Smuggling Taskforce had was that it was in international waters.

A. But the Indonesian search and rescue zone as I understand these things to operate does include international waters ... Look what are people alleging? Are they alleging that the navy just stood there and allowed people to drown? That is basically what this is coming to and I think this is appalling ...

In claiming here variously that the boat sank 'in an area near the Sunda Strait', 'between Java and Sumatra' or, finally, 'in the Indonesian search and rescue zone' (which extends to south of Christmas Island), Howard was finally saying that SIEV X could have sunk anywhere.

This period of media drama was to be the highwater mark of mainstream press interest in SIEV X. From then until the end of June, hard-hitting critical articles by senior journalists and commentators appeared almost daily—for instance, by Robert Manne, Kirsten Lawson, Margo Kingston, Mark Forbes, and Cameron Stewart. The CMI committee's session scheduled for 21 June, at which Admiral Gates and AFP Commissioner Keelty were to have testified, was abruptly cancelled. Keelty wrote a letter to the committee, saying that it might be difficult for him to answer questions without prejudicing continuing AFP investigations into SIEV X and other people-smuggling cases.[33] This did not explain the cancellation of an appearance by Admiral Gates. I think the real reason Gates was being kept away was that the government sensed its growing vulnerability, and wanted time to let the media buzz die down, and to develop a more credible public counter-strategy. It had crucial advantages—it could control the nomination of official witnesses and the timing of their testimony before the committee.

Pandora's box had spilled wide open, but the government was getting ready to close it again.

Chapter Ten

Defence Strikes Back

A HARD-HITTING COMMENTARY by Robert Manne in *The Age* on 24 June provided the peg for the launching of a government counter-strategy. Manne wrote:

> Just as Bonser's evidence had discredited the April testimony of Smith, so did the [PST] taskforce minutes discredit Halton's suggestion that information about SIEV X had not reached her committee before knowledge that the boat had sunk. The minutes also undermined a claim maintained by the government since John Howard had first raised it on October 23—namely, that there existed solid information for the proposition that SIEV X had gone down in Indonesian waters and thus outside the Australian air-surveillance zone. According to survivor testimony outlined to the [PST] taskforce on October 23, SIEV X was 'likely to have been in international waters south of Java' when it sank.
>
> Last week, Bonser ... revealed that, before 10am on October 20, he [sic] had passed on to defence a warning

sent by an officer of the Australian Federal Police in Indonesia to the effect that SIEV X was, in his [sic] opinion, grossly overloaded and, thus, in grave danger of sinking.[1] Despite this clear warning from the federal police in Indonesia about the dangers facing SIEV X, the Senate inquiry has established that, on October 20, no information was forwarded to the Australian Search and Rescue authorities. Even more importantly, despite this clear warning, the Senate inquiry has also established that no Australian aircraft were ordered on October 20 or later to fly over international waters south of the Sunda Strait in search of SIEV X.

The case concerning SIEV X can be summarised, with precision, like this. It is now clear that no Australian aircraft or naval vessels spotted SIEV X before it sank. It is highly unlikely, although not impossible, that if aircraft had been sent to survey the waters south of Java on the morning of October 20, any lives could have been saved. Yet it is also clear that on the morning of October 20, at a time when the government had learnt from an entirely reliable Australian source that 400 asylum seekers were in deadly peril, and at a time when no one knew whether or not they were still alive, no decision was taken to issue a warning or to mount a search and rescue operation of any kind.[2]

On 27 June, Hill's response to Manne appeared in the letters columns of the *Sydney Morning Herald* and *The Age*:

Manne assumes that there is no doubt that SIEV X had exited Indonesian waters and entered the surveillance zone of Operation Relex. *There is simply no evidence to support this assumption.* There have been varying estimates as to how far the boat may have travelled and its possible course, but by their nature they are at best speculative. The best advice that Defence can provide is that all indications point to the boat sinking in the vicinity of Sunda Strait. [my italics]

Manne claims that 'the Senate inquiry has also established that no Australian aircraft were ordered on October 20 or later to fly over international waters south of Sunda Strait in search of SIEV X'. Defence has confirmed that P-3 Orion aircraft made their scheduled forenoon surveillance flights over an area of some 34,600 square nautical miles of these waters on October 18, 19 and 20. Each flight spent four to five hours in the surveillance zone, including comprehensive coverage of the key north-west sector. A further P-3 Orion surveillance mission was flown on the afternoon of October 19 to compensate for the unserviceability of HMAS Arunta's helicopter. This flight concentrated on the role usually played by the helicopter over the southern sector in response to naval tasking. It should be noted that poor weather prevented surveillance of the north-west sector on this flight. Defence has confirmed that this extensive aerial surveillance did not detect any vessel in distress nor detect any distress calls on international frequencies. There is no doubt that when presented with a situation involving safety of life at sea the navy would take all actions necessary to assist.[3]

Suddenly, the Defence Minister was flooding the public with new and detailed surveillance information, before the CMI committee had seen any of this. I commented the next day:

As to RAAF surveillance: senators have heard inconsistent and unclear testimony from admirals Smith and Ritchie on this. Hill told senators on June 5 that a review he commissioned into SIEV X was being finalised and that he expected results within a few days. Yet he cancelled Admiral Gates's scheduled June 21 Senate testimony. Now Hill offers selective details on air surveillance activity in the press, details of which have not in the past three months been put before Senate committees investigating these matters. If this is not contempt for the Senate, what is?[4]

The same day, Margo Kingston ran a *Sydney Morning Herald* piece asking more questions:

> The Defence Force did no aerial surveillance of waters south of Indonesia on the afternoon of October 19 last year when the ill-fated SIEV X sank, drowning 353 asylum seekers. The Defence Minister, Senator Hill, made the admission yesterday ... [that] there was no afternoon surveillance of the [north-west] sector on October 19. Most evidence points to SIEV X sinking about 50 nautical miles off Indonesia, 20 nautical miles inside international waters covered by aerial surveillance. It sank at 3pm on the afternoon of October 19.[5]

Hill's office was now plentifully leaking RAAF surveillance flight data to the media. On 29 June, *The Australian* ran a front-page story by Cameron Stewart based on detailed briefing from Hill's chief of staff, Matt Brown.[6] It was illustrated with numerous RAAF surveillance maps of flight paths and vessel detections in the Operation Relex area over the days 18–20 October 2001— maps that were to be part of the Gates review that Hill sent to the Senate five days later.[7] Stewart wrote:

> An Australian P3 Orion spy plane flew over the area where survivors were clinging to the debris of their boat after it sank in October last year, drowning 353 asylum seekers. But the navy says the plane did not spot any survivors and was unaware that the boat, known as SIEV X, had sunk. In dramatic evidence to be presented to a Senate committee next week, the navy has revealed full details of its surveillance of the waters off Indonesia where SIEV X sank on October 19 last year. The Government hopes the evidence will debunk claims the navy turned a blind eye to the fate of the overloaded SIEV X after it embarked for Christmas Island.
>
> It shows—contrary to earlier Senate testimony—that the navy sent P3 patrols across the stretch of ocean known as Charlie Northwest, where SIEV X probably sank. These

flights, on October 19 and 20, were routine patrols and were not sent to the area specifically to look for SIEV X. They show that on the morning of October 19, the day SIEV X sank, a P3 flew in arcs as close as 24 nautical miles to the coast of Java. The flight detected 30 vessels in international waters—eight merchant ships and 22 fishing vessels—but not SIEV X. The overloaded boat sank five hours later, raising the tragic possibility it entered the Australian-monitored zone after the P3 had left the area.

The next morning—with survivors still clinging to the wreckage—another P3 flight passed through the area but was unaware of the tragedy and did not spot any debris or survivors.

The Government says it is possible SIEV X was not spotted because it sank in Indonesian territorial waters before it reached the navy's surveillance zone. However, the government's intelligence at the time said SIEV X was likely to have sunk in international waters—inside the navy's surveillance zone.

The evidence to be presented to the committee confirms the controversial admission by the navy that it did not step up its routine daily surveillance to search for SIEV X and its human cargo. The navy received intelligence information on October 18 and again on October 20 that SIEV X had left Indonesia for Christmas Island, and that the boat was dangerously overcrowded. The Australian Federal Police officer conveying the intelligence on October 20 told Coastwatch personally that he feared for the safety of the boat. However, the navy says it did not change its surveillance patterns to look for SIEV X because intelligence information about the departures of such boats was notoriously unreliable and because it believed its existing aerial patrols over the area were sufficient.[8]

Stewart here had accurately foreshadowed the main lines of subsequent committee evidence. But, remarkably, Stewart appeared to have accepted at this time that SIEV X had sunk in Operation Relex waters. Five days later, the Gates review was to say this was unknowable. In an accompanying analysis piece, Stewart commented:

> The truth about the SIEV X tragedy might boil down to some desperately bad luck and a dubious judgement call by the Australian navy … Ritchie told a Senate committee this month that [the] navy would not have changed its pattern of searching even if it knew that 10 SIEV Xs were on the way. Was this simply because Ritchie had absolute faith in the navy's existing surveillance of the area? Or was it a sign of a surveillance policy which was unresponsive and not alert to the possibility of a humanitarian disaster?[9]

Margo Kingston commented the next day: 'I guess the strategy is to get the news out of the way through one paper, so it can't run big in other papers now, and will be old news for all the media by the time the Defence Force honchos take the stand next week.'[10]

Kingston was right. But I believe that in addition to news pre-emption a deeper information strategy was being employed by Hill, one that relied on the subtle persuasive power of maps. Those detailed official maps of flight routes and boat detections sent a subliminally reassuring message: 'Here in these maps is proof that we really searched hard out there—yet we could not find the boat. Perhaps it wasn't even there.'

It would not have occurred to me at that time to consider whether any of those official maps misrepresented flight routes or detection data. Like everyone else, I simply assumed the maps to be accurate. The public concern immediately began to subside.

On 4 July, Senator Hill sent the long-awaited Defence (Gates) review—including 11 maps of four P3 Orion flights in the period 18–20 October—to the CMI committee. His covering letter noted that Defence had reviewed the P-3 Orion flight data on the crucial days, and from this was able to chart indicative flight paths. (I paid no attention to the adjective 'indicative' at the time.) The review included detailed notes on weather and surveillance conditions encountered in each flight. It all read entirely convincingly.

The committee chair kept pressing, but Hill kept putting off, and finally denying, his approval for Gates to testify. On 11 July, Colonel Patrick Gallagher, who was current head of the Australian Theatre Joint Intelligence Centre (ASTJIC), but had not been in that position at the time of SIEV X, testified at Defence's direction in place of Gates.[11] Gallagher was given only 36 hours notice to prepare his testimony. Faulkner was scathing about the minister's unsuitable nomination of Gallagher:

> It is not good enough—it is a cover-up. The minister ought to allow the appropriate witness—Rear Admiral Gates—to come before us, given that Rear Admiral Gates has been tasked to prepare information and background for the committee in relation to SIEV X—I know it, you know it and every reasonable person knows it. To shoehorn this colonel in, in relation to these matters, is just an outrage as far as the minister is concerned.[12]

Gallagher handled his unfamiliar brief competently. He said most of the SIEV intelligence input into ASTJIC came from daily Department of Immigration and Multicultural Affairs (DIMA) intelligence reports, supplemented by Coastwatch OPSUM reports and occasional reports from other sources. Australian Federal Police material usually came in via Coastwatch—ASTJIC had no direct link with the AFP. So ASTJIC got its intelligence on boats 'at third hand', after primary information had been processed in DIMA or Coastwatch. ASTJIC then sent intelligence briefs (known as INTSUMS) out to all of Operation Relex, including the ADF's Northern Command (NORCOM) in Darwin.[13]

At 1000 on 20 October, ASTJIC issued a departure report, based on the telephoned advice from Coastwatch at 0950 of the AFP telephoned report, that the boat had departed overcrowded, with more than 400 people onboard. Unlike earlier SIEV X reports, this was 'a specific immediate intelligence report', so

ASTJIC dealt with it immediately.

Gallagher did not know why it took another two days for Defence to accept confirmation of departure. Senator Jacinta Collins queried the fundamental contradiction: ASTJIC essentially on 20 October had assessed the departure of SIEV X as being confirmed, but the CMI committee had received other evidence previously and then in the Gates review that Defence only reached this conclusion on 22 October. Yet, she said, these were two crucial days in the lives of 400 people. She asked to see the wording of the 20 October ASTJIC assessment (and this was later provided —see page 194).[14]

Brandis gave his own view of it all, with a characteristically crisp summation of the uncertainties:

> **Brandis**: Colonel Gallagher, of course, because of the conflict of reporting as to the likely port of departure, that would have produced different conclusions on the question of whether or not, at a given point in time, the vessel was overdue ... in terms of the intelligence reporting, we can say two things with reasonable certainty, can't we ? First of all, there was never a report that the vessel was in distress ... and, secondly, there was never any conclusive signal or report to suggest at any material time the vessel was overdue.
> **Gallagher**: In a formal sense, no. There were only people's judgements or assessments that the vessel might be overdue.
> **Brandis**: Might be, depending on where its point of departure was, which was itself a matter of complete uncertainty.
> **Gallagher**: Yes, that is correct.[15]

The final ADF witness, on 30 July, the last day of the committee's public hearings, was Air Commodore Philip Byrne, Commander, Maritime Patrol Group, RAAF (who had led and flown in the P3 Orion surveillance flights). Byrne testified and later gave written additional answers.[16] His oral and written testimony, in summary, was that the intelligence briefing material provided to crews that flew missions in the period 18–23 October at no time contained information to indicate any potential safety-of-life-at-sea problem. The first indication in intelligence of a small and overcrowded vessel that had left the west coast of Java was on 20 October, and this was used to brief crew for the flight on 21 October. That report to crew (at midnight on 20 October) did not include any information that would lead to safety-of-life-at-sea concerns or tasking. Byrne testified that a report of a small and overcrowded vessel does not, of itself, indicate a safety-of-life situation: all of the SIEV vessels were small, and all were more or less overcrowded.

Because no safety-of–life alert was issued, it was purely radar surveillance. No safety-directed air search took place from 18 October to 23 October. A search under safety-of-life-at-sea protocols would have used different techniques—for instance, visual inspection and beacon search. No distress signals were received by any of the surveillance flights.

Byrne testified that he had looked exhaustively at all the post-flight contact reports for the period 18–22 October. He saw no contact report of anything remotely like SIEV X, or other ships reported by survivors to have been at the disaster scene. He had been unable to make any sense of those survivor reports

> If you look at the radar contacts from the flights of the morning of the 19th and the 20th, they do not shed too much light on the concentrations of ships, particularly merchant ships, in the vicinity of that latitude and longitude which was mentioned on the *Dateline* program ... I have looked to see if there is a concentration of vessels in the vicinity of the point at which the *Dateline* program indicates that the SIEV X went down. I could not find anything.

Byrne agreed that none of this information threw any light on the claims that were made in relation to largish vessels and lights shining on survivors—'not that I have seen'.[17] He concluded: 'We do not know where SIEV X sank.'[18]

A few days after Byrne's testimony, Rear Admiral Gates—the officer whom Robert Hill had declined to allow to testify in the committee, despite Gates's leadership of the Defence taskforce—spoke freely to the media in Perth.[19] Gates said that the overloaded SIEV X boat was one of nine boats the navy was tracking at the time, and information about it was scant: 'It was certainly not enough in my opinion as an operational commander to start to move assets to that effect ... let me stress to you it wasn't an oversight by the navy.' Gates said he did not believe it was necessary for him to testify at the committee's inquiry: 'My information was second or third hand and he [Hill] could get for the inquiry the people who had the information at first hand.'

The committee's chair, evidently irritated by these statements, said the inquiry was considering issuing a subpoena for Gates to appear. But nothing ever came of this.

Seven weeks after Byrne's final witness testimony, the committee on 20 September received replies to a detailed set of written questions it had sent to Brigadier Silverstone, Commander NORCOM (Darwin), who had the command responsibility for alerting Relex ships and aircraft to any safety-of-life-at-sea situations in the area. Silverstone's replies were the final link addressed in the committee's exploration of the information chain from the AFP through Coastwatch to ASTJIC to Relex operational command to RAAF surveillance. Yet Silverstone's written answers were not examined orally in the CMI committee or later in Estimates committees.[20] Silverstone had testified once already in the committee, on 4 April, on the 'children overboard' matter. He could have been recalled.

Silverstone wrote that SIEV X intelligence had been no different to intelligence on other SIEVs (Question W71). He claimed that the intelligence on 20 and 22 October was 'single-source AFP information received third-hand, which NORCOM determined as having low credibility and requiring corroboration' (W72). This claim differed strikingly from Davidson's, Smith's, and Bonser's earlier testimony as to the multi-source nature of AFP reports on 20 and 22 October (see chapter 8), and also from the 18 October

Defence Strikes Back

PST minutes noting the expected arrival at Christmas Island of two boats, one of which was SIEV X, based on 'multisource information with a high confidence level'. Multi-source information of high credibility had somehow, by the time it got to NORCOM, become single-source information of low credibility.

Silverstone wrote that at no stage did NORCOM consider SIEV X to be a confirmed departure from Indonesia (W73). NORCOM was not aware of the AFP liaison officer's concern orally conveyed to Coastwatch on 20 October for the vessel's safety (W75, W76). On 20 October, NORCOM considered that 'due to the SIEV's overcrowding and the need for it to maintain stability, the vessel may be limited to a slow passage and therefore a later time of arrival' (W76). On 22 October, NORCOM assessed that 'the boat had returned to Indonesia because the weather was bad and the crew would not risk a passage (and their lives) if the vessel was insufficiently seaworthy to make a passage in the prevailing weather conditions' (W82).

NORCOM knew nothing of any DSD radio intercepts (W79).

Silverstone's written testimony indicates that the crucial Operation Relex command judgement—not to conduct a special air search for SIEV X on 20 and 22 October under safety-of-life-at-sea protocols—was made at his NORCOM headquarters. There is no indication whether or not NORCOM consulted Operation Relex higher command, or Rear Admiral Smith personally, in coming to these judgements. However, Silverstone testified that NORCOM did go back to Coastwatch to discuss the AFP reports of 20 and 22 October (W75, W80, W81).

Even in hindsight, Silverstone did not consider that NORCOM could have done more to save lives, in terms of the quality of the information and options available to him at the time (W84).

This was the best explanation the CMI committee received as to how the AFP liaison officer Kylie Pratt's 20 October phone comment to Coastwatch, expressing her personal concern about the effects of overloading on the safety of the passengers, got lost in the Coastwatch and Defence information processing system— despite Coastwatch's immediate phone call to ASTJIC and that organisation's immediate action in response. The Relex command system just did not seem able to absorb or act on this piece of information.

Defence gave the CMI committee a blacked-out copy of the 20 October ASTJIC signal.[21] At least in its clear sections, all it said about the boat was: 'The vessel is described as a small boat and may be carrying up to 400 passengers.' (W76) That is why the RAAF Orions were never given any tasks under their safety-of-life-at-sea obligations. Stewart's two articles on 29 June had it exactly right: routine daily surveillance was never changed.

THIS WAS an Australian border-protection system whose chain of command had a perception problem in registering potential safety-of-life situations on SIEVs. Was this in part because it had been trained to regard SIEV departure reports—especially about boats connected with Abu Quassey—as inherently unreliable? Operation Relex operated in a very narrow framework: if a SIEV did not arrive, it had probably not left, or it had turned back. SIEVs became 'real' only when they came within operational interception range of navy ships, in the approach funnels to Christmas Island or Ashmore Island. If they did not get that far, Relex had little interest in their existence or their fate. Certainly, Relex would have observed the letter of the safety-of-life-at-sea law if any such ship had sent out a radio distress-call or activated distress positional beacons inside the Relex area. But if neither of these things happened, these boats were simply not there as far as Operation Relex was concerned. Cruel? Yes. Criminal? On the face of it, no.

The other possible factor in decision-making is that the navy's two fast frigates in the area were busy doing other things on 19 October 2001. HMAS Warramunga had its hands full near Ashmore Reef, forcibly escorting SIEV 5 back to Indonesia. HMAS Arunta was intercepting SIEV 6 near Christmas Island. Any signal about a possible safety-of-life situation on SIEV X would have been operationally very difficult at the time. Arunta, in order to go looking for a possible Quassey boat in distress, would have had to leave SIEV 6 free to land its passengers on Christmas Island. One can imagine the prime minister's reaction to that news in the middle of the election campaign.

Yet I am still searching for answers to the central moral question—why Operation Relex, with all its resources, could not or would not mount an air search for the people on SIEV X, even after the AFP-sourced report on 20 October. It seems clear that Relex did not really want to find them. There were operational incentives not to do so—rescue by the navy of 400 people up north near Indonesia would have seriously complicated an already stressed border-protection mission, and there would have been no thanks from the defence minister or the prime minister. Did Operation Relex learn from its unpleasant HMAS Adelaide and SIEV 4 experience at the hands of Howard and Reith to be 'rescue averse' in grey-area scenarios where it was under no legal obligation to search for possible SIEVs in distress? I think so.

FAST-FORWARD AGAIN. The RAAF maps obviously impressed the committee as important and credible evidence: they were even reprinted in the committee's report.[22] The Australian Defence Force was duly exonerated by the CMI committee, and I thought that was all there was to it as far as the ADF part of the SIEV X story was concerned.

Starting in August 2002, Marg Hutton set about a closer study of the maps for the morning of 20 October 2001. She knew that fishing boats had picked up 45 survivors that morning between 7.00am and noon (see chapter 4), so she plotted the Jakarta harbour master's rescue coordinates (as obtained by *Dateline*) onto a combined template of the Defence maps of Orion flight paths and detections on that day (see Map 2). What she found was remarkable. The Orion had flown directly over those coordinates during the five hours of survivor rescue. Indeed, it had made three passes in the northwest quarter, all within easy radar-detection range. Yet it reported no boat detections within a measured 24 nautical miles of the rescue coordinates.

The Defence review text had stated that 100 per cent surveillance coverage of the northwest sector was achieved, and that contacts were visually identified. It did not report any poor weather on that day (as it did for some other days). One therefore had to assume that the weather and observation conditions were fairly normal on 20 October.

There was only one possible conclusion: RAAF observations of the fishing boats rescuing survivors in the area on the morning of 20 October had been removed or relocated, in the preparation of the Defence review map. Yet Air Commodore Byrne had testified that he had looked at all post-flight contact reports for 20 October 'in the vicinity of the point at which the *Dateline* program indicated that the SIEV X went down. I could not find anything.' What possible explanations are there for this striking discrepancy?

The CMI committee asked one specific question relevant to Hutton's major discovery, in writing, of Rear Admiral Ritchie: 'Did the Operation Relex surveillance flight on the morning of 20 October 2001 detect the fishing vessel responsible for picking up the SIEV X survivors? The name of the vessel is reported to have been Indah Haya Makmur.' Ritchie's answer was, 'No'.[23]

Hutton and I also began to discern other instances of 'lack of fit' between claimed Orion flight paths and times, and places and times of detections on that day (see Map 2). We noted, for example, that the Orion had apparently taken nearly two hours to fly a distance of about 250 nautical miles from the detection of surface vessels at 0828 (in the northwest) and next at 1021 (in the northeast) — indicating a speed of about 125 miles per hour. But Orions fly at 200–330 miles per hour. The aircraft should have taken only one hour to fly this distance. What was it doing during the unaccounted-for hour of flying time? Could it have been looping around the rescue boats, perhaps outside visual range, monitoring by radar the rescue of survivors?

Hutton also noted other mismatches between the claimed flight route and the claimed detections.

In July 2003, pursuant to Hutton's analysis, Senator Collins put to Defence a new, detailed question on notice. The reply in

Defence Strikes Back

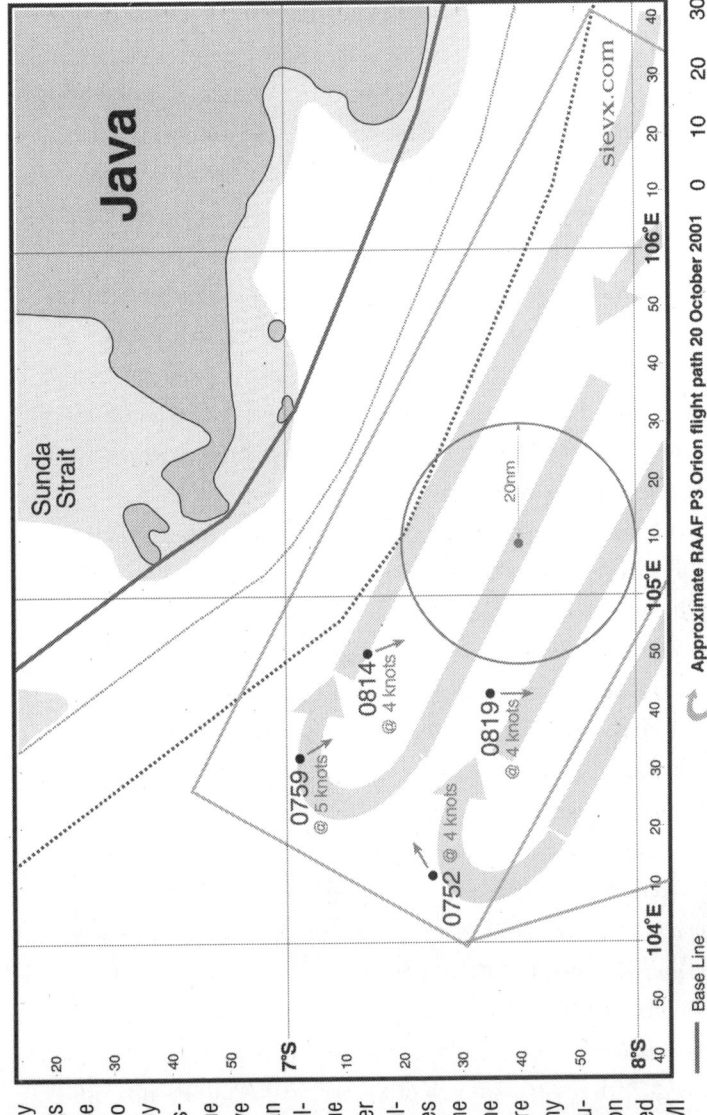

Map 2: This map, developed by Marg Hutton, dramatically casts into question both the Defence Review of Intelligence Related to SIEV X submitted on 4 July 2002, and part of the ADF's testimony on 30 July 2002. The map shows that, during the five hours 7.00am–12 noon that an Indonesian fishing boat was collecting survivors at the rescue location shown on 20 October 2001, an RAAF Orion surveillance aircraft made three passes within 20 nautical miles —one directly overhead. Yet the Defence maps claimed there were no radar detections of any surface vessels within 24 nautical miles of the rescue location —a claim apparently supported in the ADF's testimony (CMI Hansard page 2169).

September 2003 warrants citation in full:

> **Question**: With reference to the ... P3 Orion maps of 20 October 2001 that were supplied to the committee, which indicate that the flight from the NW end of the flight path to the NE end of the flight path, some 250 nautical miles away, took 2 hours:
>
> Is it the case that the flight should have taken only one hour between these two points if the plane was flying at a rate of 200 to 330 [miles] per hour.
>
> (2) Can the department indicate why the flight of 20 October 2001 took longer than the normal one hour to fly this path.
>
> (3) What were the names of the crew on the P3 Orion flight on 20 October 2001.
>
> (4) Can any of the data recorded for, or by, the crew members on the P3 Orion flights between 18 and 20 October 2001 (under Operation Relex) be made public, for example, sortie green, inflight REDS, Port Mission Form PURPLE, and mission tapes.
>
> **Senator Hill**: The answer to the honourable senator's question is as follows:
>
> (1) It is correct that a P-3C Orion travelling in a straight line could travel 250 miles in one hour. However, when conducting a search, a P-3C is rarely flown in a straight line. Typically, the aircraft is manoeuvred left and right of the search path to avoid bad weather or to position the aircraft for visual identification of contacts. Furthermore, at times the aircraft will loiter in an area in order to confirm the identification of weak or fleeting radar contacts, which may turn out to be sea life (whale, dolphin, and school of fish), or simply cloud. It is more realistic to view the NW to NE path presented in the maps provided as the intended track of the search, the actual track of the search aircraft is left and right of that path. The Defence submission which accompanies these maps clearly notes that they represent

'the approximate path' of these flights. In the interest of a thorough search the actual distance flown over a search leg is often much longer than the straight line distance. For this reason, the aircraft's cruising speed is not directly relevant to the time taken to complete a search leg.

(2) The P-3 flight of 20 October 2001 took longer than one hour for the reasons given in part (1). The crew post-flight report states 'environmental conditions for this patrol were assessed as very poor due to cloud and rain in all areas' and poor environmental conditions can exacerbate the need for the aircraft to manoeuvre either side of the search path.

(3) Defence will not release the names of the P-3 crew as this information is classified.

(4) All of the data recorded by the P-3 crew that could be declassified has been, and put on the public record, including full details of all vessels sighted. The remaining source data, such as sortie Green, inflight reports, Form Purple, and mission tapes are classified and cannot be released. [24]

So, in the end, the RAAF maps of flight paths and detections on 20 October were nothing more than approximations. Detection data that was politically inconvenient might have been left out — I note the significant qualification in Hill's answer (4): '... full details of all vessels *sighted*' (my emphasis). Even the weather data seems retrospectively changeable. Weather that had not been remarked on as unusual either in the Defence review or in Byrne's testimony was now claimed to have been reported at the time as 'very poor due to cloud and rain in all areas'. In any case, the Senate could not see any of the original data, or know who the crew members were. Another possibly promising door to the truth had been closed.

I no longer have confidence in the integrity of the surveillance maps and accompanying text presented in the Defence review. If the data presented for 20 October was so suspect, the data for other key days must also be suspect — in particular 19 October, when I am convinced SIEV X was inside the Relex surveillance zone for several hours before it sunk (see the analysis on page 100). The use in the Defence review and in Hill's covering letter of the phrases 'approximate path of this flight' and 'indicative flight paths', phrases I did not attend to at the time, may have been a prudent precaution in case this data is ever re-examined by an independent inquiry. Once again, the committee had been served up misleading evidence.

Looming behind all this, the question that was never asked is: what did the ADF's hugely powerful long-distance radar JORN detect? (see Glossary) JORN must have been in use in these crucial days, and it must have registered the movements of SIEV X, the boats that came to look but did not help, and the rescuing fishing boats the next day. JORN would have recorded all of it.

As of now, the CMI's committee's central conclusion that it 'cannot find grounds for believing that negligence or dereliction of duty was committed [by the ADF] in relation to SIEV X' is cast into doubt by the questions hanging over the completeness and accuracy of information in the Defence review of SIEV X intelligence.[25] The committee relied heavily on that questionable information in coming to its important conclusion.

Chapter Eleven

Questions about Disruption

How far does disruption go? What are the limits, if any?
— John Faulkner in the Senate, 26 September 2002, Hansard, page 5007

Disrupt v. tr.
1. to interrupt the flow or continuity of;
to bring disorder to. 2. to separate forcibly; to shatter.
— *Oxford English Reference Dictionary*, 2nd edition, 1996

ON 3 JULY 2002, *The Australian* ran a strong SIEV X editorial, headlined 'Boat people tragedy must be explained'. It stated:

> The Prime Minister could begin by explaining why his account changed. Jane Halton, the bureaucrat who headed his people-smuggling taskforce [PST], should be recalled to explain why her PM did not receive [the 23 October intelligence] assessment that SIEV X was likely to have sunk in international waters.

More importantly, we need to know why the ADF stuck to its decision not to increase its routine daily surveillance, even after it had had received specific intelligence that SIEV X had set sail and was dangerously overcrowded. There is no evidence that the navy, or the ADF generally, was placed under 'intense political pressure to avert their eyes'. But this doesn't mean there isn't scope to inquire into whether the ADF was unresponsive to intelligence reports and made a bad judgement. We must also ask whether it had a duty of care to do more. Of course, the responsibility for the deaths of these people lies with Indonesian people-smugglers who sent them out on a small, leaky boat. But given this calamitous situation, if the boat did come into our zone of surveillance, could we have done more than what we did? We need to know a lot more.

Such questions dominated the CMI committee's agenda in its final three months, from July to October. It held only two more public hearings, on 11 and 30 July, and spent the rest of the time sifting through a large quantity of oral and written official evidence. It failed to summon the one potential witness from the Australian Defence Force who by this stage must have known more of the story than anyone else — Rear Admiral Raydon Gates, head of the taskforce that reviewed the SIEV X intelligence available to Defence. Legally the committee could have compelled Gates to appear, but it chose not to. Margo Kingston was furious at Labor's acquiescence in Robert Hill's witness-denial strategy: '[Labor's] decision to capitulate to systematic government obstruction rather than do everything in its power to force the main players in the scandal into the witness box is a stain on the Senate and an awful blow to the accountability of government to the people.'[1]

The committee still had three important groups of witnesses to examine in July: Australian Federal Police Commissioner Mick Keelty; a senior DIMIA team responsible for the then DIMA–AFP People Smuggling Strike Team; and Jane Halton, in respect of her chairing of the People Smuggling Taskforce in the Prime Minister's Department. By early July, Labor's CMI committee senators may have concluded that its inquiries into ADF conduct were unlikely to produce any more surprises. Arguably, Labor may have taken a political decision not to put the ADF under any more pressure, after Hill had finally put up a plausible public defence by means of the Gates review and the flight-path maps. Labor senators may also have concluded that central to the ADF's botched safety-of-life-at-sea response to the Quassey boat was the contradictory and misleading intelligence coming in to Australia from Indonesia in the weeks and days preceding the tragedy.

The agencies most likely to have answers on that intelligence history were the two members of the People Smuggling Strike Team, DIMIA and the AFP. I don't know whether Labor senators expected to get proper answers, but they certainly tried hard during and after the CMI committee. With both agencies, Labor senators hit brick walls — legally unchallengeable refusals to answer questions.

MICK KEELTY'S TESTIMONY on 11 July became the defining moment in the SIEV X inquiry.[2] Senator Faulkner's questioning was intense, sometimes aggressive. Keelty was excruciatingly slow and cautious in framing his replies. Often, the two men went head to head. Faulkner's desire to find out what AFP intelligence had reported back about Quassey and SIEV X was frustrated from the outset by Keelty's firm brief that he was not to speak on these matters, for fear of prejudicing possible criminal prosecutions of Quassey (whom Keelty at no stage named, but to whom he was clearly referring as 'the alleged organiser of SIEV X ... currently in custody in Indonesia'). Keelty was accompanied by federal agent Brendon McDevitt and legal counsel Michael Chilcott, whom he consulted frequently.

Keelty held out two tantalising scenarios for the prosecution of Quassey. As it happened, neither was ever achieved:

> I believe that, based on the evidence available to the AFP, we can establish that the alleged organiser of SIEV X, whose actions led to the deaths of 353 persons on board, could possibly be charged with offences associated with those deaths ... *The criminal prosecution may not be dictated by where the vessel sank but it may be determined by the vessel's intended point of arrival. We are currently seeking legal advice to clarify this question.* If we can establish that Australian charges can be laid then we would seek further first instance warrants for the arrest of the alleged organiser. If we are able to proceed with such charges, dual criminality [for homicide] does exist with Indonesia and we would, therefore, be seeking extradition.[3] [my italics]

Alternatively, Quassey could be charged as a people smuggler in respect of SIEV X. Keelty noted that the AFP had obtained three warrants against Quassey for people-smuggling offences relating to earlier vessels. However, 'Seeking his extradition is a delicate matter as extradition requires dual criminality which does not exist at the moment in Indonesia because people smuggling is not an offence there.'

Keelty then said: 'the AFP does not wish to put any of these legal processes at risk by virtue of evidence provided to this committee ... given that the AFP is aware of the alleged perpetrator of this crime.' Thus he was unable to answer questions on:

> what information the AFP held about the departure, seaworthiness and ultimate fate of SIEV X; the manner in which the AFP came into possession of that information; and the specific actions taken by the AFP with that information, including whom we told and when ...
>
> I am aware that my inability to answer those questions goes to the very heart of my credibility as a witness as well as that of my organisation in your eyes and potentially those of the public but, on the advice provided to me, I simply cannot go further.

The only evidence he volunteered on SIEV X was:

> In relation to the SIEV X matter ... the AFP passed all relevant information to the appropriate authorities. All information that may have led to a conclusion that the passengers of SIEV X were in danger was obtained after the vessel had in fact sunk. Much of that information was actually obtained from interviews with survivors conducted by the Indonesian National Police. I would also like to point out that no one in the AFP was or is aware of the precise location of the sinking of the vessel.[4]

Were Keelty's claimed grounds for non-disclosure valid, and were they well-advised? The subsequent history of the AFP's failure to prosecute Quassey casts them into question. The following is a summary of that history.

On 12 December 2002, Justice Minister Chris Ellison (by now under public pressure to bring Quassey to Australia on SIEV X homicide charges) told the Senate:

> The Australian government is working with other governments in the region to seek to apprehend Abu Quassey [then imprisoned in Indonesia on minor passport offences but due for release on 1 January 2003] in relation to his alleged involvement in people-smuggling activities and bring him to Australia to face the charges. As people smuggling is not currently an offence in Indonesia, the dual criminality required for Australia to request his extradition from Indonesia does not currently exist. Australian authorities are continuing to work towards criminalisation of people smuggling in the region and Indonesian authorities have indicated that legislation would be introduced into the Indonesian Parliament this year criminalising people smuggling.
>
> *In relation to a potential murder charge in either the Australian or Indonesian jurisdiction, the AFP has not been*

able to establish the location where SIEV X sank, therefore, it is not possible to establish the relevant jurisdiction for any prosecution relating to the deaths on board. Four first instance arrest warrants have been sworn in Australia in respect to Quassey for alleged offences relating to organising suspected illegal entry vessels (SIEVs). The first three warrants for his arrest were sworn on 3 June 2002 and span alleged offences that occurred between February 2000 and August 2001. The latest warrant for his arrest is in relation to his alleged involvement in organising SIEV X in which 353 people died when it sank in October 2001 ...

The swearing of first instance warrants means an Interpol alert can be issued and it will ensure that the Australian government can seek to extradite Abu Quassey should circumstances allow. Australia respects that Indonesia, as a sovereign state, must make its own decision whether or not to investigate any particular matter.[5] [my italics]

Ellison's words revealed that, by December 2002, the untrue but vital Defence review finding that 'Defence can only speculate where the vessel foundered', which had been endorsed in the CMI committee's report, had now become the legal shelter for a claimed Australian inability to charge Abu Quassey with homicide in Indonesia or Australia—even though the boat had departed from Indonesia, and Australia was its destination. Keelty's original testimony that he was awaiting legal advice on the possibility that the criminal prosecution might be determined by the vessel's intended point of arrival was never clarified in the CMI committee or subsequent estimates committees (up to to April 2004).

Had Keelty been badly advised? Both possible avenues for prosecuting Quassey that he outlined in his 11 July testimony—as justification for his refusal to give any SIEV X testimony—turned out to be legal mirages.

Since December 2002, Ellison's public position has consistently been that Australia has no homicide jurisdiction in cases where the location of death at sea is outside Australian sovereign waters. This view was fully supported by international law specialists Professor Gillian Triggs and Dr Jean-Pierre Fonteyne.[6] Triggs said: 'Our criminal laws relating to either murder or negligent manslaughter of one kind or another do not apply extra-territorially … our criminal laws are confined to the territory over which we have sovereignty.' Fonteyne said: 'Australian authorities would be unable to prosecute Quassey [for homicide] whether the boat had been in international or Indonesian waters.'

This seems to be Criminal Law 101. Shouldn't the AFP have known it on 11 July 2002, when Keelty in his main testimony told the CMI committee that no one in the AFP was aware of the precise location of the sinking? Did the AFP consider at that time that the intended destination of SIEV X was a legal way around this roadblock? On whose legal advice did the AFP base that view? What was that advice? When and how was it found to be incorrect? We still don't know.

The other expressed hope—Quassey's extradition from Indonesia as a people smuggler—remained unachievable. There was never any serious prospect that Indonesia would pass a law against people smuggling, as this would run counter to the Islamic ethical duty to help travellers in distress.

During January 2003, Ellison, under pressure from an effective public campaign led by www.sievx.com, claimed that the government was 'pursuing all possible avenues to secure Quassey's prosecution' for people smuggling and for organising the SIEV X voyage. But Australian law-enforcement authorities mishandled an actual possibility in January 2003 to extradite Quassey, as a special case under the discretionary clause in the Australia–Indonesia extradition treaty.

On 1 February, the Indonesian Minister of Justice, Yusril Mahendra, announced he had decided to deport Quassey to his native Egypt. Yusril alleged to the *Sydney Morning Herald* that Australia had not seriously tried to extradite Quassey, and that he believed there were important questions about the disaster that Australia might not want answered.[7] Matthew Moore reported: '[Yusril] said no Australian minister had been in direct contact about the matter and he was suspicious about the reasons why Canberra had not made a more determined effort to bring Quassey to Australia.' Asked why he believed the Howard government might not want Quassey in Australia, Yusril told Moore: 'I don't know ... I don't want to talk about it, I have a lot of intelligence reports but I don't want to talk. That's the big question for me.'

Senator Collins scrutinised this matter closely in Senate legal estimates a week later.[8] Unusually, Ellison handled most of her questions himself. His replies were unclear and evasive, taking refuge (as had Keelty in the CMI committee) behind a claimed intended prosecution of Quassey if captured. But, at one point, an official from the Attorney-General's Department volunteered:

> It was not until 3 January [2003] that our officials in our embassy in Jakarta were advised that Indonesia would in principle have no objection to the Australian request for extradition. That was based on two policy changes. The first was that *Indonesia would extradite under the discretionary clause in the Australia–Indonesia extradition treaty* ... The second would involve being able to establish dual criminality for Abu Quassey's conduct, based on offences other than the people-smuggling offences.[9] [my italics]

It would have been a simple matter for Australian authorities to quickly put together a brief of testimony for dual criminality offences of alleged murder or manslaughter, based on accessible multi-source survivor accounts of the voyage, and to ask Yusril thereby to allow the discretionary extradition of Quassey. The AFP had had 15 months in which to prepare such a case, but no such request was made. Was this laziness, incompetence, or an undeclared reluctance to have Quassey face an Australian court?

Quassey flew to Cairo in April under Egyptian police escort. Thus the AFP's claimed determination to use Interpol agreements to arrest Quassey in transit was never achievable.

Quassey was arrested on arrival in Egypt on 25 April. He was charged, apparently first with manslaughter, later reduced to 'accidental manslaughter'. The AFP contributed the main body of written evidence to the Quassey trial, which took place in a semi-secret national security court. The Australian embassy closely observed the trial. The sentence was purely notional: five years for accidental manslaughter, two years for people smuggling—and subject to defendant appeal. There seems to have been no serious effort by Australian authorities (or anyone else) to put SIEV X survivors before the court to testify on the public-record evidence set out in Part One. This evidence could have tested a charge of deliberate homicide.

I handed over an early draft of Part One of this book to the Egyptian embassy in Canberra to assist in the prosecution. I was never told whether it was used. I also tried, without success, to persuade the UNHCR and the governments of Canada, Finland, New Zealand, Norway, and Sweden—countries where I knew SIEV X survivors were now living as permanent refugees and might have been willing to testify in Cairo if guaranteed protection by their host countries—to take an interest in the Cairo trial.

The scant public information about the Cairo trial suggests it was part of a whitewash to put the Quassey story finally to rest.[10] Under the principle of double jeopardy, there now seems little if any possibility of bringing Quassey to Australia on any SIEV X charges. He keeps his secrets about whom he worked with and to what ends. I would be surprised if he served his full sentence, or if he will be accessible to legal process thereafter.

Keelty in July 2002 did not have the gift of foresight as to this botched history of Quassey's prosecution. But his withheld testimony on SIEV X blocked progress in the Senate's investigation of the sinking. His refusal reinforced the misrepresentation in the Defence review, that claimed uncertainty as to where the boat sank. The combination of these two testimonies left the CMI committee with nowhere to go. As the ADF had sheltered behind claimed unclear AFP intelligence of the boat's departure, Ellison and the AFP now sheltered behind a claimed ADF uncertainty as to where the boat sank.

Such blunt questions must be asked here, because the ADF and AFP are accountable organisations under Australian law. The subsequent Quassey history casts into doubt the quality of the testimony Keelty gave as AFP Commissioner on 11 July 2002—no doubt under the advice provided to him at the time.

To this day, not one of the committee questions about the AFP and SIEV X—set aside by Keelty as matters he could not talk about—have been answered. The government continues to ignore the Senate's repeated demands for a judicial inquiry into these matters. The excuse of intended prosecutions against people smugglers seems to be infinitely extendable, and real justice for the SIEV X victims thereby infinitely delayable.

IN MAY 2003, Senator Ellison opened a surprising new judicial front. On 23 May, he announced that Khaleed (Khaled) Daoed [Abu Quassey's former bookkeeper, later established in media reporting from Sweden to be Mandaean] had been arrested the day before by Swedish police, following an 'Australian request' and an 'international investigation'.[11] Ellison thanked Sweden 'for tracking down and arresting Mr Daoed' under an extradition request for people smuggling on SIEV X and an earlier Quassey vessel.

This news was completely unexpected. Until then Daoed had figured in the SIEV X story only in a minor way. However, in August 2002, Ghassan Nakhoul's SBS Radio documentary *Five Mysteries of SIEV X* had exposed an interesting mystery about Daoed. Why were Daoed and Quassey's two other assistants, the brothers Maysam [also known as Miythem] and Maysar, arrested by Indonesian police weeks after SIEV X, then after UNHCR intercession released for lack of evidence of wrongdoing and later found secure refugee places in Europe? Daoed gained residence in Sweden in March 2002 as part of that country's refugee quota allotted by the UNHCR.[12]

Daoed's name had not come up in CMI committee evidence, or in any subsequent Senate estimates evidence in 2002–03, prior to his arrest on 23 May 2003. Three days later, Collins asked in an estimates committee why the AFP was only now pursuing Daoed.

Ellison replied that Daoed had been the subject of a 'longstanding' investigation by the AFP and [DIMIA], but he could not go into detail because it was 'operational'.[13] There is no public record that Australian law-enforcement authorities had taken any interest in Daoed after SIEV X, while he was still in Indonesia and while the UNHCR arranged his release from Indonesian prison and refugee entry to Sweden.

When and why did the AFP and DIMIA decide to seek his extradition from Sweden? A reasonable conclusion is that Ellison and the AFP may have decided to pursue a Daoed arrest-strategy early in 2003 because, embarrassed by their failed pursuit of Quassey (whether by accident or design), they were looking for a plausible, alternative SIEV X people smuggler to bring to Australia for trial in order to restore their damaged public credibility. In other words, they sought a scapegoat. They may have got the idea of extraditing Daoed from Nakhoul's *Five Mysteries*' reportage of Daoed's alleged role.

Despite Daoed's tearful public protestations that he was innocent and that Quassey was the real criminal, and the support of the Mandaean Iraqi refugee community in Sweden, the Swedish High Court, after considering Australian secret evidence, ruled in September that Daoed could be extradited to face people-smuggling charges in Australia. The Swedish government approved his extradition on 8 October. Ellison, who welcomed the news, was interviewed on the ABC *PM* program:

> **Louise Yaxley**: He comes to face people-smuggling charges. Some have suggested there should be manslaughter charges over SIEV X. What do you say to that?
> **Chris Ellison**: He's been extradited in relation to people smuggling charges, that's the basis on which we've prepared our brief. I would remind those people who think we should be looking at manslaughter charges that the maximum penalty for people-smuggling charges [is] 20 years' imprisonment. Now, *that is a substantial period of imprisonment, which would be on par with a manslaughter charge in any*

event. Now, he's facing 13 charges. I can't pre-empt what a court might do or what might not do in the event of a conviction, but certainly we have very heavy penalties involved in the legislation ...[14] [my italics]

Daoed arrived in Brisbane under arrest on 7 November. His lawyer, Peter Russo, protested at Ellison's allegedly pre-emptive statements on the case. A spokesman responded that the minister was entitled to outline information that was already on the public record.[15]

I then asked the Swedish embassy in Canberra whether Sweden considered that it still had any consular welfare responsibility for Daoed, having accepted him as a refugee on UNHCR'S recommendation. The embassy replied in writing that his fate lay with Australia: Sweden took no further responsibility for him.

A three-day committal hearing was held in Brisbane on 5–7 April 2004, and was reportedly due to resume in July, after this book went to press. Up to 20 witnesses had still to give committal testimony. Daoed has pleaded not guilty to the people-smuggling charges. Survivor testimony has been heard that ranges far beyond evidence necessary to test people-smuggling charges—that is, simply to establish whether Daoed sold tickets to passengers. The court has heard dramatic survivor testimony about Quassey's false promises of a large, safe boat; about violent forced loading by Quassey with the help of armed Indonesian police or soldiers; about engines and pumps that failed; about mystery 'metal' boats in the night that did not try to rescue survivors; and about a circling aircraft.[16] The issue of how much Daoed may have known about such matters has not yet been judicially addressed, and I don't know whether it will be, unless the relevance of such matters to the charges against Daoed is admitted in the prospective trial itself.

According to news reports, AFP officer Andrew Warton told the court on 7 April that he had evidence of Indonesian soldiers and immigration officials being involved in international people smuggling, and he had 'no idea' why attempts were not made to identify Indonesian officials accused of taking bribes from people smugglers. Warton said: 'That's a matter well beyond my bounds ... Certainly, some of the witness statements contained those facts ... those allegations were certainly raised ... but the focus of the investigation was on the principal offenders.' He said no attempt was made to investigate the claims by earlier witnesses of an Indonesian immigration official's involvement. He said he was not aware of any investigation by anyone else in the AFP.[17]

As I write this, the magistrate has yet to decide whether Daoed has a case to answer. By the time this book is published, the case, if it proceeds, is likely to be *sub judice*.

KEELTY'S TESTIMONY (and his subsequent written answers on 30 July) usefully exposed important new information on the previously mainly covert AFP-conducted people-smuggling disruption program (PSDP) in Indonesia. Under the PSDP, 20 Australian-selected Indonesian police officers were organised in five four-man regional teams, the INP SIU, or Indonesian National Police Special Intelligence Units. In October 2000, these 20 officers were given one week's intensive AFP training in disruption activities at a hotel in Denpasar, Bali. The training included 'investigation techniques, surveillance, information management and financial acquittal procedures'. The units were subsequently equipped with 'surveillance kits', and five patrol boats were promised for delivery late in 2002. The AFP funded the work of these teams, but Keelty said that the 'AFP did not engage in a 'fee for service' arrangement with INP, and AFP–INP transactions were regulated, transparent and above all else, legal.'

Cooperation took place under the legal cover of a people-smuggling protocol, signed in September 2000, that hung off an existing memorandum of understanding for AFP–INP cooperation against organised crime. Keelty said: 'The protocol allowed for the AFP and INP to provide advice regarding target selection, technical and management support of operations, informant management, information facilitation and assistance in financial reporting.' Three SIUs were located in the Bali–Lombok–Timor eastern region, and two in the West Java–Jakarta region, corresponding to the INP administrative regions of Bali, NTT, NTB, Metro Jaya, and Jawa Barat. 'These teams were involved in the ongoing gathering of information, arrests and prosecutions of Indonesian-based people smugglers and their networks.'[18]

It proved hard for senators to pin down in oral examination of Keelty what 'disruption' actually meant—as it had been carried out either by the DIMA–AFP Strike Team or by the Indonesian police Special Intelligence Unit teams. Keelty suggested that the former mainly involved public education and intelligence-gathering (using informants like Kevin Enniss), and the latter included Indonesian National Police action to disrupt the embarkation of boats at point of departure, rounding up passengers and delivering them to IOM or UNHCR, and arresting organisers. But he gave no examples, and I have found no media reports of any such activities. All the evidence on the public record that is set out in chapters 2–4 suggests that INP local units were habitually involved in helping favoured people smugglers run bus convoys and embark boats, using armed force when necessary.

Thus, members of the INP seemed to be facilitating rather than disrupting people-smuggling networks. Maybe the SIUs were not involved in any of this. Maybe other Indonesian police were doing these things while the SIUs were trying to stop them. If so, they were notably unsuccessful. We cannot find out, because we have not been told the names and ranks of the 20 INP personnel—presumably senior officers—who were selected by the AFP for training, equipment, and funding. Until evidence shows otherwise, it is reasonable to ask whether the SIU members were using their training and funding to help them organise such lucrative people-smuggling support activities. Was this their preferred way of disrupting people smuggling: penetrating the industry, making a healthy profit out of embarking asylum-seeker boats, while arranging to sink or disable the boats?

This question gains added force from remarkable admissions by Keelty towards the end of a long and gruelling examination by Faulkner and Cook.[19] He said, under questioning from Cook, that

INP disruption activities could have been 'autonomous' and 'covert', and outside AFP knowledge; that the AFP 'obviously knew when they [INP] arrested people or detained people, but we are not aware of how they did the other things that they did'; and that the INP could have paid people to disrupt people smuggling, but the AFP did not know of any specific instances, and payment of that type was not made by Australians.

Keelty summed it up thus:

> The AFP, in tasking the INP to do anything that would disrupt the movement of people smugglers, has never asked—nor would it ask—them to do anything illegal. If we became aware that they were doing something illegal or something that was inhumane ... we would ask that they not do it that way. The difficulty is that, once we ask them to do it, we have to largely leave it in their hands as to how they best do it, but it has not come to our attention that they were doing anything unlawful or inhumane. I simply do not have any advice on that at all. If we did know that, we would change the method of operation.

The clincher came moments later: Keelty admitted that if boats failed to reach Australia as a result of covert illegal INP disruption, the AFP would not necessarily find out. He agreed that the AFP would not necessarily find out about illegal INP activity, such as that suggested by Cook: 'if, on a dark night, someone slipped down and put some sugar in the fuel tank or some sand in the engine ...' Or, Cook might have added, if someone loosened a few planks in the hull, added a destabilising upper deck, forced an excessive number of people on board, and fitted a tracking device to trace the vessel's voyage and sinking location. The logic is exactly the same—the AFP might not have known.

And one recalls now Keelty's opening statement, with a feeling of less than reassurance: 'All information that may have led to a conclusion that the passengers of SIEV X were in danger was obtained after the vessel had in fact sunk.'

THESE WERE MOMENTOUS DISCLOSURES. Even though Keelty revealed almost nothing about SIEV X, he had disclosed the potential workings of Indonesian police disruption, plausibly deniable in terms of what Australian authorities would have known at the time when boats sank, that at last began to make some kind of sense of the perplexing mysteries of SIEV X.

Marr and Wilkinson reassured us in the first edition of *Dark Victory*: 'Australia did not kill those who drowned on SIEV X.' Probably not, at least in any direct sense. But it becomes a different issue if we consider how Australia, a year earlier, had designed, set up, and financed an indirect disruption system under which their own selected, trained, and funded Indonesian police teams and those teams' agents might have arranged for SIEV X to sink, and that this could all have taken place before Australian authorities were given information that would lead to a conclusion that the passengers of SIEV X were in danger.

The question becomes: why would the Australian Federal Police not have had timely access to such information, given that the boat had embarked with around 400 passengers on board, over 33 hours before sinking? Had there been an innocent 'breakdown in communications'? More darkly, might the AFP's training in 'information management' have taught the Indonesian Special Intelligence Units how to delay or withhold reports of criminal covert disruption activities so that the AFP would not be compromised by knowing things too soon?

I now see two possible AFP accountability scenarios here, equally disturbing, as both could have had lethal consequences: either a deliberate AFP 'plausible deniability' scenario, or 'it all got out of our control'. As to the first: there is a long Cold War history of illegal American covert operations conducted in plausibly deniable ways through local military, para-military, or police agencies, for instance, in Central America. At worst, Keelty's testimony could be construed in this way. There is no reason to think the AFP (or ASIS) would lack the ability to design a plausibly deniable covert people-smuggling disruption system in Indonesia, using selected undercover agents and selected sympathetic Indonesian local police. Remember, people smuggling was seen in Canberra in 2000–01 as a serious national security issue. Substantial resources were being dedicated to combat it. My speeches late in 2002 and in 2003 focused on this darker scenario.

My alternative 'loss of AFP control' scenario is equally lethal in its effects, although perhaps less ethically confronting in terms of Australian intention. The AFP came under pressure from the Howard government early in 2000 to develop more effective people-smuggling disruption strategies in Indonesia. A few months later, the AFP–INP people-smuggling protocol was signed, and the Indonesian police disruption teams (SIUs) were selected and trained. Perhaps this new disruption system then slid out of the AFP's control; maybe the AFP had unintentionally created a monster. Keelty's testimony can be read in that way, too.

This is not a guilt-free scenario. If the AFP continued in 2001 to collaborate with agencies that were suspected to be engaging in criminal activities — whether informants like Kevin Enniss or Indonesian police officers — it arguably cannot avoid legal accountability. Senator Faulkner, in the second of three speeches about the government's people-smuggling disruption program in Indonesia, on 24 September 2002, said (pp. 4781-82):

> The AFP have admitted that Kevin Enniss, in conjunction with the Indonesian police agency POLDA, was engaged in strategies designed to interdict asylum seekers where possible before they could depart for Australia ...
>
> Commissioner Keelty also told the CMI committee that AFP informants were only paid to provide information about the location of passengers and the activities of organisers. He said 'no money has been paid to anybody specifically empowered to intervene' in people smuggling. But as a result of an investigation into the activities of Enniss, the AFP confirmed that they were aware Enniss purported to be a people smuggler in Indonesia. They also admitted to knowing that Enniss had taken money from asylum seekers on at least one occasion ...

Faulkner asked whether such activities — 'sinking boats, taking asylum seekers' money and purporting to be a people smuggler' — were illegal. As noted above, the AFP, in a subsequent media release on 26 September, said that, in a formal interview with them, Enniss had emphatically denied any involvement in the sabotaging of vessels. Even so, Faulkner's questions about the legality of the AFP's informant relationship with a man who by the AFP's own testimony had taken asylum-seekers' money and purported to be a people smuggler still await answers.

FAULKNER AND COOK focused much of their questioning in the committee on the dubious legality of the whole disruption system.[20] They established clearly that the AFP was training and paying Indonesian police to combat an activity (moving people in boats out of Indonesia into international waters) that is not against Indonesian law. In effect, the SIU personnel were Australian mercenaries, doing things that lay outside their responsibility to police the laws of their own country.

Questioning established that the people-smuggling protocol had been cancelled, or 'set aside', to use Keelty's preferred euphemism, on 12 September 2001, at the request of the Indonesian Foreign Ministry. Keelty was not sure why, but he thought it might have had something to do with 'disquiet' among other Indonesian police units over the favoured budgetary treatment of SIU members. He did not know whether it reflected resentment of Australian interference in the work of Indonesian police, or Australian bullying of Indonesia after the Tampa crisis. (Later, DFAT also professed not to know why Indonesia revoked the protocol).

Keelty made it clear that disruption-program cooperation continued informally after the setting aside of the protocol, but it was more cautious and on a case-by-case basis. Full formal cooperation resumed only eight months later, when the protocol was absorbed into a new memorandum of understanding negotiated in mid-2002 after the Bali conference on people smuggling.

It follows from this testimony that, at the time SIEV X sank, there was no legal basis for the continuing 'informal' AFP–INP cooperation in people-smuggling disruption. It was a free-floating activity, outside the bounds of current Indonesian law, and relying only on previously established personal connections. Imagine how Australians would feel if a foreign police or intelligence agency (for example, the FBI or CIA) set up and maintained such a dubious commercial working relationship in Australia with chosen AFP officers. No wonder Keelty was careful during this committee testimony—he was walking through a legal and diplomatic minefield.

There are other things worth mentioning. Keelty spent a full five minutes conferring with his colleagues before responding that he could not answer Faulkner's apparently simple question: 'Did the AFP consider there might be a possible SOLAS [safety of life at sea] situation?'[21] This question arose in the context of committee discussion of the personal view that the AFP liaison officer Kylie Pratt expressed to Coastwatch along with her AFP telephoned report on 20 October 2001—that the vessel might have been subject to increased risk due to the numbers reportedly on board. What may be important here is that Pratt was apparently assigned to the AFP–DIMA people-smuggling strike team. Is it credible that DIMA, as would soon be claimed in its CMI committee testimony, knew nothing about Pratt's AFP report to Coastwatch, or her personal opinion that she had added to it?

It was clear from Bonser's evidence that the DIMA–AFP strike team had been monitoring Quassey for a long time. They knew his history of sending three grossly overloaded, ill-equipped, or unsafe boats (ADF codenames 'Donnybrook', 'Gelantipy', and 'Yambuk') to Australia.[22] The AFP–DIMA strike team might have anticipated that this latest Quassey voyage would be similarly unsafe, and this could have been the basis of Pratt's anxiety. Kylie Pratt never testified.

Keelty told the CMI committee that the AFP was not a maritime surveillance agency and did not have the expertise to plan or mount maritime operations.[23] He said: 'We did not know about the departure of SIEV X until after the vessel [that picked up survivors] had returned. We had no way of surveilling SIEV X … we had no way of receiving any distress call.'[24]

But this does not sit easily with Bonser's earlier testimony (see chapter 8) about the two AFP reports. If the AFP had no way of surveilling SIEV X at sea, by what means could it have concluded on 22 October what it will not admit to concluding two days before—that SIEV X might represent a threat to life? Had the AFP received firm information by 22 October, perhaps from DSD, ASIS, an AFP informant, or Indonesian police SIUs, that SIEV X had sunk? Did the AFP or ASIS have direct knowledge of the sinking through a tracking device on SIEV X?

The issue of whether the AFP placed tracking devices on SIEVs, or supplied devices to Indonesian police or others, has been explored without clear answers in Senate questioning subsequent to the CMI committee's inquiry. On 20 November 2002, in Legal and Constitutional Estimates, Keelty—under direction from Ellison—took on notice an apparently simple reiterated question from Faulkner: was Keelty personally aware of any practice to place tracking devices on people smugglers' boats? Faulkner's question went to the nub of whether tracking devices were part of the tradecraft of the disruption program in Indonesia.

Marg Hutton commented that she sensed from Faulkner's persistent questioning that he had a strong suspicion that such a device was attached to SIEV X. She wrote: 'If this proves to be true then it will totally collapse the government's claim that it has never known where SIEVX sank.'[25]

The next day, Keelty wrote to the Legal and Constitutional Committee chair, Senator Marise Payne, claiming public-interest immunity from answering Faulkner's questions:

> The questions call for an answer which may disclose lawful methods for detecting, investigating or dealing with matters arising out of breaches of the law, the disclosure of which would, or would be reasonably likely to, prejudice the effectiveness of those methods. I propose recommending to the minister [Ellison] that he make a claim of public-interest immunity in relation to information sought by these questions.

In March 2003, it was claimed in *Dark Victory* (page 41) that 'at AFP direction, the Indonesians attached tracking devices to many of the boats before they set out for Australia'. Then, in May 2003, in an often fiery session of Legal and Constitutional Estimates, yet more hairs were split by Keelty and Ellison.[26] Keelty said: 'I can confirm to you that, to the AFP's knowledge, there was no tracking device placed on SIEV X.' Ellison took on notice a question as to whether tracking devices were placed on SIEVs 'by Indonesians, in the knowledge of the AFP'. The eventual AFP reply was 'No'.[27] Ellison claimed public-interest immunity and refused to answer a Faulkner question 'whether tracking devices were placed on asylum-seeker vessels by the Indonesians at the request of the AFP or supplied by the AFP'.

This vexed history of unresolved questioning about tracking devices offers only one example of studied 'blockage' in Senate estimates committees subsequent to the CMI committee, covering a great many issues that might help throw light on possible Australian disruption activity in relation to the sinking of SIEV X. None of the following lines of questioning have been fully and credibly answered by the AFP or their minister, Senator Ellison: regarding radio messages from SIEV X; photographs of SIEV X; the name, home port, and ownership of SIEV X; lists of passenger names; and sources of intelligence on the embarkation and sinking. There are far too many such rejected or incompletely answered questions to recount their Senate history fully in this book. This history is in the Hansard transcripts and subsequent written replies to estimates committees in 2002–04 archived in www.siev.com. Other questions are yet to be asked.

Senate efforts to obtain answers from the AFP have produced little more than evasion or ministerial refusals, at times truculent, to answer. Such blocked questioning has sometimes generated considerable heat.[28]

We may not yet see the glow of fire, but there is a great deal of smoke coming off these Hansard pages.

BY SEPTEMBER 2002 Faulkner saw what seemed to him a secretive and out-of-control Australian system of people-smuggling disruption in Indonesia. He had no assurance that the sinking of SIEV X was not an outcome of that system. Unlike me, Faulkner has always been careful to avoid 'hypothesising' or proposing scenarios. Yet he made four powerful and impassioned Senate interventions on 23–26 September 2002, raising serious questions about the disruption program and SIEV X.[29] He dramatically concluded the last of three adjournment speeches, on 25 September, with the following:

> I ask these questions. Was Enniss involved in the sabotage of vessels? Were others involved in the sabotage of vessels? Do Australian ministers, officials or agencies have knowledge of such activities? And what about the vessel now known as SIEV X, part of the people-smuggling operation of the notorious people smuggler Abu Quassey? That vessel set sail on 18 October 2001 and sank on 19 October 2001, drowning 353 people, including 142 women and 146 children. Were disruption activities directed against Abu Quassey? Did these involve SIEV X?
>
> I intend to keep asking questions until I find out. And, Mr Acting Deputy President, I intend to keep pressing for an independent judicial inquiry into these very serious matters. At no stage do I want to break, nor will I break, the protocols in relation to operational matters involving ASIS or the AFP. *But those protocols were not meant as a direct or an indirect licence to kill.* [my italics]

The next day, Faulkner returned to the attack in a final adjournment debate:

> How far does disruption go? What are the limits, if any? I want to ask, and I want an answer to, precisely what disruption activities are undertaken at the behest of, with the knowledge of or broadly authorised by the Australian

government. I want to know, and I think the parliament and the Australian public are entitled to know, what directions or authorisations ministers have issued in relation to disruption ... Who tasks the Indonesian officials or others to disrupt people smugglers or the clients of people smugglers? ... We also want to know whether Australians are involved in disruption activities in Indonesia. And it is perfectly reasonable for us to ask about the accountability mechanisms that are in place in relation to these activities, particularly when the [memorandum of understanding] governing these particular matters collapses. The commissioner for the AFP and the minister cannot say why; the commissioner cannot even say he asked why that occurred. We want to know whether Kevin Enniss was actually involved in the sabotage of vessels, as Kevin Enniss has claimed. We want to know if others were involved in the sabotage of vessels, and we want to know why the government is avoiding an independent inquiry into these very important issues.

Did Faulkner have a whistleblower giving him secret information on the conduct of the disruption program by AFP and/or ASIS? Did he therefore have reason to suspect that Keelty's evidence may have been less than the whole truth? It is hard to explain in any other way Faulkner's determination, or the indignation of his senior Labor colleague, Senator Ray, who said in the 26 September 2002 debate:

> If ever I have seen an evasive witness, it was him [Keelty] at the estimates hearings and at the [CMI committee] inquiry. Why doesn't he front to give straightforward evidence? Why have all these officials got such selective memories or a lack of intellectual rigour, that would force them to probe certain issues that they should be pursuing if they hold responsible jobs?

Faulkner's passion for getting to the bottom of the disruption program carried over to his individual comments in the CMI committee's report four weeks later (see below, pages 244–45). The report contained in its first chapter a short but highly critical discussion of disruption and deterrence activity in Indonesia, culminating in a recommendation (which I think bears Faulkner's drafting hand) calling for a full independent inquiry.

> The Committee recommends that a full independent inquiry into the disruption activity that occurred prior to the departure from Indonesia of refugee vessels be undertaken, with particular attention to the activity that Australia initiated or was instrumental in setting in motion through both its partners in the Indonesian government and its own network of informants.[30]

Despite the subsequent passage of four Senate motions and persistent estimates committee questioning of Ellison and the AFP, little more came to light in 2003–04 on the disruption program. Faulkner restated all his September 2002 concerns in a Fabian Society speech in Melbourne on 23 July 2003,[31] and again in an article for a Labor Party journal in January 2004.[32] Faulkner has never resiled from his strong questions. Government refusal to answer them remains central to the SIEV X cover-up.

Unanswered questions on the AFP's conduct of the disruption program, and its withheld intelligence reports on SIEV X, continue to cloud that organisation's public reputation. As I wrote this chapter, Mick Keelty had just emerged (with his professional integrity intact, he said) from a bruising encounter with Prime Minister John Howard over Keelty's entirely reasonable publicly stated opinion that Australia was more exposed to terrorist attack after the Madrid train bombings (March 2004). After a change of prime minister, Keelty and the AFP might welcome a judicial inquiry as an opportunity to clear the air and set the record straight on the AFP's disruption program and SIEV X.

Alexander Downer uttered a dismissive one-liner on 30

Questions about Disruption

December 2003 when asked about the SIEV X Senate motions: 'That is just a political stunt', he said.[33] In the long run, this will not satisfy anybody as a government answer to opposition senators' concerns about people-smuggling disruption activity in Indonesia, and the role this program might have played in the loss of 353 lives.

A final word is appropriate here on the question of the relevance of the AFP–Kevin Enniss history, as so far known, to SIEV X. At no time has any senator ever alleged that Kevin Enniss might have been involved in the sinking of SIEV X. Nor have I.

At the conclusion of the Senate exchanges on disruption, in his final personal explanation on 26 September (Hansard, page 5014), Faulkner firmly rejected the first two dot points in the AFP–Keelty media release of 26 September ('Senator Faulkner has got it wrong'—see page 133):

> Dot point 1 is: 'Kevin Enniss was operating out of Kupang some 1300km from the departure point of SIEV X, and had nothing to do with either the vessel or its passengers.' So what? I have never alleged that Enniss was involved in sabotaging SIEV X. In fact, I have never alleged that SIEV X was sabotaged. I find it extraordinary that that statement appears in the commissioner's press release.
>
> Dot point 2 is: 'Kevin Enniss ceased his operations with the Indonesian National Police at least two or three weeks prior to the departure of SIEV X.' Again, so what? I have never drawn any link between Enniss and SIEV X, and I do not know at this stage what other Australian agencies Kevin Enniss may have been working for. I do not understand why that dot point has been included by the commissioner in this release.

The importance of the Enniss case for Faulkner, as for me, has been what it suggests about weak accountability-mechanisms and safeguards in the AFP people-smuggling disruption program in Indonesia.

Chapter Twelve

Out of the Loop

> The role of the [PST] taskforce is not to sieve though intelligence.
>
> — Jane Halton, chair of the People Smuggling Taskforce, Department of the Prime Minister and Cabinet, CMI committee Hansard, page 2100

TO ROUND OUT the SIEV X evidence of the Australian Defence Force and the Australian Federal Police came witnesses from the two civilian agencies most involved in border protection: the departments of Immigration and Multicultural and Indigenous Affairs on 11 July, and Prime Minister and Cabinet on 30 July. Their evidence left unresolved one of the big inconsistencies hanging over the story: how these two major agencies happened not to be in the AFP–Coastwatch–ADF information loop on SIEV X intelligence during 20–22 October 2001. Also, it raises the question of what their apparent exclusion in these two crucial days says about the handling in Canberra by these two agencies of the earlier, still unknown, intelligence about the Quassey boat.

A high-level DIMIA witness team comprised acting secretary

Ed Killesteyn, acting deputy secretary Vince McMahon, and assistant secretary (border protection branch) Nelly Siegmund. Killesteyn and McMahon had been frequent participants in People Smuggling Taskforce meetings. Siegmund's branch produced the then DIMA's daily intelligence notes (DINs) on people-smuggling boat activity.

With three such authoritative witnesses in attendance, one might have expected substantial explanatory testimony; but this team was uninformative. These three officials, who in 2001 had worked at the centre of DIMA's operations against people smuggling, seemed to have seen nothing, heard nothing, and said nothing about SIEV X during the crucial days of 18–22 October. They were out of the loop, at least insofar as any of them could remember.

Siegmund said her branch oversaw the Intelligence Analysis Section (IAS), which was the key reception point for primary intelligence reports about people smuggling.[1] IAS analysed and distributed this intelligence, in the form of DINs, to a range of agencies. IAS drew material from open sources, and from Australian intelligence and law-enforcement communities.

Her branch also provided the five DIMA members of the 15-person DIMA–AFP People Smuggling Strike Team, which worked out of the AFP in Canberra. The strike team's role was 'to undertake investigations which will hopefully lead to the prosecution of people involved in organising people smuggling'. Siegmund and an AFP equivalent (unnamed) comprised a board of management that oversaw the strike team's operations and priorities.

The DIMIA witnesses had little to say about the disruption program. As requested, DIMIA later supplied a trilingual leaflet (of unspecified date) as an example of 'the information material disseminated in Indonesia as part of the disruption strategy'. It included these chilling words:

> If you get on a boat in Indonesia you will: expose yourself and your family to great danger; lose your money; fail in your objective to get to Australia. The boats used by people

smugglers are overcrowded and dangerous. *Too many people have died trying to enter Australia by boat. Stop. Go back. Don't get further into the trap.*[2] [my italics]

Siegmund testified that DIMA 'was not part of that intelligence loop' in respect of the 20 October 2001 SIEV X report from the AFP to Coastwatch that the latter had immediately phoned through to the Australian Theatre Joint Intelligence Centre.[3]

Killesteyn and McMahon, who had both attended the PST meetings on 20 and 22 October 2001 (with DIMA secretary Bill Farmer) had little specific memory of whether there was any discussion of SIEV X on those days. DIMIA witnesses noted that PST minutes were 'cryptic'. They said they could not throw real light on them.[4] Nor could Siegmund explain, despite frequent reference to the set of classified DINs she had with her, why the DINs of those days did not cover information being discussed in PST about the Quassey boat's expected arrival, and safety-of-life-at-sea concerns about it.

There was frustratingly little in all this DIMIA testimony that senators could grasp hold of. A general vagueness and lack of memory prevailed. Senator Collins commented with some asperity:

> We have yet to get to the bottom of why it took the time it did for intelligence that is clearly from the departure on the 18th [October] to reach us on the 20th. That is an issue aside from this. But the next point, too, is that that information arrived on the 20th when these people were still in the water and there was limited response to it. And from your department's point of view, you did not even get that information in your own intelligence unit [IAS] until after the 22nd. There are some very serious communication issues here.[5]

DIMIA witnesses remained mute. Killesteyn then assured Senator Faulkner that a recent statement put out by secretary Bill Farmer to all DIMIA staff, reminding them of their obligations as employees to avoid inappropriate public comment that might compromise the department's work, would not have prevented staff from providing honest and open advice to a committee such as this.[6]

DIMIA's later written advice was hardly more informative. About three-quarters of the text in the DINs that the CMI committee had asked to see—including the consecutive series dated 17, 18, 19, and 22 October 2001—was blacked out. There were only two visible references to Abu Quassey's boat.[7] The 19 October DIN said: 'Abu Quassey's boat carrying up to 250 passengers that reportedly departed from probably Cilicap [sic] on Tuesday night [16 October] has not yet been sighted. It was expected to arrive in the vicinity of Christmas Island late Thursday [18 October].'

The next DIN on 22 October (DINs were not issued on weekends) said: 'The other vessel believed to be heading for Christmas Island, organised by Abu Quassey and carrying up to 400 passengers, has not yet been sighted but should be in the vicinity of Christmas Island if it was able to depart successfully from the Cilicap [sic] area on Friday morning [19 October].'

The next DIN on 23 October, on the now public sinking, was more informative. It contained most of the information in the (as yet unknown to senators) 23 October 2001 cable from the embassy in Jakarta. It was, I surmise, largely based on that cable. But it made one very important and precise statement that was not in the cable: it said that the boat sank 'approximately 60 NM south of the Sunda Strait'.

I don't know where DIMA got this specific intelligence of '60 NM south'. It could not have been construed from the cable, which refers only 'to the south of Sunda Strait' and 'no further south than eight degrees south latitude on a direct line from Sunda Strait to Christmas Island'. Nor was it in any public source at that time. The 60 NM figure is proof that DIMA had access to another, independent intelligence source. Was this the still-secret AFP reporting, or was it something else? Might this 60 NM have come from ASIS or DSD reporting? Or from JORN data?

Other questions: how could an agency that so prided itself on being at the centre of people-smuggling intelligence and distribution have been conspicuously left out of the AFP–Coastwatch–ADF intelligence loop on the Quassey boat in the days 20–22 October? It was the weekend, but senior officers have weekend phone numbers. And why did none of the AFP, Coastwatch, or Defence attendees seem to have spoken about the AFP 20 October report on SIEV X's departure with Farmer, Killesteyn, or McMahon at the PST meeting on 20 October (Saturday afternoon) which all attended, just a few hours after Coastwatch had relayed the AFP report to ASTJIC? Why were the DIMIA witnesses unable to remember any discussion in the PST meetings on 20 and 22 October about the expected arrival of SIEV X—meetings which, unusually, were attended by three very senior DIMA officers (the secretary, deputy secretary, and division head) — especially when PST minutes and Halton's testimony (see later in this chapter) would confirm that there was such discussion? Why did Faulkner so pointedly ask about the possible 'gagging' effect of the DIMIA secretary's circular to staff, in the context of this remarkably uninformative DIMIA testimony?

JANE HALTON testified in the CMI committee for a second time on 30 July.[8] A determined and spirited witness, she danced skillfully through a full day of intense questioning, never once losing her poise or train of thought. She showed a well-developed capacity for giving general answers to specific questions, reframing them in her own terms. Her evidence must be read with care to glean its precise significance.

Labor senators by 30 July had a clear idea of what they wanted from Halton. First, they wanted to test her understanding of the PST minutes against the evidence already in from the AFP, Coastwatch, Defence, and DIMIA as to action taken or not taken subsequent to AFP reporting on the Quassey boat.

Second, why had the prime minister on 23 October 2001 not used intelligence known to have been received by PST on that same day that the boat was likely to have sunk 'in international waters south of Java'? (PST minutes, 23 October 2001) Why had he falsely claimed, and maintained over many weeks, that the boat sank in Indonesian waters? Why hadn't PM&C ever corrected his factual error? Why was he even now claiming it was uncertain where the boat sank, despite mounting public evidence that it had sunk in Operation Relex waters? Labor sensed good political points to be scored here. It was not wrong. But had it known the contents of the DIMA intelligence note of 23 October 2001, which it only saw on 20 September 2002, and the Jakarta embassy cable, which it was not to see until February 2003, it could have nailed the prime minister's false statement immediately.

Faulkner and Collins first briefly asked about the disruption program. Halton firmly replied that disruption activities in Indonesia were outside the PST's terms of reference: it neither ordered them nor knew much about them. 'The essence of the disruption activity was not, as I have just said, canvassed in this forum [PST] in any kind of detail. It was as peripheral colour and movement on a couple of occasions, as a rhetorical question ...'[9]

She stressed the imprecision of PST knowledge of boats: 'For every time we were told that a boat was leaving, about to leave, had left, what have you, I would say probably one in 10 turned up.' SIEV X 'could have been part of the panoply of vague maybes, sometimes more likelies, in the suite of things that might turn up'.[10]

Collins questioned the apparent inconsistency between the very detailed PST note about SIEV X on 22 October, 'Not spotted yet, missing, grossly overloaded, no jetsam spotted, no reports from relatives', and Halton's testimony now that the PST usually only had vague, limited, non-categorical knowledge of these boats until they arrived. Halton replied that this discussion on 22 October was based on multi-source intelligence and thus was more reliable than usual.[11] But, she said, there was still a question on that day as to whether this boat existed. 'The context was, "Did it leave? Is it really on the water?"'[12] She recalled that the conversation was between PM&C and DIMA. She could not recall 'active participation' by the AFP. Halton testified that on 22 October she (like DIMA) was not aware of the AFP confirmation of departure that had been passed to Coastwatch and Defence on 20 October.

Halton was asked about the reference in the 18 October PST minutes to 'multi-source information with high confidence level' of 'two boats with total 600 PUAs [potential unauthorised arrivals] expected at Christmas', with 'some risk of vessels in poor condition and rescue at sea'. She said that this multi-source information had come from the ADF, DIMA, DFAT, and the Attorney-General's Department.[13] I note here that the ADF covers the Defence Signals Directorate; DFAT covers ASIS; and Attorney-General's covers ASIO, which may have been monitoring SIEV X-related telephone calls between Indonesia and Australia.

On 19 October, PST minutes noted a forecast from DIMA that the next boat to Christmas Island [SIEV X] could have 250 people on board.[14] Halton said that the PST afternoon meeting on 20 October (which Bonser attended) did not receive any report of the information—known on that morning to the AFP, Coastwatch, and Defence—that the Quassey boat had reportedly departed, that it was grossly overloaded with 400 people on board, and that an AFP officer [Kylie Pratt] had offered a personal opinion to Coastwatch that the vessel might have been at increased risk due to the numbers reportedly on board. Halton's response was, 'No, certainly not at that level of detail at all.'[15]

Halton went on:

> What I can tell you is that I do not think—and it is consistent with what is reflected here [in PST notes]—that there was any direct report of such advice ... I have absolutely no recollection that we were told that a particular vessel had categorically left.

She added she would have remembered any such reporting in the PST meeting on 20 October, because:

> The notion of a vessel of 400 ... would have set every alarm bell ... ringing, because we had a huge accommodation

problem … the notion that a vessel that we had been told was likely to be of the order of 250 might all of a sudden have blown out to 400 would have got every alarm bell going in the place.

The NORCOM intelligence summary (INTSUM) of 20 October, which was based on the 20 October AFP report, and which was quoted in the Defence (Gates) review submitted to the committee on 4 July, said that 'there is a high probability of the vessel arriving [in the vicinity of] Christmas Island from 21 Oct 01, and that due to its overcrowding and need to maintain stability it may be limited to a slow passage, and therefore a later time of arrival could be expected.' Halton testified that this intelligence was not presented to the PST on 20 October,[16] and such information was not canvassed at the next PST meeting on 21 October either.[17]

Halton was quizzed again about the dramatic 22 October reference to SIEV 8 [SIEV X]: 'Not spotted yet, missing, grossly overloaded, no jetsam spotted, no reports from relatives.'[18] She said it was only on 22 October that she learned the boat had 400 on board, which made it 'grossly overloaded'. It was part of the intelligence given in the PST on that day, and she could not be categorical about which agency reported it.

On 23 October, she learned about the sinking through a 2.00am phone call from Shane Castles (AFP). He gave no details, but said that a cable was coming from Jakarta.[19] Someone read out from that cable at the PST meeting that afternoon, and this was the basis of the PST 23 October minute. The prime minister was advised on 24 October as part of a general 'status update' prepared in PM&C.[20] The advice to him said: 'Boat capsized and sank quickly south of the western end of Java with loss of possibly 352 lives.' Halton added:

> But I should be quite clear here: there is a heading here which says 'Boat sunk in Indonesian waters'. It does not say territorial waters. There had been a conversation about

Indonesian safety in its search and rescue zone. That is just a heading.

She said she could not provide the committee with this 24 October status report to the prime minister, which had been prepared by PM&C on the basis of advice from DFAT, DIMA, Transport, Attorney-General's, and Defence. She took on notice a request to obtain it. This was to take another eight months.

Collins asked about the inconsistency between the advice in PST minutes of 23 October that the boat sank in international waters, and the heading in the 24 October PM&C status report, which Halton had said referred to the boat sinking in Indonesian waters. Halton said:

> [I] will have to take that on notice. What I can say to you is: the comment about 'south of the western end of Java' was not contained, as I understand it, in the material that was read to us on that afternoon of the 23rd. The point I was making to you about the source of the information that was contained in that minute was that there had been, as there always was—before PM&C sent a brief to the Prime Minister, which was a state of play brief—a canvassing of the individual agencies which were relevant to the particular subject matters.

She said the additional detail in relation to 'south of the western end of Java' had come from one of those agencies. The original information in the PST on 23 October had not been passed to the prime minister. He got only the PM&C status report of 24 October.

We now know that the prime minister was named on the distribution list for the DFAT priority 'First Sensitive' cable from Jakarta of 23 October—which makes this whole discussion surreal. The prime minister's office knew from the morning of 23 October, from this cable, that the boat sank 'no further south than eight degrees latitude, on a direct line from Sunda Strait to Christmas Island'. If the prime minister did not see the cable himself, one can reasonably surmise that his international affairs adviser at the time (Miles Jordana) would have seen it, and briefed him on it.

ANOTHER FAST-FORWARD HERE. The Senate, after a great deal of official delay and prevarication, finally got to see the 24 October 2001 PM&C status report, or 'state of play' brief to Howard, on 21 May 2003—fully ten months after Halton testified. All that it said, in a short paragraph, was: '[Section Heading] Boat sank in Indonesian waters ... the boat capsized and sank quickly south of the western end of Java ...'[21]

There had never been any additional intelligence after 23 October. The PM&C status report was simply a compressed collation of the Jakarta cable and the DIMA intelligence note of the previous day, with a misleading title 'Boat sank in Indonesian waters' tacked on by PM&C—a title for which there had never been any intelligence basis. Halton's testimony left the committee with the impression (later shown to be without basis) that the prime minister had received some updated stronger intelligence on 24 October that the boat had sunk in Indonesian waters.[22] The misrepresentation was not finally exposed until the public release of the 24 October status report.

However, Halton had covered herself in her testimony:

> The information in the brief [to the Prime Minister on 24 Oct] ... came from the relevant agencies. In terms of the information about Indonesian waters, it does not say 'Indonesian territorial waters'. In terms of the likely location —that is, south of the western end of Java—that material would have been provided by one of the line agencies.

As to the Jakarta cable, she intimated it had somehow been overtaken by more reliable information that came in on the next day:

the advice that we got as the cable was read to us was that this was *a preliminary report from, my memory is, the AFP*. I think it says they had had a conversation with a 19-year-old survivor and they were making *a very early assessment of the facts* in relation to this issue. Certainly I think our understanding was that [by the next day, 24 October] *the agencies concerned had had time to reflect on this issue in a more considered way*.[23] [my italics]

Halton had here perfected the art of giving testimony that was 'not quite a lie'. She had covered every base. She even challenged any necessary inconsistency between the cable and the next day's PM&C status report, relying on a professed definitional uncertainty about what 'Indonesian waters' actually meant:

> No, we would not have said that there was a particular inconsistency. As much as anything else, our experience of the description of Indonesian waters right throughout this period was, to say the very least, confused. We have the Indonesian search and rescue zone, we have what would have been their contiguous zone if they declared it and then we have their territorial waters. Right throughout this period there was a lack of precision about what the legal definition was … In my experience, right throughout this period you found that people used all this terminology quite interchangeably …

In the end, Halton argued firmly, the PST carried no responsibility for what happened to SIEV X:

> At the end of the day, the surveillance was being undertaken under Operation Relex, which was not the responsibility of this [PST] taskforce … this taskforce was responsible for dealing with the issues about when they [SIEVs] actually hit the edge of the contiguous zone … Explicitly and deliberately, the taskforce was not part of the line command

arrangements ... The surveillance was a matter for Defence and Coastwatch operating in conjunction. At the end of the day, our understanding had been that this vessel had sunk quite close to Indonesia ... the notion that we should suddenly take responsibility for something which was not within our remit is unreasonable'[24]

Collins asked: 'Then whose responsibility do you believe it is to ascertain whether this ship sank in regions where we were conducting comprehensive surveillance?' Halton replied: 'It seems to me that is a question that should be put to Defence.'

So, in the surreal game of musical chairs that the CMI committee's inquiry had become, every player had found a chair: there were no potential culprits left standing. In the end it seemed that, so long as one did not look too closely, nobody was to blame.

Chapter Thirteen

Can We Handle the Truth?

Evidence n.

1. the available facts, circumstances, etc, supporting or otherwise a belief, proposition, etc, or indicating whether or not a thing is true or valid.

2. (Law) *a* information given personally or drawn from a document, etc, and tending to prove a fact or proposition. *b* statements or proofs admissible as testimony in a lawcourt.

3. clearness, obviousness.

— *Oxford English Reference Dictionary*, 2nd edition, 1996

The struggle of the people against power is the struggle of memory against forgetting.

— Milan Kundera, Czech dissident author under the former communist regime

THE CMI COMMITTEE called no more witnesses after 30 July, but it received substantial additional written evidence about SIEV X from the Australian Federal Police, Jane Halton, the Department of Immigration and Multicultural and Indigenous Affairs, and the Defence Department, right up until 20 September—by which time it would have been well into preparing its report, which it tabled in the Senate on 23 October 2002.[1] I witnessed the tabling debate. There was an angry and bitter feeling in the air.[2]

In my opinion, the committee's report was seriously deficient in respect of SIEV X in terms of its methodology, findings, and recommendations. I am on safe ground in saying this, because opposition senators during and since the presentation of the report have in effect offered a range of comparable criticisms—in the tabling debate, in personal statements forming part of the published report, in related statements elsewhere in the Senate, and in Senate estimates questioning thereafter.

Senate reports are agreed committee products. This one was clearly deeply contentious, and many cracks must have been papered over in its negotiation. The fact is that sustained detailed questioning on SIEV X and disruption activities has continued throughout the almost two years since the CMI committee's report, in estimates committees and in questions on notice. There has been further questioning of all the main agencies that testified in the CMI committee's inquiry—PM&C, Defence, AFP, DIMIA, DFAT, Transport (AMSA), and Customs (Coastwatch), demonstrating that for non-government senators (and they are the Senate majority) the CMI report did not close the SIEV X case. Finally, there are the public benchmarks of four highly critical Senate motions on SIEV X passed in December 2002 and October 2003. (For the text of these, see the Appendix.)

The CMI committee faced a body of refused, blacked-out, incomplete, or inconsistent official evidence, both as to the intelligence available to the system on SIEV X (CMI committee report, chapter 8), and as to what was done or not done with that intelligence (chapter 9). The committee could have admitted defeat. It could have said that, with the limited powers available to it for compelling the production of evidence, it could not come to any reliable conclusions on the conduct of the agencies involved, and it therefore was recommending a full-powers judicial inquiry into the SIEV X disaster and the disruption program. There would have been no professional failure or dishonour if the committee had taken this course. I wish it had.

Instead, the committee in these two chapters tried to cobble together a broadly exculpatory explanation of the government system's response to SIEV X intelligence. It strained mightily to produce vaguely plausible explanations of serious gaps and inconsistencies in evidence presented by different agencies. It did not criticise any officials or agencies, although it left a few public questions over the conduct of Coastwatch and its head, Rear Admiral Bonser (who was harshly singled out, in my view—was he being punished for having upset the first Defence cover-up?). It firmly set aside my concerns as having been tested and found to be without foundation.

Like a diligent student sitting a tough examination, the committee seems to have felt obliged to come up with solutions and answers, even if they were the wrong ones. An admission of unease or dissatisfaction—along the lines of 'We don't understand the conflicting and incomplete information we were given, and we are not satisfied with this evidence'—apparently was not considered feasible.

Why? Did committee members think the public reputation of the Senate committee investigative system depended on producing answers? Was a political deal struck between the government and the opposition: that the government would wear the blame on 'children overboard' if the opposition allowed SIEV X to be pretty much whitewashed and set aside? Was a political calculation made by Labor: did it fear an ADF backlash if it had dared to return a majority verdict on the lines indicated above, which Liberal senators would have vehemently challenged in a minority report? There was a possible underlying validity in Senator Mason's jibe at Labor during the tabling debate: 'In the famous words of Jack Nicholson in the film *A Few Good Men*, "You want the truth? You can't handle the truth."'[3]

On the basis of the contradictory and incomplete evidence reviewed in chapters 7–12 of this book, the CMI report reached conclusions on SIEV X that are entirely different from mine. It was not a case of me finding the glass half empty and the committee finding it half full: the committee saw an almost full glass; I see an almost empty one.

Long before the SIEV X chapters in the CMI report, chapter 1 includes a substantial section on disruption and deterrence activities.[4] The Keelty testimony on disruption arose in the context of the Senate pursuing the SIEV X questions I had raised (it could not have arisen otherwise), yet these paragraphs do not mention SIEV X. Nor, except for one fleeting mention, do the later SIEV X chapters (8 and 9) refer back to disruption.[5] There seems to have been a deliberate de-coupling of the SIEV X and disruption issues in the negotiation and writing of this report.

The disruption section concludes with the first agreed, very important, CMI committee recommendation calling for a full independent inquiry into disruption activity in Indonesia that Australia initiated or was instrumental in setting in motion (the full text is noted above on page 224, in chapter 11).

Government senators did not oppose this recommendation. But their very different view on SIEV X was memorably set out in the preamble to their minority report:

> [paragraph] 13. In regard to SIEV X, government senators support the general conclusions and findings in Chapters 8 and 9. In particular we agree with the finding in paragraph 9.142, which states, 'On the basis of the above, the committee cannot find grounds for believing that negligence or dereliction of duty was committed in relation to SIEV X'. This should be all that is said in relation to this part of the inquiry, which took up an inordinate amount of time to attempt to deal with the submission of one person, Mr Tony Kevin, based upon dubious information and scant knowledge of the facts. We cannot help but wonder, though, whether the conspiracy theories so sedulously fostered by other senators in relation to SIEV 4 may have nurtured the febrile climate of suspicion in which Mr Kevin's fanciful

allegations were able to establish a foothold of credibility. The exhaustive nature of the public hearings into the scenario promulgated by Mr Kevin and the conclusion and findings of this committee should put an end to further public speculation.

Crucially, as discussed extensively in previous chapters of this book, the report accepted official advice from Defence, the AFP, and PM&C, in concluding that 'The exact location where the boat sank remains in doubt, with speculation that it might have gone down in the Sunda Strait within Indonesian waters.'[6]

The committee noted that it faced a problem of what it politely called 'limited' evidence.[7] It noted that much of the intelligence material was 'heavily censored'. Consequently, 'gaps exist in the intelligence picture on SIEV X'. The committee 'was interested to understand the relationship between the disruption activity and the circumstances of SIEV X'. But, 'despite extensive questioning of official witnesses on the disruption strategy', it got 'limited information'. The committee also complained of 'the piecemeal manner in which information was provided to the inquiry'. Official witnesses initially 'took a blanket approach of reassuring the committee that Australian authorities had acted properly in respect of SIEV X'. The report complains, 'The committee continued to experience difficulty in receiving a full account of the SIEV X episode throughout the inquiry'.

Finally:

> The committee considers that the intelligence community should ... review its approaches to the provision of information to parliamentary inquiries to better balance the flow of information to Parliament with the need to protect intelligence capabilities and sources.

For this report to propose the very notion of 'balance' in the context of SIEV X raises an abiding moral question: how many human deaths may be deliberately left unexamined, in order to protect intelligence capabilities and sources? How high does the body count need to get before the Australian Senate is duty-bound to challenge government secrecy about intelligence, on the grounds that so many deaths on Australia's watch cannot properly be left unexplored'? I would have thought that 353 deaths was well above that threshold.

The Senate's mildly worded but significant rebukes about the poor quality of evidence on SIEV X were as good as it got. From there on, the report generously glossed and parsed the official SIEV X evidence all the way.[8] The committee looked at the scant official evidence (and it determinedly did not look deeply into any other potentially available evidence) like a child gazing at drifting clouds and trying to imagine what they might resemble. Every time I read these two chapters of the report, my head reels at the heroic sophistry of the arguments offered and assumptions made, as the authors try to convince readers (or perhaps themselves) that, despite all the questions left unanswered in the CMI committee, a plausible and honourable explanatory pathway may be found through this morass of refused and misleading witness testimony and blacked-out documents.

I can also see, however, that people of goodwill, without detailed knowledge of the public history of the sinking and the inquiry, and operating under a presumption of official regularity, might conclude from reading these chapters: 'Yes, there were clearly some sad administrative glitches—honest errors at a time of stress—but everyone did all they could properly do at the time, and nobody is to blame.' Such non-partisan readers would not necessarily share the government senators' view that my raising of the SIEV X issue had wasted the committee's time, but they would perhaps accept that the committee had properly investigated a complex matter and had resolved it reasonably satisfactorily, in pragmatic Australian style.

Such is the seductive power of this superficially plausible report. And perhaps government senators might have hoped on 23 October 2002 that they had really pulled it off—that this report might 'put an end to further public speculation'.

But let us now compare this consensus report with what non-government senators wrote into the report and said on the day in their individual capacities. The chair's foreword by Senator Cook is strongly worded,[9] and his tabling statement is even stronger:

> SIEV X was a genuine tragedy. Many of the issues we are concerned about have not been fully resolved, but they need to be. We recommend that there be an independent inquiry into all the events surrounding SIEVX, including the extent of the so-called 'disruption activities'. Since our inquiry concluded, more information has come into the public domain through media reports. Senator Faulkner has spoken about this in the Senate. To do the job properly a full judicial inquiry is necessary.[10]

Senator Faulkner's written comments in the report are extraordinarily strong.[11] Here are a few examples:

> The evidence received by [this seems in context to mean 'from'] the AFP at the CMI committee and Senate Estimates, regarding active disruption has been, at times, contradictory and misleading.
>
> Foreign Affairs Minister Alexander Downer has also not confirmed whether he authorised the Australian Secret Intelligence Service (ASIS), either prior to or following the commencement of the Intelligence Services Act, to engage in disruption activities. If such authorisation occurred, the minister should explain what sort of disruption activities took place in Indonesia as a result of any such ministerial authorisation.
>
> Australian ministers who have been questioned about the disruption program have so far provided unsatisfactory responses. It is not enough for ministers to dismiss the suggestion that illegal activities might be occurring, as a result of the disruption program, when there is obviously no system in place to ensure that this is not occurring.

So far none of the ministers involved in the people-smuggling disruption program [Ellison, Downer, Hill, Ruddock] has categorically ruled out if the disruption program in Indonesia ever involved anyone sabotaging a people-smuggling vessel.

It is still unclear what occurred in Indonesia before SIEV X departed. However, given the evidence from survivors, the government should make a public statement about [its] full knowledge of the conditions surrounding the departure of this vessel. Furthermore it should reveal whether disruption activities were directed at this vessel and if so what those activities entailed. Other people-smuggler vessels that left Indonesia for Australia and sank en route should be included in such a statement.

Beyond Mr Enniss, serious questions remain about the disruption program. For example, it is still unclear whether anyone, as a result of Australia's disruption policy, was directly or indirectly involved in the sabotage of vessels in Indonesia and whether Australian ministers, officials or agencies have knowledge of such activities. There are many unanswered questions about the policy of disruption and what it actually meant for those embarking on voyages to Australia.

An independent judicial inquiry into Australia's disruption program in Indonesia is necessary to comprehensively investigate what has actually happened in the disruption program, what the outcomes of the program have been, the legality and propriety of the methods employed, and what accountability mechanisms ought to be instituted for the future.

Finally, Senator Bartlett, consistent with the strong moral perspective he contributed to the committee, criticised the border-protection regime's lack of respect for human life:

I believe that the SIEV X incident, like the 'children overboard' affair, is symptomatic of flaws inherent in the new

> border-protection regime policy, and that it exposes major failures in the implementation of that policy. Fundamental to the new border-protection regime is an underlying lack of respect for the value of human life and human rights.
>
> ... the response of Australian officials to the SIEV X intelligence reveals the inherent bias, noted already, pervading the government's border-protection regime in its totality — a bias that is skewed towards 'detecting, deterring and denying' asylum seekers rather than reacting to warnings of the danger to people attempting the passage to Australia in unseaworthy vessels.
>
> It does not require 20–20 vision in hindsight to recognise that 400 passengers on a vessel belonging to a people smuggler, well known to Australian officials as using smaller than normal vessels, was a tragedy in the making.[12]

If this Senate committee inquiry was a kind of coronial investigation into the death by drowning of 353 people on Australia's watch, it was a very strange coroner's court indeed. Three of the seven 'co-coroners' considered there was no case to be answered on SIEV X. Witnesses representing Australian government agencies were able, at will, to refuse to answer questions, and their agencies were free to decide how much of the documentary evidence they submitted would be blacked out. The inquiry heard no evidence from survivors of the sinking or from bereaved family members, though many were in Australia and could have been invited to testify.[13] With due respect to the senators involved, this was a coroners' court that would have challenged the imaginative powers of Gilbert and Sullivan, or Lewis Carroll.[14]

AFTER THE REPORT was tabled, the SIEV X story entered a strange, contradictory phase. The year 2003 was difficult and testing for me, with confusing signals all round.

On the negative side, Labor seemed ready publicly to distance itself from my work.[15] SIEV X was never raised in the House of

Representatives. After October 2002, media interest in SIEV X fell away precipitously. It became harder to re-ignite Labor's interest despite important new evidence and judicial developments during 2003. As new people-smuggling stories emerged in 2003 and 2004, essential news context from the SIEV X events in 2001 and 2002 seemed forgotten.[16]

My reputation took hits. Even some well-informed and well-motivated commentators, with high public standing in the debate on human rights for asylum-seekers, expressed views in public and private that I had 'gone too far', or that I had not come up with any new evidence to support my hypotheses — even that I was shaping facts to fit my preconceptions. It was suggested that a simple explanation, of greedy and ruthless people smugglers helped by a few bribed Indonesian police, was more likely than any kind of Australian disruption-program linkage to the sinking. The publication in March 2003 of *Dark Victory*, with its dismissive, partly exonerating judgement that 'Australia did not kill those drowned on SIEV X but their deaths can't be left out of the reckoning entirely', did not help the public credibility of my case.[17] Sometimes in 2003 I felt that the SIEV X story, despite its great evidentiary power and authenticity, was running away in the dry sands of mainstream scepticism and indifference. In the struggle of memory against forgetting, memory seemed to be losing.

Against these negatives, there were some important positives. Labor, Democrats, and Greens senators continued to ask pointed, highly focused questions in Senate estimates committees and questions on notice. The increasingly evasive, truculent, and unconvincing government answers were meticulously analysed and archived on www.sievx.com. The fact that the media did not report this quiet detective work did not render it unimportant: all these Senate questions and answers are part of the evidentiary trail that will be reviewed when SIEV X goes to a full-powers judicial inquiry.[18]

About $14,000 in public subscriptions was collected over two weeks by www.sievx.com to fund a national condolence message that ran in *The Australian* on the first anniversary of the sinking,

19 October 2002 (see Appendix).[19] Memorial observances were held in 12 cities and towns around Australia, involving thousands of people. These events were a form of reassurance that people wanted to bear witness that we cared.

A brilliant website advocacy campaign by Marg Hutton throughout December 2002, using the device of an on-line clock counting down to the final date of Abu Quassey's six-month token prison sentence in Indonesia, embarrassed Australian law-enforcement authorities into a semblance of trying to bring Abu Quassey to Australia in January 2003. The cynicism of Quassey's unchallenged return to Egypt in April 2003 brought home to many people — perhaps more than anything else had in the SIEV X story so far — the ruthless extent of the SIEV X cover-up.

From September 2003 onwards, www.sievx.com and my public advocacy on my own new website, www.tonykevin.com, helped to maintain interest in the highly suspect Quassey trial in Egypt that was being facilitated by the AFP and the Australian embassy in Cairo. The name and eventual fate of Quassey will now certainly not be forgotten. Nor will the fate of his book-keeper currently on committal in Australia, Khaled Daoed.

I picked up some morale-boosting community recognition along the way in 2003: International Whistleblower of the Year from the London-based non-government organisation Index on Censorship; Just Australian of the Year from the human rights organisation A Just Australia; and one of the Newsmakers of 2003 from *The Bulletin* magazine. Such honours helped deflect overt and covert government efforts to discredit me as a febrile conspiracy theorist whose arguments were not to be taken seriously. Victoria Laurie wrote a balanced, finally positive, review of my work for the *Weekend Australian Magazine*.[20]

Encouraged by this recognition of the importance of the issue, I gave talks about SIEV X in numerous cities and towns around Australia. The support of many individuals, and especially of that fine organisation Rural Australians for Refugees, affirmed that this issue matters to many ordinary, decent Australians.

THIS BOOK has frequently referred to the high significance of the two delayed pieces of official evidence that appeared in 2003. The 23 October 2001 Jakarta embassy cable released on 4 February 2003 gave the final lie to the Defence review's claim that one could only speculate where SIEV X sank. On this, Cook spoke sadly in the Senate on how the CMI committee had been misled, concluding:

> What I think is more important than all of that is what this cable says, because we may now be in a situation in which this cable, which was before all of those officers who appeared before our inquiry before they fronted to give evidence—and they gave evidence to our inquiry after swearing an oath before the inquiry to tell the truth, the whole truth and nothing else but the truth—reveals information which is not entirely consistent with the evidence that was given by some public servants and with the evidence that was adduced by the inquiry.[21]

The by now notorious PM&C status report to Howard of 24 October 2001, when its text was finally released in May 2003, was found to be an empty vessel.[22] There was not a word in it to substantiate the impression that had been left by Jane Halton's testimony on 30 July 2002—that new evidence had been reported to the prime minister on 24 October 2001 that the boat sank in Indonesian waters (see chapter 12).

It was disappointing that the two new sievx.com maps published in full colour in the *Canberra Times* in July 2003 (and republished in this book as Maps 1 and 2) had almost no public impact.[23] Those maps demolished Defence's July 2002 claim of not knowing where SIEV X sank, and of having thoroughly patrolled the Relex zone without finding evidence of the sinking. But the news caravan had by now well and truly moved on.

However, the forensic work of establishing that SIEV X sank in the Operation Relex zone had been done. Its worth was recognised in the text of Senator Brown's 15 October 2003 Senate motion which, as Brown proposed it, noted that SIEV X 'sank 100 kilometres south of Indonesia in international waters that were being closely monitored by Australian air and naval forces'.[24] Labor appears to have insisted that this be replaced by the words 'and that the Government has still failed to establish where the boat sank' as the price for their support of the motion.

In the end, I see the strongest concrete achievement since the CMI committee's report as being the set of four Senate motions in 2002–03 (the text of which is reproduced in Appendix 1). For two years, the Senate majority has reaffirmed its shared multi-party concerns about SIEV X, the disruption program, and the history of government failure to meet its accountability and humanitarian obligations to the survivors and the bereaved. The agenda of these motions broadened in 2003. The fact that the three non-government parties and the Senate independents voted in common for all four motions, and that the government ignored them, speaks volumes about the Howard government's contempt for the value of human life—and its contempt for the watchdog role of the Senate. Those things will be remembered, too.

WHAT, THEN, WAS ACHIEVED? What is left from this always powerfully contested story that is of durable national significance ? In fact, a great deal was achieved. Despite all the government's and its friends' efforts at suppression, the story of SIEV X has quietly crept into the hearts and consciences of many Australians. Our refugee-rights movement and our arts and literature communities have absorbed the story, and it is becoming part of our folk history.

There are memorials—the public observances that have drawn Australians of all beliefs together, and the spreading knowledge of the story. The website 'Jannah the SIEV X Memorial', an online condolence book created in September 2002 by Mary Dagmar Davies and dedicated to compassion and remembrance, has recorded hundreds of moving messages. Psychologist Steve Biddulph has involved 150 schools across Australia in designing a physical memorial, planned to be built on the shores of Canberra's

Lake Burley Griffin during 2005. The moving and poetic short educational film *Untold Tragedy*, narrated by Anne Simpson of RAR, is being shown in schools across the country, as well as to community and service clubs, many of whom are encountering the SIEV X history for the first time.

There are stories based on SIEV X by fine writers such as Eva Sallis and Arnold Zable, poems and songs, the play *A Certain Maritime Incident*, forthcoming documentary and feature films, music, dance, painting, and sculpture.

Honouring the memory of the victims of SIEV X is becoming one of the ways in which we can uphold the values of a truly inclusive and generous Australia—an Australia that rejects sterile and life-denying doctrines of paranoid nationalism. We can mourn for the broken families of SIEV X, in a similar way that we mourn for Australia's broken Aboriginal families and communities. Recognising the huge tragedy of SIEV X, not hiding from it, 'owning' it, will help us to release our sense of what will be possible in Australia when we find the courage to rediscover delight in our common humanity.[25] Out of this terrible grief can come joy; out of these deaths, new life.

Efforts by some powerful news agenda-setters to banish the memory of SIEV X will only harden the resolve of others to keep the memory alive. Every time Australians use the word SIEV X in public discourse, we are remembering something that is important to remember. So we must go on doing this.

THERE IS GROWING public scepticism over periodic new government allegations about people smuggling. Exposure to at least some of the truth about the Tampa, the 'children overboard' fraud, and SIEV X has helped to vaccinate Australian society against new outbreaks of 'Tampa-itis'. I have been able to ask serious questions about the peculiar circumstances of recent 'people smuggling' arrivals in Australian territory. These include the boat Hao Kiet, which turned up on 2 July 2003 off Port Hedland in WA with 53 Vietnamese on board;[26] the Indonesian boat Minasa Bone, which turned up at Melville Island on 4 November 2003 carrying 14 male Kurds;[27] and the unidentified boat that abandoned 15 Indonesian workers at Ashmore Reef early in March 2004.[28]

Some of my questions are:

- Why did all three boats reach land destinations (two on or near mainland Australia) apparently undetected, and certainly not intercepted? Why did the latest boat in March 2004 drop off passengers at Ashmore Reef and return to Indonesia undetected? What were Australia's border-protection systems doing? What about JORN radar, now officially fully operational ? How did the border-protection systems deteriorate from a 92 per cent detection-rate in 2001 (12 out of 13 claimed as detected; only SIEV X was missed) to an apparent zero detection-rate in 2003–04 (none detected out of three known boats)? Were they all asleep at the wheel? No boats have been reported as intercepted and returned to Indonesia since December 2001.
- Were these three boats, even assuming they were autonomous ventures (see below), allowed to go through to Australian territory in order to send domestic political messages that people smuggling is still a security threat?
- In the Minasa Bone case, why did this well-equipped modern boat with navigational aids go to Melville Island (remote and conveniently excisable—it was excised later on the day the boat arrived) when it could just as easily have sailed directly into Darwin? The passengers wanted to claim asylum, not to hide. So why did the crew take them to Melville Island, which was difficult to access from Darwin? Why were such extraordinary steps taken to deny media access to the boat?[29] And why did the boat and crew disappear as soon as the navy towed the boat back to Indonesia? Why weren't the crew arrested as people smugglers? Why, when such questions started to be asked, was a Turkish kebab shop owner in Sydney, Ali Cetin,

suddenly produced in a diversionary series of media exposes as the alleged organiser of the Minasa Bone voyage, despite his pleas of innocence? Why has he not been charged since?
- Why did the third boat disappear, with no information about who sent it? Why did this boat, the first in eight years to carry Indonesians seeking illegal entry to Australia, suddenly appear in March 2004?

None of these voyages was lethal, but all three raise questions as to whether they might have been Australian-encouraged disruption operations. Were these SIEV arrivals intended to send political messages in Australia, for example, that the government has to go on treating detained asylum-seekers harshly to deter possible new waves of boat people — Vietnamese, Middle Eastern, or Indonesian? Might more such provocative incidents occur around the time of the 2004 Australian federal election?

AFTER THE THIRD BOAT, late in March 2004, Labor's spokesman for homeland security, Robert McClelland, put a little-noticed set of 34 searching questions on notice to four ministers (Defence, DIMIA, Justice, Agriculture) responsible for different aspects of border security: Customs, Coastwatch, Defence, fisheries, policing and prosecution, and migration processing of passengers and crews. The questions concern procedures for the detection, interception, and handling of people on SIEVs, and performance monitoring of those activities. The range and rigour of these questions is remarkable. They can only reflect deep suspicions in the Labor Party that Australia's border-protection system is not working efficiently, transparently, or ethically.[30]

As I see it, the point of such questioning is not that it will necessarily bring full and honest answers — the answers, as in the past two years regarding SIEV X and the disruption program, will no doubt rely on the usual camouflage and word plays. But such questions are a warning to all those working in an intimidated and subservient federal public service and national security system.

Labor's questions send these public servants a quiet but clear message: the opposition (which, as I conclude this book, seems within striking distance of winning government) recognises a deep, systemic problem of official corruptibility under government pressure in relation to border protection and people smuggling.

The work of preparing answers to such questions is a reminder to border-protection agencies and staff that, eventually, they will be held publicly accountable. If any government tries again to play the border-protection card in Australian elections, the people will be alerted. Without the Senate's work in beginning to expose the truth about Operation Relex, SIEV X, and the disruption program, this could not have happened.

The spell of the 'presumption of official regularity' has been broken. The public has seen how ready the Howard government is to 'spin' and to lie on matters of national security. The SIEV X history is not yet widely known and understood, but the 'children overboard' fraud and the manipulation of intelligence about Iraq's 'weapons of mass destruction' certainly are. The exposure in 2002–04 of so many unanswered questions about SIEV X has left thoughtful Australians properly sceptical of any government claims in the area of border protection.

Chapter Fourteen

Epilogue

> Without justice, there can be no peace. He who passively accepts evil is as much involved in it as he who helps to perpetrate it.
>
> — Dr Martin Luther King, Jr

I HAVE OFTEN BEEN ASKED why I persevered so stubbornly and for so long with my SIEV X work, at considerable cost to my public reputation and family finances. I have two answers. First, this is the kind of investigative work I happen to be skilled at. As a diplomat and foreign policy analyst for 30 years, I was trained in the dispassionate critical analysis of policies and actions of all kinds of governments and their bureaucracies. I developed a professional nose for hidden government agendas, and learned how to smell bureaucratic rats. I am more at home in this sort of work than, for example, in humanitarian support for asylum-seekers or public advocacy for refugee rights — although I deeply admire those who do these sorts of much-needed work.

The second answer goes to the nature of the issue. I have often said that SIEV X is a test of the kind of country that Australia wants to be. I have tried in this book to let the facts of what other people have said and written about SIEV X—survivors, politicians, government officials, journalists, and newspaper editorialists—speak for themselves. Readers of this book by now will have formed views on the massive questions that surround this tragedy that happened on our doorstep three years ago. If we tried to sweep so confronting a set of questions under the carpet, SIEV X would go on eating away at our national conscience and self-esteem.

A nation like Australia has to have a conscience. I don't believe that democratic states can or should behave amorally. As Thomas Jefferson wrote in 1792 (and I think it is still true of the United States and Australia), 'A nation, as a society, forms a moral person, and every member of it is personally responsible for his society.' I did not fully understand that truth during my 30 years working on Australian foreign policy. I understand it now.

It is also true that, as Martin Luther King said, 'Our lives begin to end the day we become silent about things that matter.' If I had walked away from this issue, once I had realised how serious it was, I could not have lived with myself. I want my children to live in a society that has had the guts to confront its dark side. There was never any choice, although there were times of deep gloom along the way.

We live in an imperfect political system, and great wrongs cannot be righted overnight by a knight riding in on a white horse. People aspiring to such roles are more often mocked as deluded Don Quixotes tilting at windmills rather than thanked as fighters for truth and justice. Progress is often made in indirect ways, and any successes achieved will rightfully have many contributors. But the trend is positive: the cause of justice for the SIEV X victims is quietly but steadily making ground. The truth will out, and it will set us free.

Epilogue

IN THE JAPANESE MEMORIAL GARDENS on the shores of Lake Burley Griffin, Canberra, on 18 October 2003, about 100 people were taking part in a remembrance service for the victims of SIEV X. It was a crisp, sunny spring day—a perfect day to celebrate God's gift of life. Anglican Bishop George Browning, Catholic Bishop Pat Power, and Canberra Islamic Centre President Ahmed Youssef spoke movingly.

I want to close this book by recalling some words spoken on that day by Bishop Pat Power:

> Those of us gathered here this morning join with fellow Australians around our country to say that we stand for something different. We grieve for the loss of 353 innocent lives on the SIEV X. We express our shame that so little has been done on an official level to find out the causes of those deaths, and to make some reparation. We uphold the value of every human life; we recognize that we belong to one human family; we say that the strong should protect the vulnerable; that the more affluent should share their resources with the needy; that every person is our sister or our brother.
>
> We come together to pray—as Christians, Muslims, members of other great religions, or maybe people struggling with faith, unable to see God's goodness reflected in the world and people around them. We come together as people of good will, wanting the best for every human being.

Amen.

Notes

Chapter One

the glory of the renaissance

Chapter One: Context for a Human Tragedy

1 *Dark Victory*, by David Marr and Marion Wilkinson, offers a compelling account of the Operation Relex mandate and methods.
2 I coined this acronym in my first published article on the subject, 'Twisting tale of dog that didn't bark', *Canberra Times*, 25 March 2002.
3 Internal review of Defence intelligence relating to SIEV X, sent to the CMI committee by Defence Minister Robert Hill on 4 July 2002. See also two highly critical Margo Kingston *Sydney Morning Herald* Webdiary commentaries: 'Off the hook: inquiry produced "big fat nothing"', 31 July 2002, and 'Labor backdown opens black hole of accountability', 1 August 2002.
4 CMI Hansard, 11 July 2002, pages 1923–84.
5 Senate Hansard, 10 December 2002, pages 7562–63.
6 Senate Hansard, 11 December 2002, pages 7757–58.
7 'Australia dragging feet on smuggler's extradition: Jakarta', Matthew Moore, *Sydney Morning Herald*, 1 February 2003.
8 'Lost at sea', Tony Kevin, *Spectrum* magazine, *Sydney Morning Herald*, 5 April 2003.
9 'New maps expose further holes in government's SIEVX story', Tony Kevin, *Canberra Times*, 17 July 2003; my feature article was illustrated by the two new www.sievx.com maps.
10 Egyptian embassy Canberra, advice to author.
11 In Australia there was scant media coverage of this trial, but see 'Caged beast', Jackie Dent, *The Bulletin*, 29 October 2003, and 'Fatal

voyage ends in 7 years' jail'. Jackie Dent (in Cairo), *Sydney Morning Herald*, 29 December 2003.

12 Senate Legal and Constitutional Estimates, 27 May 2003, pages 301–29.

13 Downer interviewed on ABC *AM*, 29 December 2003.

14 Senate Hansard, 11 August 2003, page 13042.

15 *Eichmann in Jerusalem: The Banality of Evil*, Hannah Arendt; *The Holocaust and Modernity*, Zygmunt Bauman; *Evil in Modern Thought*, Susan Neiman, Scribe Publications 2003; and a review article on Neiman's book, 'The Big E', Mark Lilla, *New York Review of Books*, 12 June 2003.

16 In Graham Greene's novel *The Quiet American*, the character Pyle, a well-meaning but lethal CIA agent, memorably illustrates the area of moral choice I am talking about here.

17 Report of Senate Privileges Committee on a person referred to in the Senate, Mr Tony Kevin — 109th report, tabled 22 October 2002.

18 Robert Manne with David Corlett, 'Sending them Home: Refugees and the new politics of indifference', *Quarterly Essay* Number 13, March 2004, Black Inc.

19 Peter Mares, *Borderline* (2nd edition, UNSW Press 2002), analyses the various policies and practices developed by the Howard government in this period, and how they were sold to the Australian public.

20 See Glossary for a summary of JORN's history and importance to border-protection operations.

21 The AFP Association annual website survey of AFP activities in 2001 said this: 'It has become obvious that counteracting sophisticated "people smuggling" syndicates is highly resource intensive for the AFP. The AFP requires the use of sophisticated methods to identify organised criminal enterprises involved in people smuggling. To this end the AFP needs to be sufficiently resourced to fund "sting" operations whereby the AFP establishes small shipping companies in strategic locations known for smuggling illegal immigrants.'

22 Channel Nine *Sunday* feature programs on the AFP–Enniss relationship were broadcast on 17 February and 1 September 2002, and in shorter programs on 24 February and 29 September. See also a Channel Nine *Sunday* news release on 24 [26] August. A more detailed account is at pages 130–3.

23 In AFP written answers to CMI committee questions on notice, 30 July 2002.

24 For examples of officially briefed articles about this time, see: 'More patrols to deter smugglers', Brendan Nicholson, *Sunday Age*, 2 September 2001; 'Warships sent to boost refugees patrol', Mark Metherell, *Sydney Morning Herald*, 3 September 2001. 'Patrols to

begin the hunt off Java', Megan Saunders, *The Australian*, 3 September 2001. 'Enhanced surveillance 'puzzling', Brendan Pearson and Paul Cleary, *Australian Financial Review*, 3 September 2001.

25 Howard in *Sixty Minutes* interview with Charles Woolley, 2 September 2001. See also Brendan Nicholson, op cit, 2 September 2001.

Chapter Two: Embarkation

1 My sources are:

(1) Media reports in days following the return of survivors to Jakarta on 22 October 2001 (this is a chronological list of sources used):

Carmody, Rebecca, 'Boat tragedy emphasizes people smuggling risks', ABC *AM* 23 October 2001. (The first media report of the tragedy.)

CNN, 'Migrant ship sinks; most of those on board killed', 22 October 2001 (this news item, based on the first report from IOM Head Office, Geneva, was broadcast towards midnight 22 October European time.

Murray, Paul, interview with John Howard, Perth, Radio 6PR breakfast show, 23 October 2001.

Sattler, Howard, interview with Philip Ruddock, Sydney Radio 2SM, 23 October 2001.

Stein, Ginny, 'Asylum-seeker tragedy: 350 drown, 44 survive', ABC *World Today*, 23 October 2001.

Stein, Ginny, 'Asylum-seekers Drowned', ABC *PM*, 23 October 2001.

AAP, 'Boat sinks in 10 minutes', 23 October 2001. (This AAP wire service item appeared in the *Sydney Morning Herald* on the same date).

UN wire service, 'Hundreds die as ship en route to Australia sinks', 23 October 2001. Greenlees, Don, 'I have lost everything', *The Australian*, 23 October 2001.

Indonesian Business website (unsigned) 'Disaster for 300 potential illegal immigrants', at www.ibonweb.com, 23 October 2001.

Murdoch, Lindsay, 'Survivors tell of horror', *The Age*, 24 October 2001.

Murdoch. Lindsay and others, 'Despair drove us', *Sydney Morning Herald*, 24 October 2001.

Greenlees, Don, 'Overload kills on voyage of doom', *The Australian* and *Daily Telegraph*, 24 October 2001.

Stein, Ginny, 'Shipwreck survivors claim they were boarded at gunpoint', ABC *PM*, 24 October 2001.

Downer, Alexander, interview with Tony Jones, ABC *Lateline*, 24 October 2001.

Hall, Raymond, interview with Tony Jones, ABC *Lateline*, 24 October 2001.

Saputra, Dianthus, 'Refugees describe capsizing', *Washington Post* (US), 24 October 2001.

Greenlees, Don and Walker, Vanessa, 'Three little victims', *The Australian*, 25 October 2001.

Greenlees, Don and Saunders, Megan, 'Forced onto death boat', *The*

Australian, 25 October 2001.

Murphy, Dan, 'Fishing boat tragedy highlights refugees' plight', *Christian Science Monitor* (US), 25 October 2001.

(No author) 'Fathers mourn lost daughters' *Daily Telegraph*, 25 October 2001.

BBC World Service news, 'Indonesia police "aided smugglers"', 25 October 2001.

Collins, Joanne, 'Indonesian police deny death boat allegations', Reuters, 25 October 2001.

Greenlees, Don, 'Darkness is a smuggler's only friend', *The Australian*, 26 October 2001.

Aglionby, John, 'Boat to nowhere', *The Guardian* (UK), 26 October 2001

Murdoch, Lindsay, 'Waves of grief', *Sydney Morning Herald*, 27 October 2001.

Mitchell, Glenn, and Dickins, Jim, 'Trading in tragedy', *Herald Sun*, 27 October 2001.

Coulthart, Ross, 'The people smugglers', Channel Nine *Sunday* transcript, 4 November 2001.

Elegant, Simon, 'Shipwrecked', *Time* magazine, 5 November 2001.

Galpin, Richard 'When hope turns to despair', BBC, 8 November 2001.

Tempo magazine, Jakarta (unsigned), 'It's impossible for us to extradite Abu Quassey' 8 November 2001.

Walker, Vanessa, 'Survivor granted asylum', *The Australian*, 21 December 2001.

Gordon, Michael, 'Searching for a place to belong', *The Age*, 24 October 2002.

(2) 'Trad survivor accounts'—Keysar Trad's English translation of Arabic-language videotaped accounts by survivors conducted in Bogor on the weekend 27–28 October 2001.

(3) *The Five Mysteries of SIEV X*, Ghassan Nakhoul, SBS Arabic language radio broadcast, 28 August 2002, English transcript. See also Nakhoul, 'The Human Tide', *Walkley Magazine*, Summer 2003.

(4) My discussions with Geoff Parish on his team's interviews with various survivors in 2002, in the preparation of three SBS *Dateline* programs relating to SIEV X on 22 May, 17 July, 21 August 2002.

(5) My discussions with Ross Coulthart of Channel 9 *Sunday*, on contents of his videotaped interviews with survivors conducted a few days after their return to Jakarta (not on sievx.com).

(6) DFAT Jakarta embassy reporting cable on the disaster, sent 23 October 2001, but not released to Senate until 4 February 2003. Because this document is crucial evidence, it is reproduced on the opening pages of this book.

(7) 'Perilous Journeys', Arnold Zable, *Eureka Street*, April 2003.

2 Sondos Ismail's story was drawn from my meeting with her and her

husband in Sydney late in 2002, and from numerous media accounts (for instance, Greenlees 23 October, Greenlees and Walker, 'Fathers mourn lost daughters', SBS Dateline 22 May 2002, Zable). Sondos's grief-stricken face became the photographic icon of the tragedy. As the news broke, this image dominated newspaper front pages around the world. Like the little Vietnamese girl running towards the camera aflame with napalm, this image—and the family photograph the next day of the three drowned daughters of Sondos and Ahmed—can never be forgotten. In Australia, these two images briefly humanised the asylum-seekers' plight: however, the public mood of indifference towards boat people, fed by months of propaganda, soon returned.

3 Generally, Middle Eastern asylum-seekers paid one set of smugglers to get them to Indonesia. From here, they engaged others to take them on potentially the most dangerous stage of their journey—the sea voyage from Indonesia to Australia's Christmas Island or Ashmore Reef. This feature of the trade made disruption in Indonesia much easier. Elegant quoted a people smuggler in Malaysia: "'My responsibility ends once they are in Indonesia. I don't concern myself about how the people make their way in to Australia.'" Then he added a chilling coda: "Many refugees fall into the hands of the wrong people in Indonesia and never make it to Australia. Many people whom I have sent to Indonesia have gone missing. They could either have drowned or been murdered for their money.'"

4 See *Five Mysteries* for a detailed description of Quassey's associates, based on accounts by survivors Rami Abbas Akram (son of another survivor Amal Hassan Nasri—both now in Melbourne), and Najah Doayer (now in Adelaide). They say Quassey usually stayed in the background, organising the boats. Few passengers met him. His Middle Eastern working associates Khaled Ishnak Dawud (Daoed), Maysam (Mithem), and Maysam's brother Maysar (surnames not known) handled most of the negotiations with passengers. Khaled made the deals; Maysam recorded them in his book. People paid varying amounts: Khaled was pretty good at working out how much people could afford. Najah and Rami Akram remember Khaled and Maysam well. Rami Akram said both men were at SIEV X's embarkation. Maysam and Maysar were in the launch, transporting people out to the boat. Quassey watched from a distance.

The survivors gave such information about Quassey's associates to the Indonesian police. A few months after the sinking, the police arrested Khaled and Maysam. A few weeks later, they were released, following enquiries as to their welfare by UNHCR in Jakarta. The UNHCR media officer in Jakarta, Kemala Ahwil, explained to *Five Mysteries* producers that because the UNHCR office had granted Khaled and Maysam refugee status before the sinking of SIEV X, the office considered the men to be under its care. Ahwil told the team: 'In the end, the police couldn't find any evidence and they were returned to us.'

The discouraged survivors, though convinced of the guilt of Quassey and his associates, made no further attempts to denounce the three men. UNHCR did not question their refugee status. Khaled, Maysam and Maysar were later accepted as refugees by European countries, on the basis of their UNHCR-approved refugee status. Later, in 2003, Khaled was extradited to Australia from Sweden to face trial as an alleged people smuggler (see chapter 11).

5 Survivors' fare information varied widely. At the high end, AAP reported one survivor (Bahram Khan, Afghanistan) saying refugees had paid US$4000 each for the journey. The same estimate comes from Murdoch (24 October). Mitchell and Dickins wrote: 'The price for passage is never less than (Aust) $2000 a head. In some cases, it's as high as $20,000. Some of the survivors from last week's tragedy said they paid up to $8000 for a berth on the boat.'

Against these inflated figures, most survivors reported much lower fares for this voyage. The UN (23 October) said passengers paid between $800 to $1900 each. *Five Mysteries* quoted Rami Akram saying he paid a total $2200 in two instalments, for his and his mother's fare; and Najah Doayer saying she paid $5000 for five people, plus the young women's dowries of jewellery. Murphy reported that Mohammad Zayer and his three cousins were approached in Cisarua by Abu Kosay (Quassay), offering to put them on his boat to Australia for $1000 each. Galpin said each person handed over at least $600. Some said they had paid more than $2000. *Tempo* reported that Quassey had been charging people between US$700 and US$1500.

Greenlees ('I have lost everything') first reported about Sondos Ismail: 'She had been convinced to pay US$1000 ($1965) to a people-smuggler by other asylum-seekers.' However, this figure was later corrected by Greenlees ('Three little victims') as follows: 'Abu Quessai, who promised them passage on a boat to Australia at a cost of US$550 an adult ...'

Sondos separately offered similar accounts of her unusually cheap fare (she quoted US$500) and said her three children were given free travel and she knew of similar experiences by other women and children passengers. She spoke to Ross Coulthart (videotaped interview soon after the tragedy, reported to author) and to Helen Newman and Tahir Cambis (recent taped interview, reported to me).

6 See 'Fathers mourn lost daughters', *Daily Telegraph*, 25 October 2001.

7 Quoted in *Five Mysteries*.

Notes

8 Mares, *Borderline*, 2nd edition, 2002, gave a clear account of how the deterrent temporary protection visa (TPV) system was developed under the Howard government in Australia—with the agreement of the Labor opposition all along the way. The final cruelty was inflicted by tighter TPV legislation passed in September 2001. In an Australian government reaction to the 'Tampa affair', unauthorised boat-people arrivals granted refugee status were ruled never to be eligible to apply for permanent residence in Australia but could only apply for indefinite TPV renewals. Under their TPVs, their immediate families abroad were never to be eligible to join them as refugees in Australia.

9 From my conversation with a senior DIMIA official in late 2001.

10 According to the head of the UNHCR Office in Jakarta, about 30 of the SIEV X victims had already been granted refugee status by UNHCR, and over 200 of them had contacted UNHCR and were registered refugee applicants on UNHCR files. There was no possibility that Australia would ever legally receive them. See Hall interview, 24 October 2001.

Because names and biodata of the victims and survivors have not been released, we don't know how many of the victims had relatives waiting for them in Australia, but I believe most of the women and children on board would have. Thus, there may be hundreds of family members grieving in Australia. But we still do not know who they are, or how many they are, because we do not know most of the victims' names.

11 Coulthart and Parish, conversations with me, based on their tapes and other knowledge.

12 Immigration Minister Phillip Ruddock on Radio 2SM with Howard Sattler on 23 October was definite: 'It didn't leave Java, it left southern Sumatra.'(We know now that Ruddock was drawing on the DIMA intelligence note of 23 October, released to the CMI committee in September 2002.)

Stein (23 October) referred to the boat 'leaving the province of Lampung in Sumatra'; AAP on 23 October said: 'Aid and navy officials said shocked survivors had told of 421 men, women and children boarding the 19-metre boat last Thursday at Lampung in Sumatra'; the UN wire service of 23 October said: 'According to the Indonesian navy, the boat left Sumatra'; Ibonweb on 23 October reported: 'according to AFP [author's note: it is not clear whether this refers to Agence France Presse or Australian Federal Police], an Egyptian organisation Quassey that successfully sent two previous vessels reaching Australian territory organised suspected illegal entry vessel (SIEV) to sail to Christmas Island. Based on the report, approximately 430 potential illegal immigrants (PIIs) departed Cipanas (South of Jakarta) and travelled to Sumatra, possibly Bandar Lampung, via

Jakarta and Merak last Wednesday'; Murdoch, 24 October, included in a listed chronology: 'October 18: The 19-metre boat sets sail from Lampung, in Sumatra'; Greenlees, 24 October reported: 'The Indonesian fishing vessel ... set sail from a port in south Sumatra headed for Christmas Island in the early hours last Thursday [18 October 2001]'; Murphy wrote: 'They'd been in danger from the moment they left Indonesia's Sumatra Island'; Aglionby wrote: 'getting on "that boat", which none of the survivors knows the name of, in the southern Sumatra port of Bandar Lampung last Thursday night'; Elegant wrote: 'a battered 19-m Sumatran fishing vessel they had been told would ferry them the 36 hours from Tanjungkarang in Sumatra to Australia's Christmas Island' and *Tempo*, reporting on Quassey's arrest, was quite specific on the land itinerary before embarkation: 'Apart from Quassey, Lembang Police officer Brig. Agus Safuan was also arrested for allegedly supervising the passage of a group of illegal immigrants to Lampung using four buses from Cisarua, West Java. After arriving in Lampung, these immigrants boarded a leaky boat for the long journey to Australia.'

13 Anticipating a possible objection that Quassey may have decided to start from further afield because police were monitoring ports along the south coast of Java, ready to disrupt voyages by arresting people smugglers and rounding up their passengers, Coulthart ('The People Smugglers', op cit) noted: 'As we discovered, Indonesian police keep a very close eye on movements out of the port, but they're looking for pirates, not boat people. Our boat was stopped seven times as we headed out to the open sea, but if we'd been boat people, this week the Indonesian navy made it clear we would have been allowed to pass. Much to Australia's annoyance, the Indonesian navy admitted it will also give asylum-seekers food to help them on their way.'

14 Sondos Ismail told me there were no interruptions or police checks of which she was aware during the bus convoy.

15 Mitchell and Dickins, 27 October, also reported Kareem Jabar's account.

16 Survivor accounts 5 and 21 (Keysar Trad, op cit). Marg Hutton has established that these survivors were Rokaya Satar and Najah Muhsin.

17 There were five media reports that 10 passengers refused to embark, and some of them noted that they paid bribes to be allowed not to. The AAP 23 October report said: '10 people had refused even to board the boat'; the Ibonweb report of 23 October said: 'The ten passengers who refused to board the boat ... remain in Southern Sumatra'; Greenlees on 24 October wrote: 'Ten people refused to embark'; On 25 October, Greenlees and Saunders wrote: 'About 10 people refused to board the overcrowded and unseaworthy ship and paid bribes of US$400 ($787) to be allowed to remain on land'; and

Aglionby on 26 October wrote: 'On seeing the overcrowded boat, some people refused to board. About 10 were allowed to stay on land after paying an additional £250.'

The embassy cable of 23 October said in paragraph 4: 'due to the size of the vessel, 10 PIIs [potential illegal immigrants] refused to embark, leaving 421 PIIs on board.'

Clearly, such detailed information about these last-minute passenger withdrawals — known to the Australian embassy, AAP, *Indonesian Business*, Greenlees and Saunders, and Aglionby — would not have come from those who went on board. Information in two reports that bribes were paid was not included in the embassy cable.

The group that stayed behind were not heard of again until April 2004, when one of them, Mahhmod Yussef who now lives in Brisbane, unexpectedly appeared as a witness in the committal hearing in Brisbane of Quassey's assistant Daoed (see chapter 11). It is not clear how Yussef came to Australia. See 'Former Iraqi soldier avoided death boat', Jasmin Lill, *Courier Mail*, 7 April 2004.

Chapter Three: The Voyage

1 There were two media accounts of Quassey following in a police boat, both quoting the same survivor witness. The BBC (25 October) reported: 'They said they were willing to kill us,' said Achmad Hussein Ali, speaking through a translator. 'The police even beat two refugees with their rifle butts.' He said a police boat then escorted the asylum-seekers' boat out of the port.' Aglionby wrote: '... "To ensure that none of the rest of us got off, Quessay followed us in a speedboat for the first four hours," Achmad [Hussein] says.'

2 The incident of the Mandaeans getting off at an island in the Sunda Strait was reported in many accounts. Their number was variously described as 21 or 24.

CNN (Jean-Philippe Chauzy, IOM, Geneva, 23 October) reported that: '21 people got off at an island'; Carmody (ABC AM, 23 October) said: '21 people asked to be put ashore. They were left on a tiny island in the Java sea [sic]'; AAP, 23 October, reported: 'A further 21 asylum seekers escaped the disaster, asking to be put ashore on an island because they feared the boat was unseaworthy, said International Organisation for Migration (IOM) local head Richard Danziger'; Murdoch ('Survivors tell of horror', 24 October) reported a survivor, Almjib, saying: 'About 9.30am on Friday [sic], they came across a fishing boat. After the captain of the asylum seekers' boat admitted it was overloaded, 21 people decided to board the fishing boat and were taken to a nearby Indonesian island.' The same Murdoch article was accompanied by this chronology: 'October 19: During the morning 24 passengers, worried about the state of the boat, ask to get off and disembark in west Java [sic]'; Greenlees, ('Overload kills on voyage of doom', 24 October) said: '... In rough seas, the boat put into an island in the Sunda Strait and 24 passengers refused to continue on Thursday night'; Aglionby ('Boat to nowhere', *Guardian*, 26 October) said: '[from survivor Achmad] ... Shortly after that the fishing boat stopped at a small island and 21 people did manage to get off; it is thought that money again changed hands'; Murdoch ('Waves of grief', *Sydney Morning Herald*, 27 October) reported a conversation with one of the Mandaean survivors who had got off: '... says 53-year-old Iraqi woman Montaha Sam Adam. Adam was among 21 people who were able to pay a passing fisherman to take them in his small boat from the doomed 19-metre one they had boarded five hours earlier off the Indonesian island of Sumatra last week'.

The embassy cable (paragraph 4) said 24 passengers were disembarked at 9.00am. It did not say they were Mandaeans.

3 The official coordinates for the southern entrance to Sunda Strait, taken from page 255, Admiralty Hydrographic Office's *Ocean Passages For the World* (1974), are 6°30¢ South latitude, 105° East longitude.

4 DIMA Intelligence Note (DIN) 83/2001, 'Assessment of Boat Activity as at 1400, 23 Oct 2001', released to the CMI committee in September 2002.

5 'Overload kills', op. cit.

6 Cross-referencing these media accounts with the Trad transcript, Marg Hutton of www.sievx.com was able reliably to assign names to many of Trad's numbered speakers. She has listed such names in the Trad transcripts, as they appear on www.sievx.com.

7 'Searching for a place to belong', Michael Gordon, *The Age*, 24 October 2002.

8 A British seafarers' term for boats taken out to sea and deliberately sunk, for instance, so that the owners can collect insurance money. Captains of coffin ships had to be well paid, given the risks they ran of dying in the process of scuttling their boats at sea.

9 'SIEVX—Key New Evidence Released!', commentary on sievx.com, 4 February 2003.

10 Senate L&C estimates, answers to Collins Questions on Notice 113–16 and 132–33, provided by AFP on 27 March 2003.

11 Zaynab is survivor 6 in the Trad accounts. Aged 12 at the time, she lost her entire family—her mother Souad, father Ahsan, brothers Mahmoud and Moustafa, and sisters Fatima and Roukaya.

12 Reply to Faulkner Question on Notice, No 135 of 27 May 2003.

13 Faulkner QoN, No 2023, asked on 11 September 2003 and answered on 27 October 2003 (Senate Hansard, pages 16461–65).

14 'People smuggler gets seven years', Meaghan Shaw and Jackie Dent, *The Age*, 29 December 2003.
15 *Dark Victory*, pages 237–38 and in footnote 42 to chapter 17, 'The boat that sank'.

Chapter Four: Rescue and Return to Jakarta

1 From Marg Hutton, in correspondence with author.
2 'Boat People: Cover-Up or Stuff Up?', 22 May 2002; 'SIEV-X', 17 July 2002; 'God's Decision—The Abu Quassey Story'—with David O'Shea, 21 August 2002. These three SBS *Dateline* programs were enormously important in terms of giving public life and credibility to the story.
3 Transcript of an email from Andrew Metcalfe (DIMA) to Susan Ball, et al, 24 October 2001, 'Re: Boat lost at sea' in 'PM & C Email traffic', CMI committee, item no. 81, page 1. This email contained a series of useful earlier email reports from DIMA staff at the embassy going back to the morning of 23 October.
4 The English-language *Jakarta Post* carried stories on the sinking that were wholly sourced to international news agencies. From the start, it was handled as an international story, not an Indonesian one. Remarkably, and embarrassingly for the Australian embassy, *Indonesian Business* in its website edition Ibonweb on 23 October carried word-for-word sections of the embassy's classified reporting cable that we learned in February 2003 had been sent on that same day. This shows that the embassy wanted the story to be read by, and have an effect on, an influential readership of Indonesian government and big business people. But whomever the embassy leaked the cable text to at *Indonesian Business* did not rephrase the material sufficiently to disguise the source. This lapse was later exposed in Senate Estimates in February 2003.
5 This document was quoted and shown in the two *Dateline* features on SIEV X that were shown on 22 May and 17 July 2002.
6 Author's conversation with Geoff Parish.
7 Author's conversation with Sondos Ismail.
8 Sondos Ismail remembers that one person, who she thought might be an Australian official and not press, interviewed her at length in private on her story, with the help of an Arabic-speaking female interpreter. He indicated that her chances of early travel to Australia to reunite with her husband were good. Yet she had to wait four months before coming to Australia in February, and then only on a five-year TPV.
9 Author's conversation with Sondos Ismail. Also, *Five Mysteries*, August 2002, quoted Rami Akram: 'After he was arrested, Abu Quassey called

us from prison and said "Don't think that I am in jail. For me the prison is a kind of rest. When I am out, I will kill you all.' He threatened us.'

10 Answer in response to Senator Collins' question No. 121 to AFP in Senate L&C Estimates, 10 February 2003, provided on 27 March 2003.

11 By cross-referencing all the available published records and accounts, Marg Hutton was able to construct a database of 31 survivor names and personal details, on sievx.com. There are still 14 survivors whose names are not on the public record, although I am sure that these names must be known to the AFP, UNHCR, and IOM.

12 Transcript of email from Andrew Metcalfe (DIMA) to Susan Ball et al, 24 October 2001, op.cit (see endnote 3 above; see also chapter 2, endnote 10, indicating that UNHCR had checked off passenger names against UNHCR files).

Chapter Five: Where the Boat Sank

1 John Howard's references to 'Indonesian waters' during the 2001 federal election campaign occurred in a radio interview with Paul Murray on 23 October; a public speech on border-protection policies, in Perth on 23 October; a radio interview with Liam Bartlett on 24 October; a radio interview with Andrew Fowler on 28 October; a radio interview with Steve Liebmann on 29 October; and in a speech at the National Press Club on 8 November 2001. These references are detailed in 'SIEV X & The DFAT Cable: The Conspiracy Of Silence', by Marg Hutton, 20 May 2003, on www.sievx.com.

2 Philip Ruddock said: 'The boat could have got 100km off the Indonesian coast before sinking', quoted by Kirsten Lawson in 'Retreat on sinking of asylum seekers' boat', *Canberra Times*, 21 June 2002. Ruddock was clearly aware of the DIMA intelligence note from the beginning.

3 Also see Amal's story in Zable — she says that at dawn on 19 October, the SIEV X crew told them the boat had left Indonesian waters. This fits my reconstructed itinerary in chapter 3.

4 Sunda Strait coordinates: 6 degrees 30 minutes south latitude, 105 degrees east longitude; *Ocean Passages for the World*, Admiralty Hydrographic Office, 1974.

5 Professor Tomczak wrote: 'Based on the climatological situation, an object or a person drifting in the South Java Current around the 22nd of October would drift in a general north-westward direction parallel to the coastline, and gradually increase its distance from the coast as a result of the coastal upwelling. Over a period of 22 hours the resulting displacement would be approximately 13–26 nautical miles (24–48

kilometres) along the coast, and the distance from the coast would increase by approximately 9–21 nautical miles (16–40 kilometres).

'If the SIEV X survivors were in the water for 22 hours before they were rescued at a location 50 [sic] nautical miles from the Indonesian coast, it can be stated quite categorically that under normal climatological conditions they could not have started their drift from within Indonesian waters (the 12 nautical mile limit).'

Chapter Six: A Presumption of Regularity

1 *Dark Victory*, David Marr and Marian Wilkinson, Allen and Unwin, 2003, gives the best account.
2 'More patrols to deter smugglers', Brendan Nicholson, *The Age*, 2 September 2001.
3 'Warships sent to boost refugees patrol', Mark Metherell, *Sydney Morning Herald*, 3 September 2001.
4 'Patrols to begin their hunt off Java', Megan Saunders, *The Australian*, 3 September 2001.
5 'Enhanced surveillance 'puzzling' ', Brendan Pearson and Paul Cleary, The Australian, 3 September 2001.
6 'Navy cuts hit surveillance', news.com.au, 1 October 2001.
7 'Possible drownings highlight dangers of illegal travel', Phillip Ruddock media release, 22 December 2000, MPS 138/2000. ABC *7.30 Report*, 15 June 2000, 'Ads to dissuade would-be boat people':

> **Announcer**: ... it's the way Immigration Minister Philip Ruddock wants the journey to Australia portrayed to those at risk of falling to what he calls the criminal trade in human misery.
> **Australian government video**: People smugglers are not interested in helping people. They are interested in taking their money ...
> **Ruddock**: They're given no information about the dangers that are involved, the possible threat to life by coming through very dangerous means.

8 'RAN doctor condemns policy on boat people', Paul Toohey, *The Australian*, 7 November 2001. HMAS Arunta intercepted three SIEVs (6, 7, and 9) between 19 October and 4 November. On 19 October, the day SIEV X sank, the Arunta began its interception of SIEV 6 in the contiguous zone just north of Christmas Island. Official testimony in the CMI committee was that had the Arunta known anything about the plight of SIEV X, it would have set aside that duty and gone to the aid of the people on the stricken boat, as required by the laws on rescue at sea.
9 'Survivor granted asylum', Vanessa Walker, *The Australian*, 21 December 2001.

10 'Overload kills on voyage of doom', Don Greenlees, *The Australian*, 24 October 2001.
11 The two submissions are in the CMI committee bound Submissions volumes; my letter is at item 26, The Senate, Select Committee on a Certain Maritime Incident, Tabled Documents 13–31, October 2002 volume.
12 For a thorough description, see briefing papers on the Senate website: No.10, 'The Role of the Senate', March 1998; No 4, 'Senate Committees', December 1998.
13 And even to furnish material for a satirical black comedy, 'A Certain Maritime Incident', that ran in Sydney in March–April 2004 (created by Paul Dwyer and the Sydney University-based theatre company, version 1.0).
14 Key CMI committee witnesses, for example, RAN Commander Norman Banks of HMAS Adelaide, former Department of Prime Minister and Cabinet deputy secretary Jane Halton, and AFP Commissioner Mick Keelty, underwent what can only be described as intensive and prolonged cross-examination (although this term is not officially used in Senate committees).
15 CMI committee Hansard, 5 April 2002, pages 575–76
16 Jane Halton was denounced in the Senate by Labor Senator Jacinta Collins on 23 October 2002, in respect of evidence she gave to the CMI committee and her conduct as manager of the People Smuggling Task Force in the Prime Minister's Department. Earlier, I had been denounced in the Senate by three government senators (Brandis, Mason, and Ferguson) on a variety of grounds on 26 September 2002. Both cases must be very rare. In my case, I complained to the Senate Privileges Committee about the remarks made about me. My complaint was upheld (report of Senate Privileges Committee on a person referred to in the Senate, Mr Tony Kevin— 109th report, tabled 22 October 2002).
17 As of 3 April 2004, the government had not responded to the recommendations of the CMI committee report adopted by the Senate 18 months earlier, on 23 October 2002 (see Senator Bartlett's question, Hansard, Senate Additional Estimates, Finance and Public Administration, 16 February 2004, page 29).
18 ABC *AM*, 29 December 2003.
19 Senate Hansard, page 5800, 23 October 2002.
20 CMI committee Report, paragraph 2.84.
21 Senate Foreign Affairs Defence and Trade (FADT) Committee Estimates, 23 February, page 183.
22 CMI committee Hansard, page 661.
23 CMI committee Hansard, page 804.

24 CMI committee Report pages 469–76. Collins's additional comment offers important judgements on the context and conduct of the CMI inquiry.
25 CMI committee Hansard, pages 250 and 300.
26 PST minutes, 12 October 2001
27 See CMI committee Hansard, totality of official testimony on HMAS Adelaide's interception of SIEV 4 and subsequent events. The most significant testimony was from Banks, Smith, Shackleton, and Silverstone.
28 Senate Hansard, pages 5803–04, 23 October 2002.
29 CMI committee Report, paragraphs 3.32–3.43.
30 CMI committee Report, paragraphs 9.147–9.154, in the chapter 'The response to SIEV X'.
31 CMI committee Report, paragraph 9.154.
32 'People Smuggling: National Security Implications', a paper by Adam Graycar and Rebecca Tailby of the Australian Institute of Criminology, presented at the Australian Defence College, Canberra, on 14 August 2000. This paper would have had an impact on the ADF at senior officer level.
33 'To Deter and Deny', Deb Whitmont, *Four Corners*, shown on ABC television on 15 April 2002 as the CMI inquiry was proceeding. It gave a harrowing view of what the navy did to asylum-seekers in various phases of Operation Relex—for example, the forced towback of SIEV 7 to Indonesia on 19 October 2001.
34 Marr and Wilkinson, op cit. Except where noted, my account of Palapa is drawn from *Dark Victory*.
35 *Dark Victory*, page 5.
36 'Man behind the people trade', Don Greenlees, *The Australian*, 1 September 2001; 'Turning tide traps people-smugglers', Don Greenlees and Kimina Lyall, *The Australian*, 27 April 2002.
37 *Dark Victory*, pages 3 and 8.
38 See PM&C email traffic with Department of Transport and with AMSA in 2001 and 2002, as received by CMI committee on 14 August 2002; items selected by Marg Hutton (items 2, 3, 4, 8, 24, 25, 26, 29, 34, 76), at http://www.sievx.com/documents/20020814PMandCEmail.html
39 CMI committee Hansard, page 1387.
40 CMI committee Hansard, page 1638.
41 See 'We were ignored by passing ships: castaways', ABC News Online, 15 September 2002 (and video clip); 'Two rescued from raft after two weeks adrift', Alex Murdoch, *The Age*, 15 September 2002; 'Loss of the NSW registered vessel Tamara—1 September 2002', Australian Transport Safety Bureau marine safety investigation report No. 185.

Chapter Seven: The Thirteenth SIEV

1. 'Who'll rescue the truth of 353 lives lost at sea ?', Tony Kevin, *The Age*, 25 March 2002.
2. 'Twisting tale of dog that did not bark', Tony Kevin, *Canberra Times*, 25 March 2002.
3. House of Representatives Hansard, 18 February 2002, page 324 (foreign minister Downer) and page 326 (attorney-general Williams).
4. Senate Legal and Constitutional (L&C) Estimates Hansard, 19 February 2002, pages 186–204.
5. 'I'm just a good spy, says our man in Timor', Lindsay Murdoch, *Sydney Morning Herald*, 4 March 2002.
6. 'DFAT testimony, 6 June 2002, Senate FADT Estimates Hansard, pages 540–41.
7. 'Call for inquiry into federal police', *The Australian*, 1 September. 'Minister rejects call for judicial inquiry', Ellison media release E114/02, 1 September 2002.
8. Ramezan Ali, an Afghan refugee who eventually reached Ashmore Reef and was later sent to Nauru, reported 'three to five cases' of failed previous voyages because of 'holes' (leaks), engine failures, stove fires, etc. See 'How did we go to Australia', by Ramezan Ali Nassery Malistany, 11 January 2004, from nauruwire.org, also in 'People Smuggling 'section on sievx.com.
9. CMI committee Hansard, pages 79–82.
10. CMI committee Hansard, pages 108–09.
11. CMI committee Hansard, pages 454–55.
12. CMI committee Hansard, pages 461–62.
13. CMI committee Hansard, pages 487–88.
14. CMI committee Hansard, pages 676–77.
15. 'RAN was nowhere near sinking boat', letter from Rear Admiral Geoffrey Smith, *Canberra Times* 16 April 2002.
16. 'Truth missing in murky waters', *Canberra Times*, 16 April 2002.
17. CMI committee Hansard, page 676.
18. CMI committee Hansard, pages 455–57.
19. CMI committee Hansard, page 470, 5 April.
20. CMI committee Hansard, page 947.
21. With Faulkner, CMI committee Hansard, page 1332; with Mason, pages 1349–50, with Brandis, pages 1355–56.

Chapter Eight: Accidental Whistleblowers

1. CMI committee Hansard, page 1360.
2. CMI committee Hansard, pages 1370–71.

3 CMI committee Hansard, pages 1360 and 1367.
4 CMI committee Hansard, pages 1449–50, 1452. Raby was then first assistant secretary, International Organisations and Legal Division. He was promoted to deputy secretary in November 2002.
5 DFAT answers to Questions on Notice, 19 June 2002.
6 CMI committee Hansard, pages 1645–49, Bonser testimony.
7 There are several references to this previously unknown Defence taskforce in Bonser's testimony: see CMI committee Hansard, pages 1646–48. It was well resourced: during CMI public sessions its numerous staff worked from the vacant parliamentary committee room next to the CMI inquiry room. They were well equipped with parliamentary television monitors, laptops and other IT resources. The Gates taskforce (also referred to as the Defence taskforce or the CDF/Secretary taskforce had no formal name but its role was to prove crucial in the CMI inquiry.
8 'Clarification of Evidence', letter dated 17 May 2002 from Rear Admiral Smith, Maritime Commander Australia, RAN, to the chairman, CMI committee.
9 CMI committee Hansard, page 1631, advice from the chair.
10 From media accounts, and in personal conversation with Sondos Ismail, who was definite on this point.
11 I owe Marg Hutton thanks for alerting me to the full significance of this matter.
12 CMI committee Hansard, page 1653.
13 CMI committee Hansard, pages 1628–79.
14 Letter from Bonser to the CMI committee, 17 June 2002 — Item 9, CMI committee 'Answers to Questions on Notice' volume.
15 See CMI committee Hansard, pages 1630, 1641, 1651, 1677. In Bonser's subsequent letter to the CMI committee of 17 June, his clarifications included: 'The primary source of information about possible departures of the SIEV X from 19 October onwards was the AFP. There were also earlier advices from the then DIMA in relation to this vessel.'
16 CMI committee Hansard, pages 1630–31, and Bonser's letter to the CMI committee of 17 June 2002.
17 CMI committee Hansard, page 1638.
18 CMI committee Hansard, page 1643.
19 CMI committee Hansard, page 1644.
20 'Defence Internal Review of Intelligence Related to SIEV X', 4 July 2002, prepared by the Defence taskforce and sent to the CMI committee by Robert Hill on 4 July 2002.
21 Following consultation between Brown and Labor senators, Brown's

proposed wording (which appeared in Senate Hansard proofs for 15 October 2003, page 16235) was amended to 'and that the government has still failed to establish where the vessel sank'. This amended motion passed (Senate motion 3, at Appendix 1).
22 CMI committee Hansard, pages 1642–43.
23 CMI committee Hansard, pages 1656–57.
24 CMI committee Hansard, page 1660.

Chapter Nine: Opening Pandora's Box
1 I had tabled Robert Hill's letter of 26 March to Simon Crean, which was forwarded to me by Crean on 23 April, during my 1 May testimony. The CMI committee then released it. It is item 27 in the CMI volume, 'Tabled Documents 13–31'.
2 'Boat people story a lie: ex-diplomat', Kirsten Lawson, *Canberra Times*, 10 May 2002.
3 'Cover up or stuff up?', Geoff Parish, *Dateline*, SBS television 22 May 2002.
4 'Cover-up or stuff-up', Margo Kingston, smh.com.au Webdiary 28 May 2002.
5 'Did Howard throw the children overboard', www.zarook.com, 1 June 2002.
6 The setting up of www.sievx.com was announced on 13 June 2002. It is being preserved by the Pandora (Preserving and Accessing Networked Documentary Resources of Australia) Archive of the National Library of Australia.
7 See 'Subversives.com?', Marg Hutton, 20 July 2003, in SIEV X Comment section of www.sievx.com, and linked articles from *The Australian*.
8 No helping hands for those in peril on the sea', Tony Kevin, *Australian Financial Review*, 24 May 2002.
9 'Drowned in indifference', Phillip Adams, *The Australian*, 1 June 2002.
10 'Probe needed on drownings', *Canberra Times*, 3 June 2002.
11 'Mass drowning case could sink navy's reputation', Margo Kingston, *Sydney Morning Herald*, 4 June 2002.
12 Foreign Affairs, Defence and Trade (FAD&T) Estimates Hansard, pages 218–20.
13 FAD&T Hansard, pages 231–32.
14 FAD&T Hansard, pages 232–33.
15 FAD&T Hansard, page 337, on 5 June 2002.
16 See endnote 1 above.
17 On www.sievx.com, 'Conspiracy of Silence', Marg Hutton, 20 May

2003, in SIEV X Comment section.
18 Defence Internal Review of Intelligence, 4 July 2002, CMI committee Additional Information, Item 28; see Attachment A (often referred to as 'the Gates review') at Item 28 in CMI Additional Information volume.
19 'Conspiracy of Silence', Marg Hutton, 20 May 2003, pages 18–20, 'The Gates Review'.
20 Letter of 6 June 2002 from Prime Minister's Department to the CMI committee, at Item 23 in CMI Additional Information volume.
21 PM&C departmental submission to the Prime Minister, 7 October 2001, 'Options for handling unauthorised arrivals: Christmas Island boat', tabled in Parliament by John Howard on 19 February 2002, House of Representatives Hansard, pages 416–17.
22 Those who attended on this day were Jane Halton, Katrina Edwards, Jenny Bryant (PM&C), Shane Castles (AFP), Warwick Gately (Defence), Mike Mrdak (Transport), John Drury (Customs), Ian Errington (Coastwatch), Rod Smith (DFAT), Bill Farmer, Vince McMahon, Ed Killesteyn, Christine Sykes (DIMA), and Bill Campbell (Attorney-General's Department).
23 See CMI committee report, paragraphs 8.82–8.97, especially 8.95.
24 Both letters are at Item 23 in the CMI committee additional information volume.
25 Item 26.
26 Item 27.
27 CMI committee report, paragraph 8.127, endnote 137.
28 Ritchie said this in FAD&T Estimates 4 June, Hansard, page 216.
29 'Moments of truth at death boat inquiry', Margo Kingston, *Sydney Morning Herald*, 14 June 2002.
30 'Judge should inquire into drownings', *Canberra Times*, 17 June 2002.
31 Hill in the Senate, Hansard, page 2160, 19 June 2002.
32 Media conference, John Howard, Canberra, 20 June 2002.
33 'Probe into doomed boat', Mark Forbes, *The Age*, 21 June 2002.

Chapter Ten: Defence Strikes Back

1 I am not aware of any evidence whether it was Bonser himself who received and passed on the AFP report. His CMI committee evidence refers only to Coastwatch receiving and actioning the AFP message.
2 'The tragedy of indifference', Robert Manne, *The Age*, 24 June 2002.
3 'Navy would always do everything possible to save life', Robert Hill, Letters, *The Age* and *Sydney Morning Herald*, 27 June 2002.
4 'Senators must have all facts on SIEV X', Tony Kevin, Letters, *Sydney Morning Herald*, 28 June 2002.

5 'No aerial surveillance as SIEV X sank', Margo Kingston, *Sydney Morning Herald*, 28 June 2002.
6 Source: various Margo Kingston Webdiary articles, in particular 'Waiting game on SIEV X saga', 3 July 2002.
7 'Defence Internal Review of Intelligence, 4 July 2002', at Item 28, Additional Information (often colloquially referred to as 'the Gates review').
8 'Spy plane patrolled ocean where 353 people drowned', Cameron Stewart, *The Australian*, 29 June 2002, page 1.
9 'Tragedy boils down to bad luck', Cameron Stewart, *The Australian*, 29 June 2002, page 4.
10 'Peeling the onion', Margo Kingston, *Sydney Morning Herald*, 30 June 2002.
11 CMI committee Hansard, pages 1884–1922.
12 CMI committee Hansard, pages 1907–09, 1915, 1918 (quotes from pages 1909 and 1918).
13 CMI committee Hansard, pages 1889–93.
14 CMI committee Hansard, pages 1910–12.
15 CMI committee Hansard, pages 1912–13.
16 Testimony in the CMI committee Hansard, pages 2154–81. Written answers under letter to the CMI committee from Matt Brown, chief of staff, Senator Hill's office, 20 Sept 2002—at Item 23, Answers to Questions on Notice CMI committee volume.
17 CMI committee Hansard, pages 2168–69.
18 CMI committee Hansard, page 2173.
19 'Commander speaks out on SIEV X controversy', AAP, *Canberra Times*, 3 August 2003.
20 Letter to the CMI committee from Matt Brown, CMI committee report, Item 23, questions W64 to W84.
21 Op cit at endnote 20 above, attached document.
22 CMI committee report pages 233–59.
23 Op cit at endnote 20 (above), Question W87.
24 Senate Hansard, 11 September 2003, pages 14367–68. Question 1639, 'Defence P3 Orion Flight'.
25 CMI committee report, executive summary, page xlii.

Chapter Eleven: Questions about Disruption

1 See Margo Kingston Webdiary commentaries, 'Off the hook: inquiry produced "big fat nothing"', 31 July 2002, and 'Labor backdown opens black hole of accountability', 1 August 2002. Both are on sievx.com under Articles: SIEV X Comment, 'A betrayal of the families of the dead', 1 August 2002.

Notes

2 CMI committee Hansard, pages 1923–84. Keelty's introductory statement is on pages 1923–29.
3 CMI committee Hansard, page 1927.
4 CMI committee Hansard, page 1928.
5 Senate Hansard, 12 December 2002, pages 7907–08, Additional Reply to Question from Senator Bartlett 'Law enforcement: SIEV X'.
6 Triggs, director of the Institute for Comparative and International Law at the University of Melbourne, interviewed by Peter Mares on 'Indonesia: People smuggler unlikely to be extradited to Australia', ABC Radio National *Asia Pacific*, 19 December 2002. Fonteyne, senior lecturer in international law at the Australian National University, Canberra, quoted in 'People smuggler to elude murder charge', Annabel Crabb, *The Age*, 14 December 2002. Both referenced in 'Discussion On Daoed', by Marg Hutton, in sievx.com Comment section, 12 December 2003.
7 'Australia dragging feet on smuggler's extradition: Jakarta', Matthew Moore, in Jakarta, *Sydney Morning Herald*, February 1 2003.
8 Legal and Constitutional Estimates on 10 February 2003, L&C Hansard, pages 138–52.
9 Robyn Warner, assistant secretary, Criminal Law Branch, page 142.
10 The Abu Quassey archive on sievx.com contains all available public reporting on the trial of Abu Quassey. The trial was thinly reported. I know very little about the evidence except that all or most of it came from the AFP documents.
11 'Sweden holds man in Australia people-smuggling case', Patrick McLoughlin, Reuters, 23 May 2003; 'Alleged SIEV X people smuggler arrested in Sweden', ABC News, 23 May 2003.
12 'Sandviken resident remanded in custody', Helena Nyman, *Arbetarbladet*, 1 July 2003 [this article translated by Helen Brooks in Sweden, is on sievx.com in People Smuggling section].
13 Senate Legal and Constitutional Estimates, 26 May 2003, pages 116–24.
14 'Swedish [sic] people-smuggler to be extradited to Australia', Louise Yaxley, ABC *PM*, 10 October 2003.
15 'Queensland: Lawyer moves to gag federal government', AAP, 7 November 2003.
16 An extensive set of media reports on the first three days in the committal hearing, by Kevin Meade (*The Australian*), David Fickling (*The Guardian*, UK), Jasmin Lill (*Courier-Mail*) and Ainsley Pavey (AAP) is at sievx.com. I have not seen court transcripts. According to news reports, survivors of the sinking—Faris Kadhem, Rami Akram, and Amal Nasri—were among those who testified at the first committal hearing.

17 'Soldiers people smuggling: agent', Ainsley Pavey, AAP, 7 April 2004; 'Federal officer testifies in people-smuggling case', ABC website, 7 April 2004.
18 Keelty letter to the CMI committee of 30 July 2002, Item 17 in 'Answers to Questions on Notice', CMI committee volume.
19 CMI committee Hansard, pages 1976–82 is the key section.
20 CMI committee Hansard, pages 1936–45, 1953–58, 1967–72, 1974–77.
21 CMI committee Hansard, page 1791.
22 Donnybrook, 1 Feb 2000, 281 people; Gelantipy, 27 March 2001, 22 people; Yambuk, 4 August 2001, 147 people. Source: 'Database of Asylum Seeker Boats' on www.sievx.com.
23 CMI committee Hansard, page 1930.
24 CMI committee Hansard, page 1926.
25 See 'Was a tracking device fitted to SIEV X?', 21 November 2002, and 'Keelty seeks immunity!', 22 November 2002, by Marg Hutton, in SIEV X Comment section on sievx.com. See also 'Keelty seeks immunity from boat questions', Kirsten Lawson, *Canberra Times*, 22 November 2002.
26 Legal and Constitutional Estimates, 27 May 2003, pages 301–29. See also 'Government dodges queries on sinking of asylum seekers' boat', Bob Burton, IPS, 28 May 2003; and 'Faulkner & Collins bat on', Marg Hutton, 29 May 2003 (both on sievx.com).
27 AFP reply to Senator Faulkner's question on notice No. 134.
28 At the 27 May 2003 Legal and Constitutional Estimates, L&C pages 301–29, Faulkner contested vigorously with Ellison and with chair Senator Marise Payne his right to ask continued questions about SIEV X and the disruption program. These exchanges were a striking example of how anxious the government was to close off such questioning.
29 Senate Hansard. Faulkner's three adjournment speeches on 23–25 September are at pages 4690–92, 4781–83, 4918–20. On 26 September, Labor put numerous questions without notice, followed by a no-holds-barred adjournment debate, all at pages 4998–5015.
30 CMI committee report, paragraphs 1.39–1.57, and Recommendation 1, Executive Summary page xx.
31 Faulkner's full text and Q&A is at sievx.com in Articles—Challenging, 'Faulkner returns to SIEV X', 24 July 2003.
32 'The sinking of SIEV X—the unanswered questions: A call for a judicial inquiry', John Faulkner, *Labor Herald*, summer 2003–04, text at sievx.com in Articles—Challenging, 5 January 2004.
33 'Alexander Downer discusses Quassey sentence', Ross Solly, ABC *AM*, 29 December 2003.

Chapter Twelve: Out of the Loop

1 CMI committee Hansard, pages 1996–97.
2 DIMIA written answers, 20 September 2002, at item 22, CMI committee Answers to Questions on Notice.
3 CMI committee Hansard, page 2012.
4 CMI committee Hansard, pages 2024–31.
5 CMI committee Hansard, page 2031.
6 CMI committee Hansard, pages 2031–34.
7 DIMA intelligence notes are at item 20, 'Answers to Questions on Notice', Senate CMI volume October 2002 (and also archived under 'Documents', www.sievx.com)
8 CMI committee Hansard, pages 2040–53. SIEV X related evidence is at pages 2086–2142.
9 CMI committee Hansard, page 2090.
10 CMI committee Hansard, page 2094–95.
11 CMI committee Hansard, pages 2097–99.
12 CMI committee Hansard, page 2124, and see CMI committee report paragraph 8.129.
13 CMI committee Hansard, page 2101–09.
14 CMI committee Hansard, page 2110.
15 CMI committee Hansard, pages 2112–15.
16 CMI committee Hansard, page 2117. Collins' question here was based on text in the Defence review of intelligence, 4 July 2002.
17 CMI committee Hansard, page 2119.
18 CMI committee Hansard, page 2123–24.
19 CMI committee Hansard, pages 2126–27—this is the source of next three paragraphs.
20 CMI committee Hansard, pages 2126–27.
21 'Unauthorised Arrivals Strategy—Update 24 October 2002', sent by PM&C on 21 May 2003 to Senate Legislation Estimates Committee, in response to request of 10–11 February 2003.
22 CMI committee report, paragraph 8.5.
23 CMI committee Hansard, pages 2130–33.
24 CMI committee Hansard, pages 2137–39.

Chapter Thirteen: Can We Handle the Truth?

1 Additional written evidence: AFP letter to the CMI committee of 30 July; Halton letter of 15 August; two DIMIA letters of 30 August (enclosing DINs) and 20 September; letter of 20 September 2002 from Matt Brown, chief of staff, Office of Defence Minister—at items 17, 19, 20, 22, and 23 respectively in the CMI committee

Questions on Notice volume.

2 Senate Hansard, 23 October, pages 5751–5804. The whole debate is well worth reading, to see how deeply divided the CMI committee was.

3 In this fine 1992 film about exposure of illegal US army punishments at Guantanamo Bay military base, Marines Colonel Jessup (Jack Nicholson) thus angrily taunts a military court trying to uncover the truth of how a young Marine died under such punishment. Jessup claims — in an argument perhaps relevant both to the story of SIEV X and to recent US use of torture in Guantanamo and Iraq — that if democratic countries want to be protected against enemies, they have no right to question methods used by those 'few good men' who defend them.

4 CMI committee report paragraphs 1.39–1.57.

5 CMI committee report paragraph 8.15 is the sole cross-reference.

6 CMI committee report paragraph 8.5.

7 CMI committee report, paragraphs 8.12–8.21; this is a section titled 'Evidence available to the committee'.

8 I rely on the OED definitions of both these verbs. I think they fairly describe the report's treatment of SIEV X.

9 CMI committee report page xvi.

10 Senate Hansard, page 5753.

11 CMI committee report, pages 453–68.

12 CMI committee report, pages 445–52.

13 I did urge senators to read the survivor accounts attached to my first submission, and I know that at least one of them (Bartlett) did so.

14 The brilliance of the play put on in Sydney in 2004, *A Certain Maritime Incident*, was in unforgettably capturing this surreal quality of the committee. The play turned life into art.

15 Faulkner, interviewed on ABC *Late Night Live*, with Phillip Adams, 6 November 2002, claimed that his approach and my approach to SIEV X were different:

> You're right to say that Mr Kevin, a former diplomat — Tony Kevin had raised certain issues, but didn't go to the disruption program. He was concerned that the Australian Defence Force, particularly the Royal Australian Navy, may not have adequately or properly conducted themselves in a safety of life at sea situation ... myself and my fellow committee members did take that issue very seriously and I've got to say to you that I haven't found any evidence to support that.

16 In a memorably context-free editorial commenting on Abu Quassey's seven-year sentence in Egypt, 'Justice, of a sort, for a people smuggler', 30 December 2003, *The Australian* managed not to mention the

people-smuggling disruption program, or Senator Faulkner, or the four Senate motions, or my SIEV X campaign, or even the very phrase 'SIEV X'. The editorial reassuringly concluded: 'But whatever the failings of the Howard government, it has not tricked desperate people into risking their lives on the high seas on vessels of doubtful safety to travel illegally to Australia ... [Quassey's] conviction will reinforce the hard line taken by the Australian government in dealing with refugee boats. The Quasseys of the world are always with us, but this conviction will encourage his peers to see that the days of making easy money from desperate people willing to place their fates in criminal hands, in the hope of safe-haven [sic] in Australia, are over.'

17 *Dark Victory*, page 288. I critically analysed Marr and Wilkinson's treatment of SIEV X in a review article, 'Lost at sea', *Sydney Morning Herald*, 5 April 2003. I am sorry I had to do this, because I greatly admire the authors' outstanding achievements as investigative journalists and their deservedly successful *Dark Victory*, which was a landmark work in helping to bring about a better public understanding of the misuse of the Australian border-protection system in 2000–01 to help John Howard win the 2001 election, and the great cruelties to people on SIEV boats that were produced by that cynical exercise.

18 All of the Senate questions and answers are tabulated on www.sievx.com in the section 'Hansard Extracts'.

19 The story of this unusual national notice is told by Marg Hutton in 'Remember SIEV X', commentary of 18 October 2002 on www.sievx.com, in 'Articles—SIEV X Comment'. Phil Glendinning and the Edmund Rice Centre helped make it possible.

20 'The whistleblower', Victoria Laurie, *The Australian* magazine, 17 May 2003.

21 Senate Hansard, 5 February 2003, pages 8585–87.

22 'Butt-covering brief finally released!', Marg Hutton and Tony Kevin, 22 May 2003, in www.sievx.com, 'Articles—SIEV X Comment'.

23 'New holes in SIEV X story', Tony Kevin, *Canberra Times*, 17 July 2003. This article, including the two maps, was also republished in 'New maps expose further holes in government's SIEV X story', commentary by Marg Hutton, on sievx.com, 17 July 2003.

24 Hansard proofs, 15 October 2003, page 16235; and see motion 3 in Appendix 1 below.

25 Raymond Gaita, in his acclaimed books *A Common Humanity* and *Romulus My Father* helped me to recognise the values I hold but previously only dimly perceived. See also Ghassan Hage, *Beyond Paranoid Nationalism*.

26 'Patrol bungled asylum boat hunt', staff reporters, *The Australian*, 3

July 2003; 'Asylum boat tip-off 'too vague'', Patricia Karvelas, news.com.au, 8 July 2003.
27 'Government secretive about Melville asylum seekers', Louise Yaxley, ABC *PM*, 7 November 2003 (sievx.com carries a full set of article on the Minasa Bone affair, accessible at the end of the people-smuggling section).
28 'Indonesians tell of con-man who left them to die', Matthew Moore from Denpasar, *The Age*, 15 March 2004.
29 David Marr on ABC *Mediawatch* on 10 May 2004 asked why did the authorities go to such great lengths to impose a near-total prohibition of media access to people on these three SIEV boats — so that whatever the Australian public was allowed to know about them came only from Immigration Minister Amanda Vanstone and government spokespersons, and so that there was no way to test the truth of any claims made by government about these groups of asylum-seekers.
30 House of Representatives notice paper, 24 March 2004, Questions on Notice 3363–96 from Robert McClelland.

Glossary and Abbreviations

Chapter One

the glory of the renaissance

ADF Australian Defence Force, comprising the army, navy, and air force. See also DEFENCE

AFP Australian Federal Police, headed by AFP Commissioner Mick Keelty

AMSA Australian Maritime Safety Authority, an independent statutory authority responsible for safety services to the Australian maritime industry. Headed by Clive Davidson. Comes under administration of Department of Transport. Oversights AUSSAR (Australian Search and Rescue authority) and RCC (Rescue Coordination Centre) in Canberra, which coordinates Australia's civilian search-and-rescue activities

ASIO Australian Security and Intelligence Organisation, responsible for domestic intelligence

ASIS Australian Secret Intelligence Service—Australia's intelligence arm overseas

ASTJIC Australian Theatre Joint Intelligence Centre, responsible for preparation and dissemination of military intelligence in the Australian theatre of operations. See also INTSUM

ASYLUM-SEEKER A person who seeks protection in a country as a *refugee*. See also PII, PUA, REFUGEE, REFUGEE CONVENTION, SUNC

AUSSAR See AMSA

BASARNAS Indonesian National Search and Rescue Authority, the Indonesian counterpart organisation to AUSSAR

CMI COMMITTEE The 'Senate Select Committee on a Certain Maritime Incident' set up in February 2002, initially to examine the issue of the misrepresented 'children overboard' photographs that had helped John

Howard's government to be re-elected in November 2001. At Liberal senators' request, this committee's mandate was subsequently broadened to include examination of 'operational procedures observed by the Royal Australian Navy and by relevant Commonwealth agencies to ensure the safety of asylum seekers on vessels entering or attempting to enter Australian waters'. The sinking of SIEV X was investigated by the CMI committee under this term of reference

COASTWATCH A division of the Australian Customs Service, headed at time of SIEV X by Rear Admiral Marcus Bonser. Coastwatch comes under the Minister for Justice and Customs. Coastwatch manages and coordinates Australia's civil maritime surveillance and response program, using contracted aircraft, adf patrol boats and aircraft, and seagoing vessels of the Customs Marine Fleet. The ADF's OPERATION RELEX took over Coastwatch's management of border protection in the Christmas Island–Ashmore Reef zone on 2 September 2001

CONTIGUOUS ZONE (CZ) The seas between 12 and 24 nautical miles from a country's coastline. The CZ is formally part of *international waters*, but in border protection operations it has a special status between *territorial waters* and international waters proper. For example, Adelaide intercepted SIEV 4 in the CZ of Christmas Island

DEFENCE Department of Defence, overseeing the ADF

DEFENCE TASKFORCE
(ALSO KNOWN AS 'SECRETARY/CDF TASKFORCE' OR 'GATES TASKFORCE') This Defence–ADF team was led by Rear Admiral Raydon Gates. It was set up in early 2002 to review ADF intelligence relating to SIEV X, in response to the Senate inquiry into SIEV X

DFAT Department of Foreign Affairs and Trade, headed by Dr Ashton Calvert. Minister is Alexander Downer

DIMA/DIMIA Department of Immigration and Multicultural Affairs headed by Bill Farmer. The name was changed to DIMIA in November 2001 when Indigenous Affairs was added to the portfolio

DIMA/AFP STRIKE TEAM See PEOPLE SMUGGLING STRIKE TEAM

DIN (DIMA/DIMIA INTELLIGENCE NOTE) Security-classified summaries of people smuggling intelligence that are prepared in the department, based on both overt and covert sources, and distributed to a range of government ministers and Australian government agencies

DSD Defence Signals Directorate, Australia's intelligence agency responsible for electronic interception of signals intelligence

HMAS Her Majesty's Australian Ship (in RAN)

Glossary and Abbreviations 287

IBONWEB The online edition of *Indonesian Business*

FIRST SENSITIVE A priority marking on DFAT cables, signifying that a cable contains politically sensitive information and is of first priority. The purpose of this sparingly used marking is to alert senior departmental and ministerial office staffs to politically important cables that should be read quickly and possibly brought to ministers' attention. This is not a national security classification (see RESTRICTED)

IGIS Inspector-General for Intelligence and Security, an independent statutory office that monitors the conduct of Australia's intelligence agencies, including ASIO, ASIS, *and* DSD

INP Indonesian National Police (sometimes referred to also as POLDA)

JORN Jindalee Operational Radar Network, designed and built by ADF to monitor 9 million square kilometres of ocean to Australia's north, without the high cost of maintaining constant maritime and air patrols. JORN cost $1800 million and took 30 years to complete. It covers all waters between Australia and Indonesia from three permanent installations in Australia, and is amazingly precise. It underwent final operational trials between 2000 and 2003, when it officially became operational. Although originally designed for military air detection, JORN was reconfigured in 1999 at Australian government request to scan for marine intruders. It was reported in February 2000 that 'more than 500 illegal immigrants have been arrested and detained in recent weeks, largely as a result of JORN intelligence passed to civilian customs authorities. JORN can also measure wave height and wind direction for meteorological reports'. I assume that most if not all interceptions carried out during OPERATION RELEX were facilitated in the first place by JORN-based detection data, thereafter confirmed by RAAF P-3 ORION detections. See Michael Sinclair-Jones, 'JORN assures early warning for Australia', *Defence Systems Daily*, 29 February 2000, web reference http://defence-data.com/features/fpage37.htm.

INTERNATIONAL CONVENTION ON MARITIME SEARCH AND RESCUE Australia became a party to this convention on 22 June 1985. Annex chapter 2.12.10 provides: 'Parties shall ensure that assistance be provided to any person in distress at sea. They shall do so regardless of the nationality or status of such person or the circumstances in which that person is found'. See also SAR ZONE, SOLAS

INTSUM Security-classified military intelligence summaries that were prepared in ASTJIC and circulated regularly to ADF and other recipients

IOM International Organisation for Migration, the UN agency responsible for migration issues. IOM works with national governments and the UNHCR, on migration, refugee and people smuggling issues

NORCOM ADF Northern Command. *Operation Relex* was conducted out of the headquarters of NORCOM, located in Darwin (HQNORCOM)

OPERATION CRANBERRY The COASTWATCH-led Australian border protection operation that was in place before Operation Relex, to detect and detain ASYLUM-SEEKERS arriving by boat

OPERATION RELEX The ADF-led border protection operation that commenced on 2 September 2001, to block the entry to Australia of ASYLUM-SEEKERS arriving by boat

OPSUM Security-classified operational summaries of intelligence relating to border protection, that are compiled from a range of sources and distributed by COASTWATCH

P3 ORIONS RAAF surveillance aircraft, equipped to conduct military surveillance, and also to assist when so tasked in maritime search-and-rescue operations

PII Potential Illegal Immigrant, ASYLUM-SEEKER. Such persons are often, though incorrectly under the law, referred to as 'illegals'

PM&C Department of the Prime Minister and Cabinet

PST People Smuggling Taskforce, a high-level interdepartmental committee chaired at the time of SIEV X by Jane Halton, then of PM&C

PEOPLE SMUGGLING The unauthorised transport of people (often ASYLUM-SEEKERS) from one country to another

PEOPLE SMUGGLING PROTOCOL, OR 'PROTOCOL' This was signed by the AFP and INP in 2000. It was 'hung off' the existing AFP/INP Memorandum of Understanding to combat organised crime. The protocol was cancelled by the Indonesians in September 2001

PEOPLE SMUGGLING STRIKE TEAM, OR 'STRIKE TEAM' A combined AFP/DIMA team of 15 officers (10 AFP, 5 DIMA) that worked from Canberra on operations to collect intelligence on and to disrupt PEOPLE SMUGGLING from Indonesia to Australia at the time of SIEV X

POLDA See INP

PUA Possible Unauthorised Arrival, ASYLUM-SEEKER

RAN Royal Australian Navy

RCC AUSTRALIA See AMSA

REFUGEE A person who 'owing to a well-founded fear of being persecuted for reasons of race, religion, nationality, membership of a particular social group or political opinion, is outside the country of his nationality and is unable or, owing to such fear, is unwilling to avail himself of the protection of that country'. Article 1A of the REFUGEE CONVENTION. See also ASYLUM-SEEKER

REFUGEE CONVENTION The 1951 Convention Relating to the Status of Refugees and the 1967 Protocol Relating to the Status of Refugees, signed by Australia

'RESTRICTED' The lowest-grade national security classification used in Australian government documents (coming below Confidential, Secret, and Top Secret). See also FIRST SENSITIVE

SAR ZONE Search and Rescue zone. The Indian Ocean between Australia and Indonesia is notionally divided into Australian and Indonesian search-and-rescue zones. The dividing line runs approximately midway between the two countries' coastlines, south of Christmas Island. The INTERNATIONAL CONVENTION ON MARITIME SEARCH AND RESCUE provides that the nearest available shipping or aircraft must attempt search and rescue, irrespective of the SAR zone in which the event occurs

SIEV Suspected Illegal Entry Vessel

SITREP Situation Report

SIU Special Intelligence Units. The four five-man teams of Indonesian police that were selected, trained and equipped by the AFP in October 2000 to assist AFP efforts to disrupt PEOPLE SMUGGLING operations from Indonesia to Australia

SOLAS Safety of life at sea (as in 'Australia's SOLAS obligations')

SOLAS CONVENTION International Convention on Safety of Life at Sea, 1974, to which Australia became party in 1983

SUNC Suspected Unauthorised Non-Citizen, ASYLUM-SEEKER

TPV Temporary Protection Visa, introduced in October 1999 granting a three-or five- year stay in Australia to persons accepted as REFUGEES. Holders of TPVs are not eligible for immediate family reunion or a range of resettlement services and social security benefits

TERRITORIAL SEA, TERRITORIAL WATERS The area of sea extending out to 12 nautical miles from a country's coast, that is claimed as sovereign territorial waters. This zone is measured out from straight-line coastal baselines, charted between capes and promontories. See also CONTIGUOUS ZONE

TRACKING DEVICE A miniaturised transmitting instrument placed (overtly or covertly) on a person or vehicle, and used to record back to a base data on the movements and location of that person or vehicle

UA Unauthorised Arrival, ASYLUM-SEEKER

UNHCR United Nations High Commission for Refugees, the UN agency mandated to lead and coordinate international action to protect REFUGEES and resolve refugee issues worldwide

Cast of Characters

ADAMS, PHILLIP Broadcast several features on SIEV X in his ABC radio program *Late Night Live*

BANKS, COMMANDER NORMAN Captain of HMAS Adelaide that intercepted SIEV 4 on 6–8 October 2001. Witness in CMI committee

BARRIE, ADMIRAL CHRIS Chief of the Defence Force (CDF) until May 2002, when General Peter Cosgrove succeeded him. Witness in CMI committee

BARTLETT, SENATOR ANDREW (Queensland, Democrats). Member of CMI committee, Leader of the Australian Democrats Party

BEAZLEY, KIM, MP (Western Australia, Labor). Leader of the Federal Opposition until November 2001

BIMANTORO, GENERAL Indonesian police chief who denied SIEV X survivor allegations of forced police loading at gunpoint. Other Indonesian police spokesmen quoted by media were Lt Colonel Prasetyo and Saleh Saaf

BLICK, BILL Inspector-General for Intelligence and Security, who reviewed ASIS and DSD documentation in relation to SIEV X

BONSER, REAR ADMIRAL MARCUS Director General, Coastwatch, Australian Customs Service (on secondment from RAN). A witness in CMI committee

BRANDIS, SENATOR GEORGE (Queensland, Liberal Party). Deputy Chair of CMI committee

BROWN, SENATOR BOB (Tasmania, Greens). Leader of the Greens Party

BYRNE, AIR COMMODORE PHILIP Commander, Maritime Patrol Group [P3 Orions], RAAF. A witness in CMI committee

Chauzy, Jean-Philippe Media spokesman, IOM, Geneva, who first announced the sinking of SIEV X

Cook, Senator Peter (Western Australian, Australian Labor Party). Chair of CMI committee

Collins, Senator Jacinta (Victoria, Australian Labor Party). Member of CMI committee

Coulthart, Ross Reporter on *Sunday*, Channel 9 television current affairs program, who first broke the story of Kevin Enniss

Crean, Simon, MP Leader of the Australian Labor Party from November 2001 to December 2003

Danziger, Richard Head of IOM Office in Jakarta at time of sinking of SIEV X

Daoed, Khaled Iraqi refugee, alleged assistant to people smuggler Abu Quassey in the voyage of SIEV X. Extradited from Sweden to Australia in 2003, now awaiting trial in Brisbane on people smuggling charges relating to SIEV X and one earlier vessel that reached Australian territory

Davies, Mary Dagmar From the beginning, a dedicated and creative activist for the cause of SIEV X justice, who used her own professional experience as a writer and media producer to open doors for me that I could not have opened myself. Created Jannah, the SIEV X Memorial website

Davidson, Clive Chief Executive Officer, Australian Maritime Safety Authority. Witness in CMI committee

Dixon, Agent Leigh AFP senior liaison officer in Australian Embassy, Jakarta at time of sinking of SIEV X

Downer, Alexander Minister for Foreign Affairs and Trade (portfolio responsibility for DFAT and ASIS)

Ellison, Senator Chris Minister for Justice and Customs (portfolio responsibility for AFP and Coastwatch)

Enniss, Kevin undercover informant involved in people-smuggling issues in Indonesia in 2000–01

Farmer, Bill Secretary, DIMA (DIMIA after November 2001). A witness in CMI committee

Faulkner, Senator John (NSW, Australian Labor Party). Member CMI committee, Leader of the Opposition in the Senate

Ferguson, Senator Alan (South Australia, Liberal Party). Member of CMI committee

Cast of Characters

FINDLAY, PROFESSOR MARK Professor of Criminal Law, Sydney University

GALLAGHER, COLONEL PATRICK Commander, ASTJIC. Witness in CMI committee

GATES, REAR ADMIRAL RAYDON Head of Defence [CDF/Secretary] Taskforce which in July 2002 submitted to CMI committee a report on defence intelligence relating to SIEV X. Appointed Maritime Commander, Australia in July 2002 (on retirement of Rear Admiral Geoffrey Smith)

GREENLEES, DON Journalist, Jakarta correspondent of *The Australian* in 2001–02. Walkley Prize winner for his articles in 2001 on people smuggling

HALL, RAYMOND Head of UNHCR Jakarta office at time of sinking of SIEV X

HALTON, JANE Chair of PST and Executive Coordinator, Department of PM&C, at time of sinking of SIEV X. Appointed as Secretary, Department of Health and Ageing, in January 2002. Witness in CMI committee

HAWKE, ALLAN Secretary, Department of Defence until October 2002. Now Australian High Commissioner to New Zealand. Witness in CMI committee

HILL, SENATOR ROBERT Leader of the government in the Senate. Defence Minister since November 2001

HOWARD, JOHN Prime Minister of Australia, 1996–2007

HUTTON, MARG Owner of independent investigative and archival website www.sievx.com

ISMAIL, SONDOS SIEV X survivor

JORDANA, MILES Was Senior International Adviser in Prime Minister Howard's Office at time of sinking of SIEV X. Appointed in July 2003 as First Assistant Secretary, National Security Division, Department of Prime Minister and Cabinet

KAYHATU, FIRST ADMIRAL FRANKY Indonesian Navy spokesman who fielded early media inquiries on SIEV X sinking

KEELTY, MICK AFP Commissioner since March 2001. Witness in CMI committee and related estimates committee hearings

KILLESTEYN, ED Deputy Secretary, DIMA [DIMIA]. Witness in CMI committee

KINGSTON, MARGO Journalist with *Sydney Morning Herald*. She closely followed CMI committee's SIEV X enquiry in 2002, and is convenor of the highly regarded www.smh.com.au/opinion/webdiary, a political-commentary website.

Laurie, Victoria Journalist with *The Australian*, wrote major feature article 'SIEV X whistleblower' which appeared on 17–18 May 2003

Lawson, Kirsten As the *Canberra Times*' Parliament House reporter, wrote several important SIEV X stories in 2002

McEwan, Agent Glen AFP liaison officer in Australian Embassy, Jakarta at time of sinking of SIEV X

Marr, David Investigative journalist with ABC *Media Watch* and *Sydney Morning Herald*, co-author with Marian Wilkinson of *Dark Victory*

Mason, Senator Brett (Queensland, Liberal Party). Member of CMI committee

Maysam and Maysar Brothers, surnames unknown, Abu Quassey's two other reported Middle Eastern assistants. Present whereabouts unknown

Metcalfe, Andrew At time of SIEV X, was First Assistant Secretary, Border Control and Compliance Division, DIMA. In June 2002, promoted to Executive Coordinator, Government and Corporate Group, Department of PM&C. By December 2002 was Deputy Secretary, Department of PM&C, chairing the National Counter Terrorism Committee and overseeing the National Security Division (headed by Miles Jordana). Witness on SIEV X in estimates committee hearings

Moore-Wilton. Max, A.C. Secretary, Department of PM&C 1996-2002. Resigned from Australian public service in December 2002 to become chief executive, Sydney Airport Corporation

Murphy, Senator Shayne (Tasmania, Independent). Member of CMI committee

Newton, Robert Australian Ambassador to Egypt at time of Abu Quassey's trial in 2003; Newton reportedly attended parts of this trial

Nakhoul, Ghassan Journalist, produced Walkley Award–winning SBS Radio Arabic-language documentary, *The Five Mysteries of SIEV X*, broadcast 28 August 2002

O'Shea, David Journalist, SBS Jakarta correspondent, discovered the Jakarta Harbourmaster's report on the rescue of survivors

Parish, Geoff Journalist, producer of three SBS *Dateline* current affairs programs on SIEV X in 2002

Payne, Senator Marise (NSW, Liberal). Chair of Senate Legal and

Constitutional Committee, whose estimates hearings in 2001–03 addressed many SIEV X questions

PRATT, KYLIE AFP liaison officer who passed AFP intelligence reporting about SIEV X on 20 October 2001 to Coastwatch, together with her personal opinion about risk to life of passengers

QUASSEY, ABU Also known as Mootaz Hasan Mohammed—his official Egyptian name. People smuggler, organiser of SIEV X and four known earlier voyages. On the evidence assembled in this book, Quassey was probably a INP disruption agent. He was sentenced in Egypt in December 2003 to seven years' gaol for people smuggling and accidental manslaughter in regard to SIEV X

RABY, GEOFF Was First Assistant Secretary, International Organisations and Legal Division, DFAT, at time of sinking of SIEV X. Promoted to Deputy Secretary, DFAT in November 2002. Witness in CMI committee and related estimates committee hearings on SIEV X

RAY, SENATOR ROBERT (Victoria, Australian Labor Party). Chair of Senate Standing Committee on Privileges. He supported Senator Faulkner's challenge to the government to disclose the full facts of the Australian people-smuggling disruption program in the Senate in September 2002

REITH, PETER Defence Minister at time of SIEV X. Announced his intention to resign from politics in June 2001, but continued to serve as Defence Minister until after the November 2001 election when Senator Robert Hill replaced him

RITCHIE, REAR ADMIRAL CHRIS Commander Australian Theatre, RAN. Witness in CMI committee and in related estimates committees

ROWE, RICHARD Australian Ambassador to Sweden in 2003, who successfully negotiated the extradition to Australia of alleged SIEV X people smuggler Khaled Daoed

RUDDOCK, PHILIP Minister for Immigration and Multicultural Affairs at time of SIEV X. Became Attorney-General in October 2003

SAFUAN, AGUS Indonesian police brigadier reported to have escorted Abu Quassey's bus convoy of 430 passengers from Cisarua–Bogor across Western Java and Sunda Strait to Bandar Lampung. Subsequently reported arrested. Not heard of since

SIEGMUND, NELLY Assistant Secretary, DIMIA, responsible for the branch that prepared DINs. Siegmund was also the senior DIMIA officer overseeing the AFP/DIMIA People Smuggling Strike Team. Witness in CMI committee

Shackleton, Vice Admiral David Chief of Navy, RAN. Witness in CMI committee

Shepherd, Marilyn Australia's most indefatigable refugee activist, who has never forgotten SIEV X

Silverstone, Brigadier Mike Commander Northern Command (NORCOM), RAN. Witness in CMI committee (and later provided written testimony on SIEV X)

Smith, Rear Admiral Geoffrey Maritime Commander, RAN (until succeeded by Rear Admiral Raydon Gates in July 2002). Witness in CMI committee

Smith, Ric Australian Ambassador to Indonesia from 2000 to November 2002, then became Secretary of Department of Defence (succeeding Allan Hawke)

Stein, Ginny ABC journalist in Jakarta who in early days broke important parts of the SIEV X story

Stewart, Cameron Investigative journalist with *The Australian* who covered the SIEV X story in key months June–December 2002

Taylor, Allan A.M. Director-General of ASIS, from February 1998–February 2003 (succeeded by David Irvine)

Tomczak, Professor Matthias Professor of Oceanography at Flinders University, Adelaide, who carried out oceanographical analysis in December 2002 of predicted ranges of current drift distances to the recorded survivor rescue coordinates

Trad, Keysar Community Affairs officer of the Lakemba Mosque, Sydney, who provided author with translated transcript of survivor meeting in Bogor a week after the sinking

Vanstone, Amanda Became Minister for Immigration Multicultural and Indigenous Affairs in October 2003 (since when three SIEVs have brought passengers into Australian territory/territorial waters — see chapter 13)

Waterford, Jack Senior Editor of the *Canberra Times*, the newspaper whose news and editorial coverage of the SIEV X story was from beginning to end the most fearless and resolute

Wallace, Dr Duncan Naval Reserve psychologist who disembarked in protest from HMAS Arunta at the height of Operation Relex's 'deter and repel' operations in October 2001

Whitmont, Debbie ABC investigative journalist whose *Four Corners* ABC television program, 'To Deter and Deny', 15 April 2002, stunned the nation with its revelations of Operation Relex cruelties towards asylum-seekers

WILKINSON, MARIAN Investigative journalist with *Sydney Morning Herald*, and co-author with David Marr of *Dark Victory*

YUSRIL, MAHENDRA Indonesian Minister for Justice who said he had been willing to deport Abu Quassey to Australia in January 2003 had Australian authorities seriously pursued this, but in the end sent Quassey home to Egypt

ZAINUDDIN, CAPTAIN Captain of SIEV X, who reportedly sent radio messages from the boat during its 36-hour voyage and was never seen again after the sinking

Website Sources

A general note on SIEV X information websites

Marg Hutton's www.sievx.com is the indispensable information archive. Most of the documents cited in this book are readily accessible through links on that site's homepage. It is worth familiarising oneself with the structure of her site, which is now very large. 'Chronology' is linked to many of the events and documents and is a user-friendly introduction to the story. 'Articles — SIEV X Comment' accesses the full set of SIEV X homepage commentaries. 'Articles — Smuggling' is an archive of the media history on people smuggling. All the crucial SIEV X official documents, for example, the CMI committee and Estimates Hansard, the CMI committee's report, and Senate questions on notice and replies, are readily accessible in the relevant linked sections. There are two powerful data bases, listing what is known about unauthorised entry boats attempting to reach Australia since 1989 and what is known about the people who lived and died on SIEV X.

My website, www.tonykevin.com (opened in October 2003), contains a personal selection of talks, published and unpublished writings on SIEV X by me and others, and related matters.

Margo Kingston's archive of SIEV X files from her former Webdiary, which was posted from 2002 to 2003, can be located at www.smh.com.au/news/opinion/webdiary/sievx.

Appendices

Appendix 1: the four Senate motions on SIEV X

1. IMMIGRATION: PEOPLE SMUGGLING

Motion passed without discussion 10 December 2002, moved by Senator Faulkner, also on behalf of the Leader of the Australian Democrats and Senators Harradine, Murphy, Brown and Nettle. (Senate Hansard, pages 7562–63):

> That the Senate —
>
> (a) expresses:
> (i) its support for the majority findings in the report of the Select Committee on a Certain Maritime Incident and calls on the Commonwealth Government to immediately implement all of the recommendations contained in that report, and
> (ii) its serious concern at the apparent inconsistencies in evidence provided to the committee and estimates committees

by Commonwealth agencies in relation to the People Smuggling Disruption Program and in relation to Suspected Illegal Entry Vessels (SIEVs), including the boat known as SIEV X; and

(b) calls on the Commonwealth Government to immediately establish a comprehensive, independent judicial inquiry into all aspects of the People Smuggling Disruption Program operated by the Commonwealth Government and agencies from 2000 to date, including:

(i) all funding and other resources put to the program, both within Australia and overseas,

(ii) the involvement and activities of all Australian Departments and agencies involved in the program, both within Australia and overseas,

(iii) the extent of ministerial knowledge of, and authorisation for, the program,

(iv) allegations raised in the media in relation to the program, including by the Sunday program,

(v) the nature of the co-operative relationship between the Australian and Indonesian Governments and agencies, including the operation of agreements and protocols, the funding and resources provided under those arrangements, and the activities of individual Australian and Indonesian citizens,

(vi) the use of Australian equipment and resources in the program, including use by persons outside of Australian agencies,

(vii) the effect of the program on persons seeking asylum from Indonesia or Australia, including the effect on means of transport, and

(viii) the circumstances and outcomes of all departures from Indonesia of all boats carrying asylum-seekers, including the circumstances of the sinking of SIEV X.

Question agreed to.

2. IMMIGRATION: PEOPLE SMUGGLING

Motion passed 11 December 2002, moved by Senator Collins on behalf of all opposition senators, the Leader of the Australian Democrats and all Australian Democrat senators, and Senators Brown, Nettle, Lees, Harradine and Murphy. (Senate Hansard, pages 7757–58)

That the Senate

(a) notes the evidence presented to the Select Committee on a Certain Maritime Incident regarding the central role played by the person known as Abu Quessai in organising people-smuggling operations in Indonesia;

(b) welcomes the statement by the Australian Federal Police that they have issued a further warrant for the arrest of Quessai, in relation to his involvement in people smuggling specifically in relation to the vessel known as SIEV X;

(c) further notes that the issue of this warrant indicates the strength of evidence linking Quessai with the people-smuggling aspects of SIEV X, including the procurement of the vessel, the recruiting of crew, the provision of passage on the vessel in return for payment, the loading of the vessel (including the gross overloading), and the departure of the vessel bound for Australia;

d) further notes that Abu Quessai is currently in prison in Indonesia for unrelated immigration offences, and is due to be released on 1 January 2003, with a high risk of him remaining out of reach of Australian legal authorities after that time; and therefore

(e) calls on the Australian and Indonesian Governments to undertake all actions necessary prior to 1 January 2003 to ensure that Abu Quessai is immediately brought to justice:
(i) on all matters relating to the outstanding warrants

relating to people smuggling, and

(ii) in relation to his involvement with the vessel known as SIEV X, including the foundering and sinking of that vessel with the resultant tragic loss of 353 lives.

Question agreed to.

3. IMMIGRATION: PEOPLE SMUGGLING
Motion passed without discussion 15 October 2003, moved by Senator Brown (Senate Hansard, page 16539)

That the Senate

(a) notes:

(i) the Government's failure to respond to the two Senate orders of 10 December and 11 December 2002 concerning the People Smuggling Disruption Program and the ineffectual pursuit by Australian justice authorities of the alleged people smuggler Abu Quassey,

(ii) that it is two years since 142 women, 65 men and 146 children perished after their boat, referred to as SIEV X, sank, and that the Government has still failed to establish where the vessel sank or release a list of names of the dead; and

(iii) that the Minister for Justice and Customs (Senator Ellison) has revealed that a list was provided to the Australian Federal Police from a confidential source, but that it is unlikely that a full list of those who boarded SIEV X or those who drowned will ever be available; and

(b) calls on the Government to produce the list and any information it possesses as to its veracity.

Question agreed to.

4. IMMIGRATION: SIEV X

Motion passed without discussion 16 October 2003, moved by Senator Bartlett, Leader of the Australian Democrats (Senate Hansard, page 16602)

> That the Senate
> (a) notes that:
> (i) on 19 October 2001, a boat known as the SIEV X, bound for Australia and carrying 421 passengers and crew, sank with the tragic loss of 353 lives, including 146 children,
> (ii) a number of those who lost their lives had close family members in Australia who are on temporary protection visas, which prevents them from fully rebuilding their lives, and
> (iii) the Commonwealth Government has not responded to the report of the Select Committee on a Certain Maritime Incident, which included an examination of the SIEV X sinking;
>
> (b) asks the Minister for Immigration and Multicultural and Indigenous Affairs (Senator Vanstone) to grant those refugees in Australia, whether they are awaiting a decision of their review or are on temporary protection visas, who suffered a personal loss through the sinking of SIEV X, permanent visas on humanitarian grounds;
>
> (c) calls on the Commonwealth Government to immediately establish a comprehensive, independent judicial inquiry into all aspects of the People Smuggling Disruption Program operated by the Commonwealth Government and agencies from 2000 to date, including Suspected Illegal Entry Vessels, and in particular the boat known as SIEV X; and
>
> (d) expresses its regret and sympathy at the tragic loss of so many innocent lives.

Question agreed to.

Appendix 2: the SIEV X advertisement

Advertisement

Remember the Victims of SIEV X

One year ago today, 353 asylum-seekers drowned trying to reach Christmas Island in a leaky overcrowded boat that capsized in international waters after its engine failed. Only 44 survived, rescued by Indonesian fishermen after 22 hours in the sea.

The Senate Committee of Inquiry into a Certain Maritime Incident tried unsuccessfully since March to establish the full facts about the sinking of SIEV X, impeded by official obstruction and evasion of evidence. The Committee's report, due on 23 October, will be contested and inconclusive.

Disturbing questions emerge from Senate investigations thus far. Did these victims die as a direct or indirect consequence of the Howard Government's determination to protect Australia's borders against boat people, at whatever human cost? Did SIEV X sink as a result of Australian disruption operations in Indonesia over which Australian Federal Police had lost control? And why was there no safety of life air search, despite clear intelligence warnings? Senator Faulkner and leading Australian newspapers have called for a judicial inquiry. We support these calls.

Only a full judicial inquiry can answer these questions.

In time, this terrible event will be acknowledged in our history as Australia's largest-ever civilian disaster. Because these peaceful and defenseless asylum-seekers were not invaders. They sought only our nation's compassion and a chance to join the Australian family. Their deaths horrify and shame us. We share the grief of their bereaved families.

Today and tomorrow, in many places around Australia, people come together to mourn the victims of SIEV X, to honour their memory, and to reach out to their families. Please join us: full details in "Events" <www.sievx.com>.

The loss of SIEV X is Australia's loss: 146 children died, some quickly others slowly; they should have grown up to be Australian - we will remember them. 142 women died, loving women who bravely traversed the world because Australia promised freedom once - we will remember them.
65 men - doctors, an engineer, linguists - fine and resourceful people we would have been proud to call Australian - we will remember them.

As we mark this first anniversary of 353 human lives lost, as this tragedy knifes its way into the soul of our nation, we remember you with burning hearts. Rest in Peace for you are not forgotten, nor will you ever be forgotten. You are part of this country and its people.

*Authorised by: Tony Kevin, Forrest ACT 2603 & other members of the SIEV X First Anniversary Memorial Notice Committee.
Thanks to the Edmund Rice Centre for managing this appeal and to all who donated.*

Acknowledgements

THERE ARE MANY TO THANK for this book: the survivors, bereaved individuals and Islamic community members I was privileged to meet; people who helped me through their own professional pursuit of the truth on SIEV X (many of these names already figure in the main text and endnotes); people whose creative work honours the significance of the SIEV X story; those who helped me by understanding what I was trying to do, and supporting my professionalism and integrity through difficult times; and my loyal family and friends.

First and foremost there is my publisher, Henry Rosenbloom of Scribe, without whose courage this book might never have appeared, and:

Phillip Adams, Norman Aisbett, Mohammed Alghazzi, Tim and Jackie Ashton, Paul Austin, the Australian Senate, John Baker, Desmond Ball, Grahame Bates, Geoffrey Barker, Basim Bazyar, Alan Behm, Param Berg, Garry Bickley, Steve Biddulph, Robert Bolton, Frank Brennan, Alison and Richard Broinowski, Greg Brown, Claire Bruhns, Joanna Buckingham, Julian Burnside and Kate Durham, Bob Burton, Tahir Cambis and Helen Newman, the Cambodian Buddhist community of Canberra, Mike Carey, Noam Chomsky, Sebastian Clark, Hugh Collins, James Cotton, Ross Cottrill, Ross Coulthart, Simon Crean, Mary Crock, Pamela Curr, Mary Dagmar Davies, Jackie Dent, Howard Dick, Marianne Dickie, Joost Dirkschwager, Phil Dwyer and the version 1.0 team, John Eddy, Anne Fairbairn, Chris Feik, Raoul de Ferranti, David Fickling, Jim Fox, Malcolm Fraser, Morag Fraser, Michel

Gabaudan, Phil Glendenning and the Edmund Rice Foundation, Belinda Goldsmith, David Golovsky, Forbes Gordon, Michael Gordon, John Gorman, Don Greenlees, Phil Griffiths, Pamela Gutman, Bruce and Jody Haigh, Andy Hamilton, Matt Hamon, Charles Hawksley, Johannah Henderson, John and Trish Highfield, Lybbie Hillman, Sue Hoffman, Brenton Holmes, Marg Hutton, Ron Huisken, Sondos Ismail and Ahmed Al-Zalime, Frank Johnson, Di Johnstone, Wio Joustra, A Just Australia, Kay Kan, Dominic Kelly, Patrick Charles Naomi Michael Margie and Cathy Kevin, Fatima Killeen, Margo Kingston, Susan Kinley, Victoria Laurie, Hugh Lamberton, Carmen Lawrence, Kirsten Lawson, Garry Linnell, Sarah Macdonald, Catherine McGrath, Jenny McGregor, Kate Mackenzie, Malcolm Mackerras, Jamie Mackie and Ann Moyal, Gerald McManus, William Maley, Robert Manne, Peter Mares, David Marr, Ian Mathews, John Menadue, Michael Merrony, Tony and Claire Milner, Marcelle Mogg, John Monfries, Michael Moore, Sophie Morris, Tessa Morris-Suzuki, Tom Morton, Lindsay Murdoch, John Murphy, Paul Murray, Ghassan Nakhoul, Helena Nyman, Terry O'Gorman, David O'Shea, U Ne Oo, Geoff Parish, Sir Richard Peek, Colin Penter, John Pilger, Pat Power, Jurek Pys, Gaby Radinger, Penny Ramsay, Margaret Rasa, Peter and Karen Reid, Margaret Reynolds, Merle Ricklefs, Jack Robertson, Cameron Ross, Ngareta Rossell, Robin Rothfield, Kevin Rudd, Eva Sallis, Alistair Sands, Morrie Schwartz, Marilyn Shepherd, Anne and Rob Simpson, Tony Simpson, Jack Smit, Moira Smith, Jane and Rick Smythe, Hans and Els Sondaal, Frederika Steen, Ginny Stein, Sarah Stephen, Cameron Stewart, Dominique and Jane de Stoop, Francis and Susan Sullivan, Helen Tait, Nikki Todd, Matthias Tomczak, William Tow, Keysar Trad, Gillian Triggs, Lauren Vandyke, Michael Visontay, Vanessa Walker, Christine Wallace, Patrick Walters, Jack Waterford, Petra Weber, Pat Weller, Gough Whitlam, Debbie Whitmont, Amrih Widodo, Kate Wildermuth, Andrew Wilkie, Marian Wilkinson, David Williams, Garry Woodard, Dick Woolcott, Tara Wynne, Brett Yeats, Ahmed Youssef, Arnold Zable, George and Tom Zubrzycki.